THE **ELECTRIC GUITAR**
SOURCEBOOK
HOW TO FIND THE SOUNDS YOU LIKE

THE **ELECTRIC GUITAR** SOURCEBOOK

HOW TO FIND THE SOUNDS YOU LIKE

Dave Hunter

THE ELECTRIC GUITAR SOURCEBOOK
HOW TO FIND THE SOUNDS YOU LIKE
Dave Hunter

For Freddie and Flo

A BACKBEAT BOOK
First edition 2006
Published by Backbeat Books
600 Harrison Street
San Francisco
CA 94107, U.S.A.
www.backbeatbooks.com

An imprint of The Music Player Network,
United Entertainment Media Inc.

Devised and published for Backbeat Books by Outline Press Ltd,
2A Union Court, 20–22 Union Road, London SW4 6JP, U.K.
www.backbeatuk.com

ISBN 10 0-87930-886-9
ISBN-13 978-0879-30886-5

EDITOR: **Simon Smith**
BOOK DESIGN: **Balley Design Associates**
JACKET DESIGN: **Paul Cooper Design**

Origination and print by Colorprint (Kong Kong)

05 06 07 08 09 5 4 3 2 1

Contents

There are plenty of good books about guitars on the market – books about the histories of different makes and models, about collecting guitars, about repairing guitars, and about playing guitars – but no quality publication to date that I know of provides the player with a comprehensive lesson on how and why the many diverse ingredients that go into making any given electric guitar all contribute to the way that that guitar sounds. *The Electric Guitar Sourcebook* takes the reader into the guts of the electric guitar, helps him or her to understand the many, many variables that make one different guitar design sound and feel so different from another, and enables the player to understand better what type of guitar might achieve the sound they seek.

To that end, this book is not intended as a history of the guitar, but as a primer on components, construction variables, and that grand enigma we all know as Tone. A little history has inevitably been covered along the way, but the intention is to inform players of the sounds currently available from guitars either made in the past or from those still being manufactured today, so I haven't taken great pains to adhere rigidly to a chronological format. Even so, a certain amount of chronology exists, as does something of an imbalance toward seminal, 'vintage' guitar models, simply because so many electric guitars of the 1950s and '60s set the templates that have continued to provide the sounds most people still desire today.

The first section of *The Electric Guitar Sourcebook* is designed to be used as a cross-reference for a more in-depth view of the ingredients listed as parts of the different models reviewed in the type-specific chapters that follow. This seems like the most logical way to make a book like this both informative and easy to navigate, without stopping at each model to revisit wood, component, and hardware details that might be common to many guitars. I would recommend reading Chapter 1 carefully in order to get a good grounding of the sound and performance of many of the different factors that contribute to electric guitar tone, as well as referring back to it to refresh your memory as you dive into the various makes and models covered in detail. Also, the intention of the model-specific chapters is not to document every relevant model of electric guitar – which, obviously, would be impossible to do in any adequate detail in the space allowed – but to present a representative selection from which the reader can extrapolate information that will readily apply to other similarly appointed makes and models not included here. Similarly, the CD included with this book seeks to offer a significant selection of sound samples from enough seminal guitar types to give a taste of the variables at play within the chapters of the book.

Be aware that in many places I am discussing the fine points of guitar components as they relate to tone, and that some distinctions made in these pages might be extremely subtle to the average ear, if detectable at all – say, the difference between the increased harmonic sparkle of a 25½″ scale length as compared with the denser, blurrier response of a 24¾″ scale on an otherwise identical instrument. Such matters, however, are the very point of a book like this: the intention is to dice up sonic distinctions to the finest degree possible, and to point out whatever nuances can be detected, however subtle. Otherwise, we might as well just put out another 'history of the…' book to slide on to the shelf alongside the hundreds of others already available. Of course, as a diehard student of tone you already know this, and that's why you're here in the first place: to find out about the nuances that make the whole of any electric guitar so much more than the sum of its parts.

1

The Components
Of Tone

Any quest to understand better the factors that contribute to the tone of your electric guitar must begin with an examination of the individual parts that make up the whole. Virtually every single thing that is glued, screwed, inlaid, or bolted into or on to the instrument plays a role in determining its sound, and the way in which these things are joined together – in other words, a guitar's design and construction format – arguably plays the biggest role of all. Also, because the sum of the whole is an interaction of many components, surprising changes in the tonal contribution of a major component – choice of body wood – for example, can be triggered by the alteration of a seemingly minor component, size of fret wire, for instance.

Given all the variables, it's not possible to come up with an equation to describe how

WOODS

Different wood types have different resonant properties, and these 'tone woods' – as they are called by guitar makers – are critical in setting a base for any electric guitar's voice. A guitar's sound begins with the transference of vibrational energy from the strings into the wood of the body and neck via different coupling elements such as bridge saddles, nut, and frets. The frequency spectrum that results from this acoustic interaction yields the sonic palette that will be amplified and modified by whatever pickups, effects and amplifiers reside in the signal chain. Certain elements of a guitar's raw, acoustic sound can be altered by the electronic stages that comprise our 'rig,' but most players are happier with their overall tone when it represents an amplified picture that's not too far removed from the sonic sketch provided by the unplugged guitar – a sketch that has its foundation in the instrument's woods. You can crank the bass, scoop the mids, tweak the treble, but by starting with the best raw tone for your sound and style that you can find you allow further sound-shaping stages to add depth, harmonics, power, and thickness, rather than bending them to the task of reshaping an imperfect acoustic template.

Both body and neck take part in setting this template, and each can be of single-wood or multiwood construction. The characteristics of most of the former are fairly straightforward to define, but necks and bodies that use combinations of wood types offer further ways of tailoring an instrument's core tone – further variables that many skilled, creative guitar makers have learned to use well to their advantage. Of course, woods of the same type cut from different trees or grown in different regions will sound slightly different, too, and have different weights and densities, different grain spacings, and so on. So the sonic variables exist not only between woods, but in subtler degrees between different guitars made from the same wood, which is part of the magic of searching for your dream guitar amid, for example, ten different Stratocasters hanging on the wall of the guitar store.

Makers will also select woods – and players select guitars to buy – based on their esthetic properties: the beauty of the grain and the way they look with a clear or semi-transparent finish applied. The first consideration generally remains the wood's sound, however, with visually appealing examples being sought out from samples of an appropriate tone wood. Some other woods that are visually appealing but lack the strength or resonance required in guitar building are sometimes used for decorative purposes, or as thin veneer tops over more appropriate tone woods. In most cases, however, workable, plentiful hardwoods that both sound and look good are the guitar maker's first choice.

Body Woods

Ash > The classic 1950s Fender body wood, ash is most desirable in the form of 'swamp ash,' wood taken from the lower portions of wetland trees from the southern states of the U.S.A. that have root systems growing below water level. The cells within the lower sections of the trunks of such trees expand to hold larger amounts of water than most trees would store. When the swamp ash is harvested and dried, the water in these cells is replaced with air, and the properly seasoned wood is therefore both light and resonant, and generally carries a broader grain besides. The 'swamp-ash sound' is a blend of twangy, airy, and sweet, with firm lows and pleasant highs, and a slightly recessed or 'scooped' midrange. Swamp ash is also considered to possess a degree of warmth as well as excellent sustain. Ash from the upper portions of the tree has also been used, as has harder ash from farther north, but both tend

An ash-bodied early-1950s
Fender Telecaster

to be denser and heavier, and give a brighter, harder sound that might be more appropriate when cutting, distorted tones are desired.

The broad, attractive grain of ash looks good under a transparent finish. There are no universals in guitar making, but as a rule of thumb the majority of Fender guitars with translucent finishes have ash bodies, while those with opaque or 'custom color' finishes have alder bodies. It's interesting to note that throughout the formative years of the 1950s and '60s Fender's decision to use ash or alder on a guitar had more to do with finish appearance than it did with factors such as weight and sound: if you wanted a blond Strat in 1957 you were aligning yourself with the swamp-ash sound – whether you knew it or not – while if you wanted a Shoreline Gold guitar, you were usually taking on the sonic properties of alder. Ash is traditionally used for single-wood, slab-bodied guitars, but has sometimes been employed by more contemporary designers in multiwood bodies, most commonly with a carved maple top or 'cap.'

Ash

Alder > This is another wood that found its place among classic electric-guitar tone woods thanks to the designs of Leo Fender. It's difficult to find any reference to the use of alder – or ash for that matter – in the hollowbody electrics that preceded Fender's arrival as the first mass-producer of solidbody electrics. Prior to the solidbody guitar, alder was mainly used for standard-grade furniture, flooring, and other domestic carpentry and cabinet-making. Alder is harvested mostly from trees grown in the north-western U.S.A. It's a medium-weight wood, although quality cuts of alder used for guitar bodies will often weigh less than denser cuts of ash. Alder has a strong, clear, full-bodied sound, with beefy lower mids and excellent lows. Its highs are slightly sizzly and rarely harsh, and it offers a decent amount of sustain.

Alder has a slightly brownish hue in its natural, dried state, and a grain that isn't necessarily unattractive, but usually isn't pronounced or particularly interesting either. It is usually used under opaque finishes, but some examples can look good under darker translucent finishes. Like ash, alder was traditionally used in single-wood, slab-bodied guitars, but has occasionally been used in more recent years in multiwood bodies, like ash, most commonly with a carved maple cap.

Alder

Maple > This is the first of the North American woods to be used commonly both for bodies and necks (see the section on necks below). Maple is a dense, hard, heavy wood, sourced mostly in the north-east and north-west of the U.S.A. and in Canada, and as such is usually used as one ingredient in a multiwood body, where it is generally partnered with a second, lighter wood. All-maple bodies aren't unheard of, although the weight of such is usually off-putting, but some makers have used solid, all-maple bodies to take advantage of highly figured bird's-eye, flame, quilt, or tiger-stripe patterns in the wood. On its own, a maple body lends an instrument an extremely bright, precise tone, with lows that are more tight than fat.

This light-colored wood, with a tightly packed grain, doesn't always carry dramatic figuring, but some examples can be quite spectacular. Electric-guitar makers first made use of its esthetic properties on the backs and sides of hollowbody archtop guitars, which were polished to a glossy, rippling, three-dimensional effect. A random percentage of maple timber – referred to as 'curly maple' – can exhibit impressive flaming, tiger-striping, and quilting, which occasionally appeared beneath the sunburst finish on the carved maple tops of Gibson Les Pauls from the late 1950s, setting the trend for its use by a great number of makers in the

Maple

Mahogany

decades that followed. Maple is also one of the most common ingredients of laminate wood stocks used for hollow and semi-hollow electric-guitar bodies. Laminated into a sandwich with other woods, maple helps to make a hollow-bodied guitar more tight and defined than it might be if made only with potentially muddy sounding woods.

Mahogany > Like maple, mahogany is a classic ingredient of the multiwood body, and is a common neck wood, too, but it is also often used in single-wood bodies. As for the classics, the Gibson Les Paul Jr, Les Paul Special, and SG were made of solid mahogany – with mahogany necks besides – and countless makers have used the wood in both solid and semi-solid designs over the years. Harvested in Africa and Central America, mahogany is a fairly dense, medium-to-heavy wood that yields quite a wide range of guitar-body weights depending upon stock sources. Used on its own, its characteristic tone is warm and somewhat soft, but well balanced and possessing good grind and bite. There is usually good depth to the sound of mahogany, with full but not especially tight lows and appealing if unpronounced highs. Mahogany is tonally different from ash, but possesses a somewhat similar openness and resonance as well as good sustain.

In its natural state mahogany has an appealing light-brown appearance with a tight grain. Under the right translucent finish it can be made to look a shimmering golden or bronze, with a surprising depth raised from the fine grain. It is most often seen as the translucent cherry back of a Les Paul or a PRS Custom, or the trans cherry or walnut finish of a Les Paul Junior or SG. Mahogany is also a popular wood for the back and sides of acoustic guitars, and therefore appears in some archtop electrics as a solid or laminated wood, but is less often used in such models than maple.

Maple-Mahogany Combination > Gibson raised the bar on Fender's slab-bodied Telecaster with the introduction of the carved-top, multiwood-bodied Les Paul in 1952, and thus ushered in what would become the most popular 'wood combo' body type of all time. Adding a solid maple cap to a solid mahogany back yields a guitar body that exhibits many of the best tonal properties of both tone woods. The solid maple-mahogany body – when quality wood stocks are selected that are well-matched and well-assembled – is characteristically rich, warm, and resonant, with mahogany's smooth, appealing lows and low mids and good sustain, with extra clarity, sparkle, definition, and bite added by the hard, dense maple cap. In other words, the mahogany smoothes out the maple's potential high-frequency harshness, while the maple adds cut and definition to the mahogany's potential wooliness. Between them, they combine for a lot of midrange punch, too.

For many players and guitar makers alike this marriage is equally appealing for its visual potential. Relatively little can be done with translucent finishes to dress up mahogany's plain appearance, but many stunning, bookmatched cuts of figured maple can be turned into real showpieces beneath sunburst, cherry, or translucent amber finishes. Both mass manufacturers and custom makers have used a variety of other wood combinations in their bodies, but maple-mahogany is by far the most common in a multiwood body, and is really the only one whose tonal properties have been etched deeply enough in tone lore to be considered a 'classic' or a 'standard' of body construction, despite some occasionally stunning results from other body combos.

Basswood > This abundant, affordable wood – also known as American linden – has emerged in more recent years and is particularly associated with mid-level or budget guitars, taking the place of alder or ash in many solidbody designs. But basswood is a good tone wood by any standards, and has been used by many high-end makers with excellent results. It is a very light and fairly soft wood, and is light in color, too, with minimal grain. Solid basswood bodies have a fat but pretty well-balanced tonality, with a muscular midrange but a certain softness and breathiness as well. On a well-made guitar basswood can yield both good dynamics and definition, and with enough grind to give the sound some oomph.

Visually it is uninspiring, but its clarity lends it to a wide range of finishes. Basswood's looks rely more on the finishing techniques applied to it than on any inherent esthetic qualities of its own.

Walnut > This dense, fairly heavy tone wood is occasionally used in electric-guitar bodies, and it has sonic characteristics similar to those of mahogany. It tends to be warm and full, but usually with a firmer low end and more overall tightness than mahogany. Walnut's rich brown color and often pleasing grain patterns means it looks good under a simple coat of translucent lacquer.

A number of custom builders have made guitars from walnut, but it has more commonly been seen in production instruments like Gibson's The SG and Firebrand models of the late 1970s and early '80s, or Fender's limited Walnut Double Fat Tele. It is a more expensive wood than the commonly available mahogany stocks used today, so it hasn't been widely used in mass production in recent years. Walnut was also occasionally used for the backs and sides of acoustic guitars in the early part of the last century, and occasionally reappears in the models of contemporary flat-top builders.

Korina > This is the tone wood of the 'space-aged Gibsons' of the late 1950s – the flashy Flying V and Explorer, along with the mythical Moderne and Futura that Gibson is said to have designed along with them, but never to have produced – which fell flat amid a generally conservative market at the time, but now fetch in excess of $100,000 among collectors. The wood probably doesn't have much bearing on the value of these guitars – it isn't as expensive as some other exotic tone woods, although it can be quite rare – but Korina is indeed a warm, resonant, balanced performer when used for a solid guitar body. It also yields great clarity, definition, and sustain.

Known generically as limba, an African wood related to mahogany, but imported under the trade name Korina, this is a reasonably light hardwood with a fine grain that is usually enhanced in the finishing process to appear as an attractive array of long, thin streaks. White limba, as used by Gibson, has a light appearance in its natural state, while black limba, used by some custom makers, has a more pronounced grain.

Rosewood > This highly prized tone wood is seen frequently on fingerboards and the backs and sides of many quality acoustics, but so rarely in solidbody electric guitars that it almost needn't be included here. Its use by Fender for the Rosewood Telecaster produced sporadically between 1969 and 1972, however, warrants a quick look. Originally produced for Beatle George Harrison as a one-off custom guitar in 1968, the all-solid-rosewood Tele has become something of an icon with Beatles fans, but the design makes for a very heavy and overly bright-sounding guitar, and an expensive one, too. (Some of Fender's later Rosewood Telecasters used two-piece bodies with hollowed chambers inside, but that in itself is a waste of a lot of good rosewood.) Other than these guitars and the occasional custom-made design, when rosewood contributes to the sound of an amplified guitar body it will usually only be as part of a hollowbody acoustic with a pickup mounted on it.

Poplar > An extremely plentiful wood, poplar is a hardwood by definition but is actually relatively soft when compared with other hardwoods. It is seen in North America mostly in the form of affordable furniture, flooring, general carpentry, and so on, but has also been used in the manufacture of many sorts of musical instruments over the years, mostly those of the 'folky-craftsy' variety. It is now surfacing more and more as a body wood used in cheap to midrange Asian-made electric guitars, and as such it displays a rather bland, characterless quality that isn't necessarily bad, but isn't overtly good either. Poplar bodies aren't particularly resonant nor do they give much sustain, and they generally don't seem to enhance any particular frequency range or overtones, but that means they are also pretty well-balanced, if dull. This is an extremely plain wood in appearance, and relies on the finish used upon it.

Some other alternative, largely exotic woods such as purple heart, wenge, koa, bubinga, and others are used by custom guitar makers, but don't feature highly in mass-production guitars or what we would call the 'vintage classic' templates. These are mostly hard, dense woods with distinctive grain patterns and sometimes appealing colors in their natural state, and they are usually used as one ingredient of many in a multiwood body. The two most common woods for the tops of acoustic guitars, spruce and cedar, will very rarely come into the picture when it comes to electric-guitar construction, and only when used primarily in guitars that are designed to be heard as acoustic instruments first.

Left to right > all-rosewood Fender Telecaster; korina Gibson Explorer; maple-topped Gibson Les Paul; mahogany Gibson SG; mahogany-backed PRS Santana Model

Neck Woods

The wood used in a guitar's neck might be considered a less obvious tone ingredient than that used in the body, but it certainly contributes to the brew. In a well-designed guitar the neck and fingerboard woods will flavor and enhance the tonal characteristics defined by the body wood, and clever makers know how to use this extra length of timber to fine tune their creations' resonance and response. While the solid maple neck offers one of the most popular of all neck types for solidbody electrics – and the only widely popular single-wood neck – there are more relevant multiwood combinations used in necks than in bodies. In the end, the overall contribution of wood to any guitar's tone is found in the marriage of its neck and body woods, which might therefore involve three or even four different woods all together.

Maple > This hard, dense wood was used in many higher-end archtop acoustic guitars prior to 1950, some of which would have been amplified, but we will forever know the one-piece maple neck in particular as 'the Fender neck,' thanks to its arrival on the Broadcaster (later Telecaster) in that year. Whether in the form of a solid one-piece neck with integral fingerboard or a neck with an added fingerboard of a second type of wood, maple is easily the most common type of wood used in solidbody guitars, and probably all electric guitars.

A one-piece solid maple neck contributes a lot of tightness and cut to a guitar, with an edge of sizzle in the highs and high mids. Its high end is usually not as over-pronounced as many people might think, although it is a characteristically bright neck-wood choice, and its lows are firm. Mids tend to have a snappy attack, with a punchy, slightly gnarly edge when the strings are hit hard but excellent clarity with light-to-medium picking. The keyword for maple is probably 'tight' – but this is a *good* tight,

one that lends to clarity and note definition, rather than any kind of uptight constipation. This is the classic 'twang' neck, especially when partnered with a body of solid ash. Maple's hardness also gives it a firm, well-defined playing feel at the fingerboard.

Maple-Rosewood > Topped with a rosewood fingerboard, a maple neck's tonal character becomes a little warmer and sweeter, with more sparkle in the highs and thicker lows, tending toward a looser sound. Mids tend to have both a little more openness and compression. In simple terms, rosewood's contribution to a maple neck-back smoothes and 'furs up' the solid-maple sound, but of course the subtleties of this blend are more complex than that. Note also that, given the excellently musical and responsive performances of both solid maple and maple-rosewood necks in well-built guitars, a player's choice of one type over the other might come down to feel or even appearance as much as to sound, although the sonic differences are certainly real and worth exploring.

In terms of touch, rosewood has a somewhat softer, more organic feel, which is partly down to the fact that rosewood fingerboards are only rarely covered in any type of finish – as most maple fingerboards are – but this also partly stems from the natural feel of the

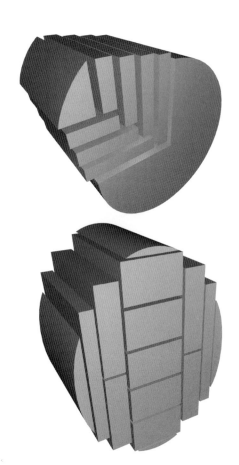

◀ Sawing timber

Sawmills cut timber in different ways, and the type of cut that has been used to turn a tree into lumber can be of great importance to a guitar maker. The two main sawing techniques are flat – or plain – sawing (left, bottom) and quarter sawing (left, top).

Flat-sawn wood is milled just as its name implies: the log is run through the saw blade so that a series of vertical cuts are made from one side to the other until a series of boards is produced. Quarter-sawn wood is far less common than flat sawn because it takes more labor to produce, but it is stronger, has a more consistent grain, and is less prone to warping, twisting, shrinking, and swelling. The key to quarter-sawn wood lies also in its name, but the technique might not be so obvious. The log is first sawn straight down the middle, then each half is run straight through the blade and cut into quarters. Each quarter is then rotated back and forth for each pass through the saw blade to produce a series of ever-smaller boards.

The visual evidence of quarter-sawn wood is a grain that runs nearly perpendicular to the surface of the board, typically at an angle between 60 and 90 degrees, and this gives greater strength along the length of the wood. Flat-sawn wood, in contrast, often displays the typical rings of wood grain that widen outward across the face of the board-like ripples on the surface of a pond. Given the method of producing quarter-sawn lumber – its very nature, in fact – you can clearly see that much larger raw logs are required to produce quarter-sawn boards of an equal size to the larger boards produced in flat sawing. Given this fact and the more labor-intensive nature of quarter sawing, such wood is both more expensive and harder to come by.

Guitar makers value quarter-sawn wood for a number of applications, but for the necks of guitars in particular, where great strength is required along the full length of a relatively narrow piece of wood.

different woods. Rosewood has a deeper, more pronounced grain, which results in a certain airy softness under the fingertip. Some players refer to it as a 'warmer-feeling' 'board, while some love the rock-solid feel of maple.

Maple-Ebony > Dense, hard, and dark to the point of near-blackness, an ebony fingerboard is seen far less on a maple neck than is rosewood, but the combination has been offered by some makers. It is a classic upscale option atop a mahogany neck, however, so let's wait and address it in more detail there. In short, ebony exhibits some of the same sonic properties as maple – tightness, brightness, and a quick attack – so the pairing doesn't offer much that the solid-maple neck can't offer other than looks and a slight difference in feel.

Maple-Pau Ferro > A fairly hard, dense, tight-grained wood which has seen increasing use in recent years, pau ferro can be considered tone wise as something of a cross between ebony and rosewood, although, of course, the fine points of its tonal character defy such easy categorization. It offers excellent clarity and definition, but has more complex highs than maple, with chunky lows, muscular lower mids, and an airy, open midrange. A pau ferro fingerboard is almost always paired with a maple neck.

Mahogany-Rosewood > The second most common guitar-neck wood after maple, mahogany is most often coupled with a solid mahogany or mahogany-maple-topped body. This more porous, open wood doesn't quite have maple's hardness, strength, or stability, however, and it isn't suitable fingerboard material. Mahogany has a warm, mellow tone as a neck material, with good presence in the lower mids. The mahogany-rosewood pairing in such a neck contributes to complex highs, thick and creamy lows, and an appealing midrange that avoids harsh honking tones, but isn't excessively punchy.

Mahogany-Ebony > This is a popular upscale pairing, in which the ebony fingerboard contributes to a little more tightness, clarity, and definition as compared with the mahogany-rosewood neck. A very dense, hard wood, ebony makes for a fast attack from the instrument and offers a muscular, controlled bass and snappy, sizzling highs. With a mahogany back contributing some warmth and openness to the brew, this can be a very appealing pairing for many players. Ebony also wears very well, and doesn't divot under years of finger-and-string pressure nearly as easily as does rosewood.

FINISH

Many players don't consider a guitar's finish a factor in its tonal makeup, but the types of finishes commonly applied to electric guitar bodies all alter the wood's resonance in one way or another. In extreme cases – for example, in the case of heavy, air-tight finishes – they can even impede the way the wood performs, and choke off its voice considerably. Therefore, we can probably consider a guitar's finish as something of a 'sub ingredient' of its wood type.

Traditional finishes include oil varnish, spirit varnish, and nitrocellulose lacquer, the latter being that used on the vast majority of vintage electric guitars and still the industry

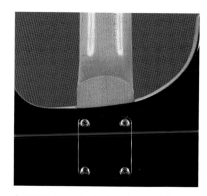

A maple neck bolted on to an alder body on a 1998 PRS Classic Electric

eugait loreet

The above examples of PRS's own color options show the variety of finish that can be created over a figured maple top.

standard for quality instruments. Nitro is hard enough to be buffed to a high gloss, but is also flexible enough to vibrate with the wood, allowing the wood to 'breathe' tonally. Nitro can also change hue with age – transparent coats generally go from clear to a golden amber, while colors will sometimes simply fade – and is prone to wear from the constant friction of player contact. However, this aged look appeals to many players, and it has become one of the tell-tale signs of the vintage guitar. Many such players – the ones in the know, at least – also agree that the amber hues and bare forearm patches are a fair trade-off for a more open and resonant instrument.

Since the early 1970s many more affordable guitars – and some quite expensive ones – have been given heavy polyester or epoxy finishes, often referred to by their detractors as 'plastic' or 'thick-skinned' finishes. These are both cheaper and easier to apply, the finishing process produces less hazard from toxic fumes, and the results survive the dings and bumps of minor abuse extremely well, so they are appealing to the budget-range manufacturer on a number of counts. But the thickness, rigidity, and total impermeability of these finishes can really dampen the wood's vibration and make a guitar – relative to one with a nitro finish – sound tight, choked, and nasal. With an awareness of this, many manufacturers have more recently used polyurethane finishes, which represent something of a compromise of characteristics.

These are fine points, of course, and the tonal contributions of other components in any given guitar's makeup will very likely jump out at you more than will its finish – and it's virtually impossible to set up A/B listening tests to plot the sole variable of finish, given that two different raw body blanks of the same type of wood might sound different unpainted anyway – but they are fine points that many sharp-eared players have detected down the years, so are worth noting. Many guitarists have sent beat-up old instruments away to be refinished and restored, only to find that they just didn't sing and resonate in the same way after they returned with their nice, new coats of paint. In some cases, a guitar buyer might find that an instrument with a heavier finish even yields a preferable tone – one with more tightness and cut when heavily distorted, for example – but in most cases it is desirable to allow the wood to resonate and impart its own natural tonal characteristics.

BRIDGE AND TAILPIECE

Having discussed the discernible voices of a number of different types of body woods, it's important to consider what lies between the vibrating string and the wood from which any guitar is made: a bridge, and sometimes a tailpiece. Any guitar's bridge – by which is meant the total structure of its bridge saddles and any plate into or on top of which they are mounted – performs double duties soundwise: it determines one end point and therefore the pitch of the vibrating string, and it also transfers some of that string's vibrational energy, which is to say the guitar's acoustic energy, into the body of the guitar. As such, the bridge forms a critical anchor point for the string, and the solidity of that anchor point is critical in determining the voice of any guitar.

Of course, by design, different bridge types differ greatly in their solidity in this regard, but any flawed or generally unstable saddle or bridge plate will clearly dissipate some of the string's energy into the sonically pointless rattling of that loose part. This solidity – in tonal terms – also depends a great deal upon the break angle of the strings over the bridge saddles, that is, the angle formed by the rising ball-end length of string from the tailpiece or mounting holes, and the 'speaking length' of the string between saddle and nut slot. A relatively steep angle is generally desired because it keeps good downward pressure on the saddle and transfers a lot of vibrational energy from string to guitar body, although in some designs too steep an angle – a thing occasionally determined by a guitar's set-up, not written in stone at the design stage – can choke the tone a little or result in too much downward pressure on the top of the guitar, something more likely to be a concern with hollow and semi-hollow instruments. Too shallow an angle will often result in a thin, somewhat dead tone, and can even result in the string feeling loose and unstable at the bridge.

In any event, it won't always be the case that the most solid coupling physically possible between string and guitar body is universally desirable. For one thing, this might not always be possible, given other design objectives of any given bridge – for example, adjustability for intonation and action, or the necessity of movement for vibrato action – but the 'world's most solid' bridge just might not be preferred tonally by some players, either. Take the case of Eric Clapton, whose preferred guitars after the early 1970s have been Fender Stratocasters with vibrato tailpieces. However, he has the vibrato arm removed and the tailpiece 'blocked off,' where a wedge-shaped wooden block is inserted between the tremolo block and the body of the guitar from the rear in order to clamp the bridge plate down firmly against the guitar body. Given this, you'd think Clapton would simply jump straight to the strings-through-body 'hard-tail' model Strat, but, in fact, he doesn't like the sound of those guitars. There's a good chance this has something to do with the touch of softness that the springs and the somewhat lesser strings-to-body coupling of this format gives him. The theory applies in varying degrees to players' preferences for a wide range of different bridge types, otherwise we'd all be playing strings-through-body Telecasters or Les Paul Juniors with wrapover tailpieces.

It's also important to be aware that tailpiece design and positioning can also considerably affect the playing feel of a guitar, in that they determine the overall length of the strings, not merely the playing length or 'speaking' length, and therefore the perceived looseness or tautness of the string against fingertip. Two guitars that are identical right down to the Tune-o-matic bridges, for example, but which have different tailpieces – a stop-tail and a trapeze – will feel slightly different to play, particularly with regard to

Top to bottom > vintage-style Fender Stratocaster vibrato tailpiece; hardtail Strat with fixed bridge and through-body stringing; trapeze-style Gibson wrapover bridge

fretting and string bending. The guitar with the trapeze will feel a little stiffer than the stop-tail example, because its strings travel a greater distance overall between ball-end and tuner post. The strings on a guitar with a wrapover bridge-tailpiece will feel a little looser still, because they have only a minimal length behind the top arc of the bridge that determines the speaking length.

Strings-Through-Body Bridge > As mentioned above, the Fender Telecaster is the classic of this breed, but many other makers have employed similar body-end string anchoring over the years. This bridge arrangement negates any need for a separate tailpiece because the strings' ball-ends are anchored in steel ferrules embedded in the wood at the back of the guitar's body. In effect, this creates a sort of double-locking anchor at the strings' body end: they are held tightly in the wood of the body, and they also make very firm contact with their most sonically significant termination point thanks to the 90-degree break angle over the bridge saddles. Relative to any guitar design or body wood, this is an extremely resonant, punchy, long-sustaining bridge format, and it suits players that want a lot of attack and a fast response from their guitars.

There are a number of variations on the strings-through-body bridge, and the vintage Telecaster bridge, while employing this design, adds its own quirks to the brew as well. This bridge still benefits from the solidity of through-body stringing, but because the stamped-steel bridge base plate is held in place by four screws at its back edge, and extends over the body rout for the pickup without being further anchored at its neck-facing edge, this bridge type produces a subtle metallic resonance and twang, which is another ingredient of the classic Tele sound. The way that the bridge pickup is suspended from this base plate, and the interaction between the strings vibrating the saddles seated on the plate, the acoustic energy transferred more directly into the body wood, and any vibration amplified by the pickup's microphony, also plays a big part in making a vintage Tele sound the way it does.

Different versions of the Tele through-body-strung bridge provide further subtle variables according to the types of saddles they carry. All vintage units had three saddles, each carrying a pair of strings, but in the mid 1970s six-saddle bridges were phased in. The production Broadcaster (later Telecaster) of 1950 had brass saddles, which impart a warm, rounded, sustaining tone with plenty of bite. However, in late 1954 steel saddles replaced brass, and brought a somewhat sharper tone, while in mid 1958 threaded steel saddles were introduced. The last change was subtle, but some players detect in it the arrival of a little more 'zing' in the Tele tone.

The strings-through-body setup of the hardtail Stratocaster is a different affair, because its bridge is clamped firmly and entirely down against the wood of the body without any portion 'floating' out over a pickup cavity as on the Telecaster. This bridge also carries an individual saddle for each string. Other models that carry through-body stringing – some otherwise Gibson-flavored Hamers, Tom Anderson's T-style guitars – use bridges that are similar to the hardtail Strat format, bolted firmly and squarely to the face of the guitar. Other more unusual configurations exist, such as the through-body stringing of Yamaha electrics, the AES and RGX series, for example, where strings emerge through the ends of six individual 'tone bars' on their way to a Tune-o-matic-style bridge.

There's plenty of solidity, punch, and resonance in each of these setups and in that of the vintage Tele bridge, but many players claim that only the latter will suffice for archetypal Telecaster twang, snap, and zing.

Wrapover Bridge > Introduced on the Gibson Les Paul from 1953 and standard equipment on the Les Paul Jr and Special after that, the wrapover bridge is considered another great standard of solid, ringing tone. It's a surprisingly simple bridge design to have been included on what was then the most intricately crafted solidbody electric guitar ever made, but the unit does its job well, and has retained a lot of fans. The wrapover bridge is essentially just a gently arched steel bar with holes along its forward edge through which the strings pass, to be wrapped tightly back over the top of the bar on their way up the neck. This bar has wide U-shaped slots at either end that fit snugly into the heads of chunky bolts that are screwed tightly into studs set into the body. Once the strings are tuned to pitch, the whole affair is tight and solid, and a great proportion of acoustic energy is transferred from the strings through the bar, bolts, and studs into the wood of the body.

There's no facility for setting the height or intonation of individual strings with this bridge – a grub screw at either end allows a degree of overall intonation adjustment via the 'a little less here, a little more there' technique, and string height is set with the mounting bolts – but fans of the format are usually happy with the compromises. In most cases, the results are good enough for rock'n'roll, and that is good enough for a surprisingly large, devoted contingent of tone-conscious guitarists. The wrapover bridge offers good sustain and punchy yet resonant sound, which introduces a good proportion of the tone of the guitar's woods into the overall brew.

A great many variations on the wrapover theme have followed in the footsteps of Gibson's original version. Gibson updated the design itself with a 'compensated' version that had a staggered, raised ridge on the top of the bridge bar to account for the different intonation requirements of individual strings. Wilkinson took the concept one better with its GB-100 bridge, which carried both the compensated ridge and an adjustable section for the G and B strings, which often require more extreme adjustment relative to the rest of the strings. PRS's Stop-Tail bridge has a gently upswept, compensated bar-top with guide slots for each string, and is a highly effective variant on the wrapover theme. In the 1970s Leo Quan offered a deluxe version of the wrapover bridge – his Badass Bridge (still available) – which was a clever amalgamation of the simple bar bridge and the more versatile Gibson Tune-o-matic (see below). With the Badass, strings still anchor in holes drilled at the front edge of the bar and wrap up and over the top, but there they are seated in six individually adjustable steel saddles. The design carries more moving parts, but provides extremely accurate intonation adjustment. A lot of players find this a good 'best of both worlds' alternative – while plenty more still are perfectly happy with the crude but solid bar of the original.

Tune-O-Matic Bridge > Gibson addressed the wrapover bridge's limited adjustment capabilities in 1954 with the release of the Tune-o-matic bridge, also known as the ABR-1 in Gibson literature. Partnered with a separate 'stud' tailpiece, which was really just a slightly modified version of the wrapover bridge without the grub screws for angle adjustment, the Tune-o-matic provided both a firm seating for the strings at the body-end termination point of their speaking length, and a facility for the adjustment of the individual length of each string via a sliding steel saddle and adjustment screw. When adjusted for the correct break angle over the saddles, this hardware combination also yielded excellent coupling between string and body, which resulted in good sustain. Overall string height, however, was still set with the two mounting bolts. The design is still with us today, in its original form and Gibson's own updates on the theme, as well as in precise or near-copies from a great many

Top to bottom > Gibson Tune-o-matic bridge with stop-bar tailpiece; three-saddle Fender Telecaster with through-body stringing; six-saddle Tele with through-body stringing

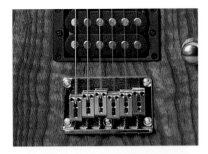

Top to bottom > a modern example of the classic Fender fixed bridge; Gibson's ultra-simple wrapover bridge; Yamaha's take on through-body stringing; PRS's adaptation of the wrapover bridge

other guitar makers, and it is one of the most popular bridge formats of all time for solidbody electrics. Devotees of the old wrapover might tell you that the Tune-o-matic design took Gibson bridges a notch further away from the solid simplicity of the single-bar unit, and the shorter string length behind the saddle that the wrapover design affords makes string bending a little easier on the guitars that carry such bridges. With most others, however, the Tune-o-matic and stop-tailpiece has established itself as an undeniable classic.

Versions of the Tune-o-matic have been used with both stud-mounted and floating setups for semi-hollow, thinline, and fully hollowbody archtop guitars. For these versions – and on some solid bodies, too, in the 1960s and early '70s – Gibson often used nylon saddles, which imparted a slightly mellower tone. The Nashville bridge was a variation on the Tune-o-matic theme, which employed a wider, heavier rectangular metal bridge base and elongated saddle slots for more extreme adjustments.

G&L Saddle-Lock Bridge > Some of the unique pieces of hardware developed in the modern era of guitar making came from the workbench of the famed father of the mass-production solidbody electric guitar: Leo Fender. After selling his company to CBS in 1965, Fender eventually moved along to Music Man guitars, then co-founded the G&L company in 1979 with former Fender colleague George Fullerton – hence, G&L, George and Leo – and, rather than retreading old pre-CBS-era Fender ground, which probably would have been a popular and financially rewarding thing to do at the time, he kept right on moving forward with the innovations for which he was already famous.

The Saddle-Lock Bridge is Leo Fender's own update of his own original design for a Fender Telecaster bridge, and takes the place of the old semi-floating steel bass plate and pickup mount arrangement on the G&L ASAT Special and Z-3 models. It is a top-mounting metal bridge unit with holes for ball-end anchoring at the back edge to eliminate the necessity for through-body stringing. But thanks to its heavy, die-cast construction and a wide notch that fits into a rout in the guitar body to anchor firmly against the wood grain, it retains the tone, sustain, and resonance of the vintage Tele bridge design, without the potential metallic ring and feedback of the plate-mounted pickup arrangement, as the G&L models carrying the Saddle-Lock have pickups mounted in the scratchplate, as on a Stratocaster. The bridge also has six individually adjustable saddles, with a tension screw at either end of the row to keep these firmly locked together once set for height and intonation in order to increase sustain and reduce tone-killing mechanical vibrations – in short, the other unique feature that gives the unit its name. All credit to the late Mr Fender for continually moving forward in his hardware design, rather than treading in the safe and no doubt lucrative water of his past successes.

Melita Synchro-Sonic Bridge > This bridge is only rarely seen on anything other than a Gretsch guitar – originals were all made in inventor Sebastiano Melita's own workshop, and it's a difficult piece to copy – but this fully adjustable design actually beat Gibson's Tune-o-matic to the punch by a full year, arriving late in 1952 and appearing on the semi-solid Duo Jet in 1953. Despite its clunky looks the Melita is actually very simple to use. Each of the six individual string saddles carries a top-mounted screw that locks it into position; to make an intonation adjustment, simply loosen the screw, slide the saddle, and tighten it down again. The Melita's stability is similar to the more famous Tune-o-matic's,

These two Gibson archtops show bridge developments that were designed to update the traditional floating bridge: a Tune-o-matic bridge on floating base (left) and a fixed wrapover bridge with trapeze tailpiece (right).

but the fact that they were mostly mounted in floating wooden bridge bases adds a further variable to their sound.

Floating Bridge > Most hollowbody electrics and many semi-hollows carry a floating bridge, a bridge that is mounted on a wooden base which in turn is not permanently attached to the top of the guitar, but held in place by the downward pressure of the strings. The performance of these depends a lot on the precision of the match between the surfaces of the bottom of the base and the top of the guitar – in other words, the accuracy of the coupling of these two pieces of wood – and, of course, the type of bridge piece that's mounted on the base.

The base itself is most commonly made of rosewood or ebony, and on guitars that have evolved from hollowbody archtop roots the one-piece bridge atop it will be made of the same material. This unit is called a 'two-piece floating bridge.' The two-piece rosewood bridge, as found on a Gibson ES-175 or ES-125TCD, for example, imparts a warmth and roundness to the tone, whereas the upmarket two-piece ebony bridge, used on the Super 400CES and L-5CES, offers a little more snap and definition, and perhaps a more immediate transference of energy into the top of the guitar. In most cases, the bridge piece, although adjustable for overall height only, is compensated to take account of each string's general intonation requirements, and of course the entire floating unit can be moved forward or backward for larger adjustments.

Many players are surprised to find a floating bridge on vintage thinline semi-solid guitars and even some solidbody models. All early Gretsch electrics carried such units, for example, even the semi-solid Duo Jets that were aiming to pass as solidbodies to rival Gibson's Les Paul, and electrics from Kay, Guild, Harmony, and plenty of others were often outfitted this way, too. In almost all cases, a floating bridge with a wooden base will impart more warmth and roundness to a guitar's tone than a steel bridge anchored right into the guitar top,

Most electric archtops have, of necessity, carried floating bridges with wooden bases, although these have been coupled with a range of bridge and saddle types.

although less sustain. One exception is the all-aluminum rocker bridge that partnered many Bigsby tailpieces; if anything, this piece usually just thins out a guitar's tone, and impedes its resonance somewhat.

Other floating bridges were complemented with all manner of otherwise standard, set-mount bridge pieces: Tune-o-matics (or similar); Gretsch's Melita; simple bar bridge or roller bridge; or the odd slotted wooden unit sometimes found on Hofner guitars, which used staggered pieces of fretwire as saddles. In all cases, the floating nature of the bridge, and its wooden base, adds a further variable to the inherent sound of the bridge piece itself, which is usually heard as an extra degree of softness or smoothness in the tone.

Interestingly, the standard bridge of semi-solid Danelectro/Silvertone guitars was somewhat the reverse of this format: a rosewood bridge piece – or one-piece saddle – mounted in a metal base plate that was screwed down to the top of the guitar.

Vibrato Bridge-Tailpiece

Aside from the obvious function of allowing the player to produce a manual vibrato, plus some more dramatic divebombing and up-bend effects on more versatile units, vibrato tailpieces also offer their own variables in energy transference, resonance, and tone as compared with set bridges and tailpieces. By and large, vibratos – by the very fact of being movable – provide a less solid connection between string and guitar body, and are therefore more likely to decouple the string's vibration from the wood of the guitar more than the average set bridge and tailpiece. The degree to which this occurs varies widely from unit to unit, and some vibratos are better than others at accounting for the loss of resonant body mass that is the inevitable result of their softer, looser connection.

Bigsby Vibrato > The first widely available vibrato tailpiece, the Bigsby Vibrato has only a limited travel for down-bends, and most players agree it lightens and thins a guitar's tone in most applications, but it does what it does pretty well, and the large fan base that has accumulated over its six-decade existence has kept it a perennial favorite. Bigsby units take the form of tailpieces that can be used with almost any separate bridge over which the strings pass from the angle of a top-mounted stop-tail or trapeze tailpiece. The simplest Bigsby types have a steel bar that rotates in bearing-loaded cups at either side of its cast aluminum frame when the arm attached to it is depressed by the player. The strings' ball ends are anchored on six grub screws inserted in this bar and wrapped backward over it on their way to the bridge, so that dipping the arm and rolling the bar forward creates a slackening of the strings over the saddles. A single, stout spring lodged between cups in the arm mounting and vibrato frame provides the pressure needed to return the bar to its original 'at-rest' position and put the guitar back in tune.

However, 'in tune' is possibly not the most accurate description, as a Bigsby can be one of the less efficient vibratos as far as return-to-pitch accuracy is concerned – although much of its performance depends upon the bridge with which it is paired, the break angle of the strings over that bridge's saddle, and the general set-up of the guitar. The two main factors involved in what you might call a Bigsby's 'flaws,' when it's working less than optimally, have to do with the strings' inadequate downward pressure upon the bridge saddles, and a tendency to hitch in the slots of those saddles, which, remember, are mounted in a bridge that's entirely separate from the vibrato unit itself. The first matter involves tone, the second, performance, and more specifically tuning stability. The two can work against each other, as well: on guitars that can handle a set-up that provides a steeper break angle over the bridge without resulting in mile-high action over the fingerboard – and thereby eke a little more resonance out of the union – the increased pressure on the saddles can render the strings even more likely to stick and fail to return to pitch.

The Bigsby company has itself sought to deal with these issues in two ways. The cast aluminum 'rocker bridge' that for a long time came with Bigsby units, and which is still available today, rocks back and forth slightly on its mounting studs to help keep the strings closer to in-tune pitch during vibrato action – and its compensated, one-piece saddle surface is slightly smoothed and 'rounded over' as well, to minimize string hitching. But it's a tonally mediocre bridge in itself, and it doesn't do anything to improve on the first of the potential flaws mentioned above. The second cure, however, addresses just that issue. Such Bigsby models as the B5 (for solidbody guitars) and B7 (for semi-acoustics) have a rolling 'tension bar' under which the strings pass on their way to the bridge, which increases the break angle over the saddles and along with it, the downward pressure of string into bridge into body. If you're a step ahead of me, however, you will already be figuring out that this 'tone cure' can sometimes increase the strings' likelihood of hitching in the saddles. So choose your poison: light tone, or potential tuning hang-ups.

But I'm being hard on the Bigsby, and I bear it no grudge. This is one cool, smooth wobbler of a vibrato, and for many musical styles and playing techniques it really is the best tool for the job. Its limited travel means you can go at it pretty heavily, with lots of emotion, without inducing seasickening dips or taking yourself right out of key, and its action is more suited than many to slight tremors of subtle shimmer. Also, it's the best sounding and functioning vibrato tailpiece that you can mount on a solidbody or semi-acoustic Gibson, Gretsch, or Guild guitar without routing out valuable wood, and that fact in itself gives it a near-monopoly for fans of the 'Big Gs.' (See Gibson Maestro Vibrola below for the Bigsby's main rival in this department.) Bigsby vibratos were frequently licensed to and branded by the other makers who used them on their guitars.

Vintage Fender Tremolo > Despite the Fender company's mislabeling of the guitar component that it originally dubbed the 'Synchronized Tremolo' – tremolo, properly speaking, being a pulsating-volume effect, whereas the slight decrease and increase of a guitar's pitch affected by such spring-loaded tailpieces is correctly named vibrato – this 50-plus-year-old design is one of the most efficient, versatile, and effective of the species. Unlike the Bigsby, which was essentially designed as an after-market component that could be

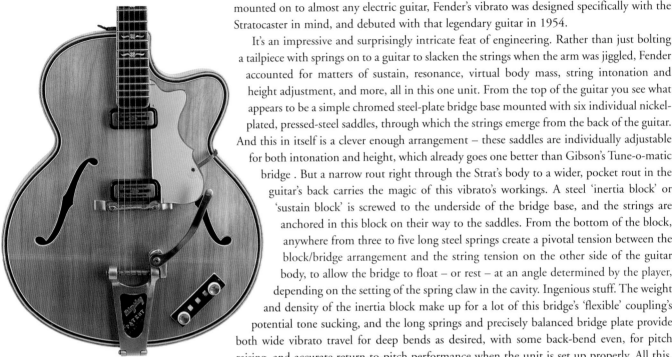

Bigsby vibratos come with (above top) and without (above bottom) a roller bar for added string tension over the bridge (note the cast-aluminum Bigsby rocker bridge in the top picture).

mounted on to almost any electric guitar, Fender's vibrato was designed specifically with the Stratocaster in mind, and debuted with that legendary guitar in 1954.

It's an impressive and surprisingly intricate feat of engineering. Rather than just bolting a tailpiece with springs on to a guitar to slacken the strings when the arm was jiggled, Fender accounted for matters of sustain, resonance, virtual body mass, string intonation and height adjustment, and more, all in this one unit. From the top of the guitar you see what appears to be a simple chromed steel-plate bridge base mounted with six individual nickel-plated, pressed-steel saddles, through which the strings emerge from the back of the guitar. And this in itself is a clever enough arrangement – these saddles are individually adjustable for both intonation and height, which already goes one better than Gibson's Tune-o-matic bridge . But a narrow rout right through the Strat's body to a wider, pocket rout in the guitar's back carries the magic of this vibrato's workings. A steel 'inertia block' or 'sustain block' is screwed to the underside of the bridge base, and the strings are anchored in this block on their way to the saddles. From the bottom of the block, anywhere from three to five long steel springs create a pivotal tension between the block/bridge arrangement and the string tension on the other side of the guitar body, to allow the bridge to float – or rest – at an angle determined by the player, depending on the setting of the spring claw in the cavity. Ingenious stuff. The weight and density of the inertia block make up for a lot of this bridge's 'flexible' coupling's potential tone sucking, and the long springs and precisely balanced bridge plate provide both wide vibrato travel for deep bends as desired, with some back-bend even, for pitch raising, and accurate return-to-pitch performance when the unit is set up properly. All this, plus string height and intonation adjustment, too… Pretty nifty.

Even when mounted in the guitar of a player who never uses it, the Fender vibrato alters the tone of the guitar somewhat from that of the hardtail, although as we see in the case of Eric Clapton and a good many other guitarists, this isn't necessarily a minus point. And the Fender unit doesn't deaden, choke, or thin out its host's tone nearly to the same degree as so many other vibratos. That inertia block does a good job of minimizing the potential for lost mass in the equation, and the six-screw connection between the front edge of the bridge plate and the top of the guitar, although both a narrow and inherently flexible – that is, not solid – coupling, does a surprisingly good job of enacting a firm, sturdy link between bridge steel and body wood. Even so, this bridge design elicits a sound that is quite different from that which a through-body bridge or stop-tail and Tune-o-matic-style arrangement would enable, and the sound of the inertia block and even the tension springs contribute an edge of compression and softness to a Strat's tone – with a hair of silky sizzle – that isn't there in a Tele's, for example. Hit a chord on a vintage-style Stratocaster, mute it, and put your ear against the plastic trem-cavity cover on the back: you can still hear those springs vibrating long after the strings are at rest. The guitar's playing feel is also a little softer and spongier thanks to these very same elements.

Working together, this bridge's chromed steel base plate and nickel-plated pressed-steel saddles yield a ringing brightness that's jacketed in decent warmth and a solid low end. In late 1971 Fender changed the saddles to chromed die-cast Mazac (an alloy of magnesium and zinc), and the steel inertia bar was replaced with one of chromed Mazac as well. The lesser density of this material versus the former steel parts brought a somewhat thinner, brighter sound to the Stratocaster bridge. Later vintage and reissue-style models returned to something closer to the original bridge of 1954–71, but players

interested in the seminal Strat tone need to check the details of these carefully to determine what they're getting.

Some more recent Fender Stratocasters have also carried an updated vibrato design known as the American Standard Vibrato or, later, the American Series Vibrato, that has been used on a variety of standard and Custom Shop models. The main differences between these and the vintage Stratocaster vibrato are seen in the block-style stainless-steel saddles and the use of two large pivot posts into which are set the knife-edge slots of the bridge base, rather than the six simple screw-style pivot posts of the older unit. These have a somewhat different sound from the vintage designs, often described by players as a distinct clarity and definition in comparison with the bridge with nickel-plated pressed-steel saddles. But the more modern designs also possess a little more warmth than the post-1971 Strat vibratos with Mazac saddles. The two-post vibratos are often considered to have a slightly smoother action and better return-to-pitch capabilities, too, although players – or techs – who know how to set up the vintage Strat units might argue the point.

Gibson Maestro Vibrola > First appearing on a variety of Gibson SG models, Firebirds, and some Epiphone guitars, the Maestro Vibrola tailpiece is even simpler in principle and performance than the Bigsby. Judging by the number of vintage guitars from which the unit has been removed, it is far less loved, too. The Vibrola is a tailpiece vibrato that acts, like the Bigsby, in conjunction with a separate bridge. It consists of a steel base plate with a flat bottom and concave top screwed flush to the body of the guitar, on to which is hooked a curved steel plate piece with string anchor slots and vibrato arm, which acts as both tailpiece and simple spring. Depressing the vibrato arm bends the curved steel piece downward and slackens the strings, and releasing it returns them to pitch – in theory, at least.

The units are solid enough structurally when not in use to provide a decent string anchor and therefore good downward pressure at the bridge, but they are perhaps a shade less stable than an immovable stop-tail. Their real problem seems to arise when the arm is in use, and as straightforward as the design appears on paper, the Maestro Vibrola frequently has real trouble returning to pitch consistently enough to enable stable tuning. A few players swear by these units, but I'd guess that far more have had trouble with them rather than success over the years. Upmarket Gibsons, such as the more deluxe reverse Firebirds, used Vibrolas

Fender continues to use the classic original vintage tremolo, as seen laid bare above. More recent Stratocasters have used the unit with knife-edge slots (top middle), while older guitars and vintage-reissue-style Strats have six-screw pivot posts (top left).

with Tune-o-matic bridges, whereas more standard models used them behind the simple wrapover bridge, which was held in position in its stud bolts by the strings' downward pressure. The latter arrangement allowed the player simply to restring the bridge wrapover style, and lift the curved-steel vibrato piece from its base block. (Pete Townshend's Gibson SG Specials of the late 1960s and early '70s usually appeared either with a partly disassembled Vibrola or just three screw holes in the body where the thing had previously been mounted.) Because of the flat design of the Vibrola's base, these vibratos were only ever mounted to flat-topped electric guitars, and never to carved-top models like the original-style Les Paul.

Floyd Rose > This seminal double-locking-style vibrato, and others of its type, became popular in the wake of Eddie Van Halen's extreme divebombing maneuvers of the late 1970s. For a time, the deep-bend effects and impressive return-to-pitch stability afforded by these units were requisites of heavy rock, and it seemed like few lead guitarists of the genre could do without a Floyd, or Kahler, or some maker-licensed version of the same.

These heavily re-engineered designs were revolutionary not for their inherent sound but for the sounds and styles they enabled. They were – and still are – pretty complex affairs compared with the Strat-style vibratos they followed, and required a lot of moving parts to do their job. To simplify, so called double-locking vibratos lock down the string at both ends (ball end and nut) for increased stability. They are also designed with a much wider travel than standard, and can usually take the strings from entirely slack to an up-bend of up to five semi-tones or so. The fact that the strings are clamped at both the nut and the saddle, however, means restringing and even retuning can be a hassle – although fine-tuners at the saddles enable simple adjustments of a semi-tone or so in either direction – and they can be extremely complex to set up, so players who aren't going to use them a lot usually don't favor these types of vibratos.

Floyd Roses and some other locking vibratos have a reputation for being either thin or bright sounding or both, but correctly installed and set up well they are mostly pretty neutral. Because the kinds of guitars that carry them are usually used for heavy, high-gain distortion sounds, tonal considerations here will usually be assessed with the amp's lead channel on. A player's decision to Floyd or not to Floyd will usually have more to do with its functionality than its sound: there was a time when, if you needed that double-locking performance, you fitted that double-locking vibrato, period.

These days, however, there are some non-locking options in smooth-functioning dual-pivot-post vibratos with wider travel than the Vintage Strat and good return-to-pitch tuning stability. The Wilkinson VS100 is one of the best-known of the breed, and it offers a less fussy design and greater ease of stringing and tuning than the Floyd/Kahler camp, with very similar results. The wide availability of locking tuners, GraphTech, or other varieties of friction-reducing nuts to use with this and other vibratos has also minimized the necessity for a locking nut, which has always been one of the real sticking points of the double-locking system for many players.

PRS Vibrato > While many heavy rockers were wanging away on their double-locking setups, Paul Reed Smith was making great strides toward improving the vintage Strat-style vibrato by addressing its two main drawbacks, which involved smoothness of action and tuning stability. At the tailpiece end, the PRS system – originally made by Mil Com – employed a smoother cast-steel base design, stainless-steel saddles, and an inertia block that had the string ball-end seats positioned deeper into the steel from the back of the guitar to reduce the potential for stretching and twisting at the dead string length behind the saddle. Also, crucially, the six pivot posts were notched to receive the knife-edge-fine holes in the base plate and yield an ultra-smooth travel.

PRS also recognized, as did the double-locking brigade, that a big part of a vibrato's efficiency has to do with the hardware at the other end of the neck, but it achieved efficiency there without the use of a locking nut. A friction-reducing graphite-style nut partnered with locking tuners to provide impressively slick action at the headstock coupled with excellent stability. When these guitars first became widely available, many players who had wrestled with vintage Strat vibratos for years – and perhaps never encountered a tech who could set one up properly for them – were amazed by how well these non-locking vibratos functioned and stayed in tune. Soundwise, these are in the vintage Strat vibrato camp, but arguably with a little more sustain – but, of course, it's very difficult to make an apples-to-apples comparison here, because none of the PRS models to which these are fitted are exactly like a pre-1971 Fender Stratocaster.

Fender Jazzmaster/Jaguar Floating Tremolo > I'm not sure how this unit 'floated' any more than most others. Despite heavy promotion of these by Fender as a great advancement in tremolo [sic] design when introduced in 1958, posterity tells us the Jazzmaster – and later Jaguar – vibrato unit was actually a step backward from the efficient unit on the Stratocaster. It certainly has some of the smooth action that was frequently boasted about in advertisement copy, but the fact that strings often hitched in the grooved bridge slots meant that tuning stability often wasn't fantastic. The bridge was supposed to rock with the vibrato action, but usually didn't go all the way back and forth with the strings' travel, so there was still an element of saddle friction to contend with as with any separate bridge-and-tailpiece vibrato like the Bigsby, and that extended length of dead string between the bridge and tailpiece didn't help matters either.

More to the point the Jazzmaster/Jaguar vibrato is tonally mediocre in most circumstances. The combination of the multitude of moving parts – which again included a rocking bridge – and a very low break angle over the saddles contributed to a thin and often slightly deadened tone, with some buzzing at extremes. These guitars can be extremely short on sustain, too. All of this seemed to go over pretty will with the surf crowd in the late 1950s and early '60s, where the percussive, staccato sound was all a part of the guitar instrumental's vibe, and the punk, new-wave, and indie/alternative players who took them up again in the late 1970s and beyond didn't raise many objections either. But players more conscious of tonal purity have occasionally been frustrated with these models, and sometimes even sought to address their shortcomings. One proven means of doing so is embodied in an after-market part called the Buzz Stop, a base plate with string-tension bar that bolts down to the Jazzmaster-style tremolo using two of the unit's existing screws. This greatly increases downward pressure in the bridge saddles, and improves these guitars' tone – and puts an end to buzzes – as a result. Of course with the similar roller-bar Bigsby models, the increased friction at the saddles risks an increase in string-hitching and therefore tuning instability when the vibrato is in use.

A wide variety of other types of vibratos exist. Some were seen regularly for a particular period of a maker's history – for example, the Burns vibratos used on Gretsch guitars for part of the 1960s, or the 'sideways vibrato' of early 1960s Gibson SG/Les Pauls – and others were one-model designs. Either way, few other than those detailed above ever came into wide enough use to establish themselves as what we could consider the 'tonal templates' of the

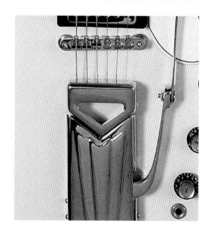

Top to bottom > Gibson Maestro Vibrola on a Firebird; Burns vibrato, as also used briefly by Gretsch; Gibson's 'sideways' vibrato system

The Floyd Rose vibrato (above) is the divebombing rocker's favorite, while Fender's Jazzmaster/Jaguar vibrato (near right) epitomizes smooth surfy wobbles. The PRS vibrato system (far right) brings improved return-to-pitch abilities to the classic Fender format.

vibrato world. Some functioned quite well, however, and even sounded pretty good. There were also the genuine oddballs, the gadgety vibrato that appeared on some beginner-level Gretsches such as the Corvette, for example, which was really just a clamp with a stubby arm that bolted on to the strings between the bridge and the trapeze tailpiece. Other reasonably smooth, decently functional designs were used by the likes of Mosrite, Hagstrom, Guyatone, National, Teisco, and their ilk. However, the vast majority of makers today that include vibratos on their guitars use a design purchased, licensed, or copied from one of the major models that we have already discussed.

NUTS

This little component at the start of the fingerboard plays an important role in the transference of the strings' vibrational energy into the wood of the guitar – and, therefore, in setting the tonal template for the instrument – but of course it has more to say in the sonic mélange when you're playing open strings than it does when you're fretting a string. During playing at any of the frets up the neck, however, the nut's condition and performance still contribute greatly to a guitar's tuning stability, if not so much to its tone.

A number of different materials can be used in a perfectly good sounding nut. Many of the quality options will all still sound just a little different, of course, but at the same time they will all sound better than inferior materials such as light plastic, the hollow plastic that is sometimes used, aluminum, or other soft, low-density materials that surface from time to time. Ivory nuts turn up on older acoustic instruments, but the most common 'vintage' nut for electrics will generally be made from bone. This has a little less density than ivory, but still provides a firm, well-defined sound with good resonance and plenty of brightness, if not quite the same degree of highs. Trademarked manmade materials such as Tusq and Corian make excellent modern replacements for bone, although genuine bone nuts are still plentiful, and offer very similar sonic performances. Keep in mind that genuine bone, being an organic material, comes in a wide variety of densities and degrees of porousness anyway, so there's no such thing as a consistent, universally quantifiable sound for a bone nut. For this reason, many manufacturers and repairmen alike prefer to work with manmade nut blanks, which allow a degree of consistency.

Many players, and those who use tremolo/vibrato arms in particular, like graphite nuts of various sorts for their ability to let strings glide back into place in the nut-slots, and therefore aid accurate tuning retention. A 'slick' nut might sound like a real tone killer, but, in fact, these types generally have very good density and transfer string resonance very well. Some players believe they even offer a warmer tone than bone or manmade bone substitutes.

Whichever of these preferred materials a nut is made from, the solidity of its seat in the neck is a crucial factor in its ability to perform tonally, and the condition of its slots are equally important in helping you avoid string hitching and tuning instability.

Another nut design that is more than 'just a nut' is that used in the Buzz Feiten Tuning System. Guitarist and inventor Feiten developed a compensated nut design that, put simply, uses staggered string slots to account for the fact that ordinary guitars very rarely can be intonated to perfect pitch, even when they carry staggered adjustable bridge saddles. It's a simple theory, but an effective one, and it has won praises both from many pro players and from some high-end manufacturers, Anderson Guitarworks for one, that use the system as standard.

Finally, a nut that isn't a nut, the zero fret is an alternative to the traditional nut used by some makers – Gretsch used a zero fret for a time, as did Framus, Hofner, Kramer, and National – mainly in the 1960s and early '70s. As it sounds, the format employs an extra fret in the 'zero' position just in front of a string-retaining nut that is used for string spacing and break-angle point only, but does not need to be cut precisely for speaking-length termination point because the zero fret is performing that job for it. The theory seems sound, and the practice gives open notes the same form of termination point at the neck end as fretted notes, but most respected contemporary makers have shunned the technique.

FRETS

When a guitar string is held down against the fingerboard the fret takes over from the nut as the anchor point that determines the speaking length of that string, and therefore in transmitting the vibrational energy into the neck and body wood of the guitar. While a great many variations in materials will affect the sound of almost every other component on a guitar, however, the shape and condition of your frets is likely to be of more concern than the steel from which they are made. Contemporary fret wire is commonly made from only two different materials: the traditional steel alloy that contains approximately 18 per cent nickel-silver – also called German silver – a silver-free alloy of nickel and copper; and the less traditional stainless steel. The former is in far wider usage, although stainless steel seems to be growing in popularity, being used as standard by a small number of makers, including Parker and John Suhr, and is a custom or refret option from other makers and repair shops.

Traditional nickel-silver frets are actually quite a soft steel, and can't be relied upon to last the lifetime of a played guitar. They have evolved as a compromise between tone and durability, and being the standard they really do hold a tonal monopoly as far as classic recorded guitar sounds are concerned, and it is thus a little pointless to try to describe 'the nickel-silver fret sound' in light of all of the other variables at play on any given guitar. Frets obviously need to be sound and well seated to do their best vibration-transference work, and they need to retain an adequate depth of divot-free crown surface to be serviceably playable. Beyond matters of age, stability, and condition, the size of fret wire – its width and height, or, taken together, its profile – will be the only slight tonal variable at play here. The three broad categories of fret profile are narrow, medium, and wide (or jumbo).

Many players are convinced that fatter wire equates with fatter tone, and there could be some logic here, considering that more metal in any fixed component usually means a greater vibrational coupling between string and guitar. Players such as Stevie Ray Vaughan, Kenny Wayne Shepherd, Rory Gallagher, and plenty of others have been known for preferring wide frets on their Fender Strats, but in many cases this is a feel thing as much as a sound thing, and wider frets are indeed easier to bend without choking out. Wider frets also present somewhat more blurred, less distinct noting than narrow frets – all this under a powerful microscope, if you will, in tonal terms, but that's what we're here for – which are more precise and can yield more shimmering harmonics. So you have to weigh the way the fret allows the string to determine pitch and to vibrate, against the way it might or might not transfer additional energy into the neck wood, against the way it bends and feels to the finger when played. In the end, the feel thing probably matters most to more players – followed closely by the 'that's the way SRV had his guitar' factor.

Stainless-steel frets, although extremely rare until recently, are in wide enough circulation now to be considered a second standard of sorts. The same considerations of profile and feel apply here of course, but stainless-steel fret wire certainly does wear a lot better than nickel-silver fret wire, and it can be expected to last a lot longer under comparable playing conditions. They also feel a little harder and slicker under the fingertip, which some players like and others don't. Some makers and players claim stainless-steel frets give a guitar a harder, harsher sound than nickel-silver frets, but many other respected luthiers will tell you that's anything from 'nonsense' to 'negligible.' In the end, the feel thing will once again probably sway players to or away from stainless steel more than any other single factor, coupled by their willingness to pay the extra cash required to install and/or service these much harder frets.

TUNERS

A tuner's main job is to, well, do its job: to wind forward or backward smoothly and efficiently to put a string in tune, and to stay where you leave it. Tuners do make their own contribution to the tonal palette, however, and many insightful guitar makers select them not only for their ability to function, but for their weight and resonance qualities, too. There are two opposing schools of thought regarding tuner weight. Many say that heavier tuners or tuner buttons mean increased mass at the headstock and, as a consequence, increased sustain; others say that a lighter headstock allows the guitar to resonate more, and that increasing the mass at that end of the guitar just soaks up the acoustic energy rather than transferring it to where it matters. In the latter camp you'll find Robert Benedetto and a handful of other very well-respected makers; in the former, Aspen Pittman, who swears by his Fat Finger device, which adds mass at the headstock to increase resonance and sustain, the same kind of thing countless players also sought to achieve by replacing the original Kluson tuners on their Les Pauls with heavier Grovers.

In the end, a lot depends on where you want the vibrations to go, and what you want them to achieve. Each practice yields different results, but those same results might mean different things to different players. Using lighter tuners to let more of the vibrational energy run down the neck toward the body might benefit some tones – particularly the more acoustic tones of a semi-hollow or hollowbody archtop electric – while increasing the ring at the headstock end might accentuate sounds desired by other players. Be aware that the difference exists, and that changing tuners won't always just alter the mechanical function of those six bits of hardware, but can change the tone of your guitar as well.

SCALE LENGTH

You could actually call this an 'invisible' component of any guitar's makeup. Scale length is a major factor of any guitar's design and, while most of us recognize a difference between the playing feels of different scales, each also has a different sound. This component of guitar design is often overlooked by players, although, it is to be hoped, not by designers and makers. At best, a player might have a subconscious awareness of the effect of scale length in his or her preference for, say, a Les Paul over a Stratocaster, but that choice is often made even without the full awareness of what's at the heart of it. Sure, being a set neck guitar with humbuckers, a Les Paul sounds different from a Strat – a bolt-on-neck guitar with single-coils – for reasons other than scale length, but it surprises many players to learn that the Strat's 25½" scale actually contributes to the instrument's bright, harmonically complex sound even before you plug the thing in, just as the Les Paul's 24⅝" scale contributes to its overall warmth and fatness.

Here's a simple way of getting a notion of what scale length does for a guitar's sonic character, regardless of any considerations for playing feel. Pick up whatever guitar you have handy, electric or acoustic, and place your finger lightly on the low E string directly over the fifth fret to play the harmonic there (a pick will bring out this harmonic more easily, and aid you in the rest of the exercise). Now run your finger down slowly from the fifth fret all the way to the nut, holding it lightly on the string and picking up and down constantly as you go. The notes produced here – which will be surprisingly pronounced in certain positions, even between frets – make up what is called the 'harmonic series.' Note that there are dead spots between these harmonics called nodes that get more closely packed as you approach the nut, and note also how the harmonics rise in pitch even though your finger is descending the string.

If you are fortunate enough to have a second guitar of a different scale length, try the same procedure with it, and notice that a guitar of a longer scale length will produce clearer, more ringing harmonics in this fifth-fret-to-nut region while that of a shorter scale will have slightly duller harmonics here, and more tightly packed nodes. Harmonics are produced in varying degrees, at various pitch relationships, every time we play a note on the guitar. Their spacing is determined by the scale length of the instrument, so scale length likewise contributes greatly to the core sound of any guitar. All guitars have these harmonics and nodes, but the string tuned across a longer scale length stretches them out, while the shorter scale length packs them more tightly together. The longer scale length gives a string's harmonics a little more room to 'breathe,' if you will, between the dead-sounding nodes, lets them ring a little more clearly, and therefore yields a tone that is more harmonically complex, characteristically more 'chiming,' 'shimmering,' you choose your own favorite adjective. This might sound universally desirable, but sometimes all that harmonic shimmer can get in the way of warmth, body, and power, and the relatively shorter scale length will be many players' choice for achieving specific sonic goals.

So much of any guitar's tone starts with the vibration of a string, and that string's composition, its length, the way it has been plucked, and so forth are among the least considered details of many a player's tone quest. If the harmonics that we are speaking of here aren't present in a string's vibration, whether or not you're even plugged in, nothing can add exactly the same sorts of harmonic elements to the sound further down the chain. Certainly different amplifiers will contribute their own harmonic sheen and help to generate overtones as products of distortion, heard even in what we think of as 'clean' sounds, but they still can't add the exact same types of harmonics found in the sound of string-generated harmonics. Likewise, if the harmonic brew is too much for your desired sound, it can be difficult to remove the harmonics from the sound without simply muddying it up or overcompensating by lowering the amp's treble and/or advancing the bass, and therefore just dulling out rather than warming up your sound.

The two most popular scale lengths are usually thought of broadly as 'the Fender scale' (25½″) and the Gibson scale (24⅝″ – often quoted as 24¾″, although it's actually a little shorter than that). Because these two makers have also established the two most copied designs for electric guitars – or four if you also bring in the Telecaster and the ES-335 – the majority of instruments tend to follow one or the other of these established scales. Others certainly exist, however: both Paul Reed Smith and Danelectro/Silvertone use a 25″ scale length, as do many high-end archtop jazz guitars made today, including those made by Robert Benedetto. Fender Jaguars and Mustangs were made to a 24″ scale, while many smaller 'student' guitars have been made to 22″ or 22½″ scales.

While we have seen how scale length affects tone considerably, the feel factor should not be ignored. As I said near the top of this entry, more players are likely to give consideration to scale length for reasons of feel than for reasons of sound – or, to be honest, because the set-neck, humbucker-loaded guitar they want just happens to have X scale rather than Y – and that's certainly a valid consideration. The shorter the scale, the easier it is to fret and bend

strings. On the other hand, longer scales that have to be tuned up to a greater tension to reach pitch have a firmer feel, often a more precise pitch when set up right, and won't be thrown briefly out of tune when you whack the strings hard. Either way, since a guitar's feel inspires our playing just as much as its sound, this is an important consideration to keep in mind, even though this book's mission is to examine the sonic variables at play in electric guitars.

BODY DESIGN

It's obvious to most players that – all consideration of woods aside – solidbody guitars will sound different than semi-hollows, but even the shapes and proportional dimensions of otherwise similarly constructed guitars can have an effect on their tone. I won't go into this in great detail here. For one thing, we'll cover most discernible aspects of this variable in following chapters when specific types and models are discussed; for another, this is a factor that's difficult to quantify in absolute terms. Generally, however, be aware that body thickness and overall mass, the directness or indirectness of the coupling of different body parts – laminates of wood in a multiwood body, top and back plates on a semi-solid, the body 'wings' on some designs – and the placement of such crucial items as the bridge, tailpiece, and pickups within the body will all affect sonic factors: resonance, sustain, and overall tone.

You might think that a slab of alder, for example, of approximately the same weight and size would yield a guitar sounding pretty much the same whether it was cut into a double-cutaway or single-cutaway shape, a V, a rectangle, a body with exaggerated horns, an offset modern shape, or what have you. But many guitar makers have identified nuances between the characteristic sounds of the shape of a Strat and a Tele body, that of a Flying V and an Explorer, that of a single-cutaway Les Paul Junior and a double-cutaway model, and so forth. Certainly, the greater amount of body wood in contact with the neck in a single-cut design will contribute to a sound that's different from the lesser amount in contact with the neck in

Elements of body design – such as the number and shape of cutaways, the position of the neck-body joint, and, perhaps more obviously, wood thickness – all play a part in shaping a guitar's voice.

Left to right > Fender Stratocaster, Fender Telecaster, Gibson Flying V, Gibson Explorer, Gibson SG, Gibson Les Paul Junior

a double-cut design, but even beyond that it seems the differing lengths and protrusions and concentrations of wood density throughout the body also play their part in shaping the way that body emphasizes specific frequencies.

Of course, we have few opportunities to try this out for ourselves in a like-for-like comparison, where body woods, pickups, and all other hardware are the same, the only variable being the shape of the wood. Comparing the single- and double-cut Les Paul Juniors and Specials might be one opportunity; the same could be done with the hardtail Strat-type and Tele-type guitars of some makers, especially those who use Strat-type pickups in their Tele-type bridge positions, and don't employ the traditional Tele-type bridges with integral pickup mounting, which itself plays such a big part in the sound of an original Fender Telecaster. It's worth experimenting if you get the chance, however, because the differences can be considerable. In comparing Telecaster-type guitars with Stratocaster types, if you can eliminate enough of the other variables to make the exercise even worthwhile, you will often find that those Strat body horns that appeared so modern and stylish in 1954 also contribute to a lot of resonance and a pretty rich tonality, as against the Tele's snappy, defined voice. In the end, we probably just need to take the word of those thoughtful makers who claim this as a significant variable. Either way, once again, players are likely to select a body shape and basic criteria involving looks and feel, rather than any discernible sonic factors, even when they do put some serious thought into elements such as wood tone.

NECK DESIGN

This is a little more quantifiable than body design, because more comparable examples exist of guitars with similar components and styles but different neck formats. Having already discussed the tonal properties of different woods used in neck and fingerboard construction, we are now talking bolt-on versus set necks. The former are usually not actually bolted on, of course, but screwed on, while set necks are those permanently glued to the body – or semi-permanently, in the case of some SGs and ES-125s. For the purposes of generalization, we can also include neck-through-body designs in the set-neck category, although there are further subtle differences between the sound and response of glued-neck and one piece neck/body-center designs.

As might be expected, glued-in or through-body necks transfer the resonance between neck and body more freely and immediately than do screwed-on necks. The result is usually heard as a little more warmth and fullness in the set-neck guitar, and a little more snap and twang in the screwed-on instrument. The lesser, slower transference of acoustic energy from the non-glued neck yields a little more pop and attack from the string – in essence, it decouples the strings from the body a little more – whereas the more efficient, more thorough transference of energy through the various parts of the set-neck guitar yields a thicker, juicier voice.

How efficiently the energy is transferred has to do with the quality of the neck join in bolt-on guitars. There are makers out there who believe that a well-executed bolt-on neck can achieve the vibrational coupling and therefore much of the resonance and tone of a set neck. Among the critical elements of this type of construction are an extremely tight neck-in-pocket fit, and very often the exclusion of any finish in the neck pocket itself. On the other hand, not all guitarists want their bolt-on guitars to sound like set-neck guitars, and the sound introduced by that slight decoupling of neck and body is a desirable and positive element in certain styles of playing.

It is partly coincidental, it seems, that so many other aspects of each of these two systems also emphasize the fat/warm, bright/snappy dichotomy of the classic Gibson versus Fender voice: the different pickups, body, and neck woods, hardware, and other ingredients of a Les Paul or a Stratocaster all contribute to differentiating further these designs. Although many makes available today blend the two – notably many PRS models, a broad range of 'super-Strat' designs available from near-countless makers, some models from such makers as Tom Anderson, Don Grosh, John Suhr, and others – the classic templates tend to run either toward the fat and warm or the bright and twangy polarities.

Another factor of neck design that will affect a guitar's tone is angle of the headstock, namely whether it is parallel to the fingerboard or points away from it at a downward angle. Both affect the break angle of the strings over the nut, and the amount of downward pressure the strings exert in the nut slots. The nuances of this will be covered in greater detail as individual models are discussed, but this is yet another detail that is readily divided along Gibson versus Fender lines. The classic Fender headstock is parallel to the plane of the fingerboard, if slightly lower to it, and in order to create enough downward pressure in the nut slots for good, clean string vibration a 'string tree' is used to pull down the highest two strings at a sharper break angle (sometimes a pair are used, one for the E and B strings and another for the G and D strings). Some modern makers using the Fender-type headstock use tuners with staggered post heights to achieve this break angle; the tuners for higher strings have increasingly shorter posts, and therefore pull the strings down at sharper angles. Gibson headstocks, on the other hand, are raked downward from the plane of the fingerboard, so that the strings break down over the nut at an angle, but still run approximately parallel to the face of the fingerboard. Both templates produce satisfactory results when done correctly, but they do have slightly different effects on the transference of vibrational energy into the neck.

PICKUPS

I can almost hear some readers shouting, "Yes, *finally*! Now we're getting somewhere!" The magic tonal properties of certain pickups have become almost a religion with many players, and an industry has been born out of guitarists' desires to alter their tone by swapping this single component. Certainly swapping pickups can result in one of the most dramatic and immediate alterations of tone of any single-component swap on the entire guitar – other than a complete neck or body transplant. Changing pickups can result in considerable increases in gain, or dramatic voice shifts from bright and thin to fat and dark, or just subtle but discernible improvements that might only be heard by the players themselves as shadings or nuances: changing a decent stock Strat single-coil for a vintage replica from a reputable maker, swapping early 1970s Gibson humbuckers for accurate reproductions of late-1950s PAFs, for instance. Whether the results are earthshaking or barely noticeable, it goes on a lot, so we can reasonably conclude that a pickup's contribution to a guitar's overall sound and character is by now an accepted fact of guitardom.

It's still important to remember, however, that a lot of a guitar's sound is shaped even before the pickup picks it up. If, because of the very parameters of its design and construction, a guitar has very little brightness or warmth in its tonality when played

unplugged, swapping for notoriously 'bright' or 'warm' pickups to induce a desired sonic shift won't achieve the expected results, or will at best only ever be partly successful. Also, it's useful to keep in mind that makers that were successful early on in the era of the electric guitar generally used whichever of one or two pickup types were their current in-house designs, and bolted those into pretty much every guitar they manufactured at that time. They had often put some thought into these pickups, certainly, but they rarely voiced them for the specific guitar. (Fender is a rare exception to this: by the late 1950s the company had two different pickups on the Telecaster, another different pickup on the Strat, and new pickups on the Jazzmaster and Musicmaster.) Contemporary makers, on the other hand, usually go to great lengths to match pickups to guitar designs from hundreds of available options to fine-tune the desired sonic results. This, of course, is partly because makers can pick and choose from pickups that emulate the designs and sounds of the products of more than 50 years' worth of electric guitar history, plus the countless hotrod variations that have taken these as their springboards over the past few decades. All of which takes us back where we started: there are a lot of pickups out there today; it's worth learning a little about some of the basic differences between the classics and the most popular types, but it would be impossible to discuss all types and models in any depth. Fortunately, the vast majority of pickups available still follow just a few longstanding templates, with, perhaps, some modifications to make them stronger, brighter, smoother, or whatever else has been widely desired by guitarists.

Players and some manufacturers generalize about pickups' power, or output, in terms of 'DC resistance,' which, in fact, is determined purely by the number of wraps and gauge of wire wound in the coil. This reading is measured in ohms on a specially designed meter, although the measurement is not usually included in a pickup's specifications. A higher resistance reading is usually considered to indicate a more powerful and darker pickup, a

The types of pickups fitted and their mounting formats contribute to making guitars from the same manufacturer sound very different from one another. **Left to right** > four Fenders with a variety of pickups and pickup mountings: an early-1960s Stratocaster; a late-1960s Paisley Telecaster; a 1959 Jazzmaster; a late-1950s Duo Sonic

lower resistance a weaker and brighter pickup. A pickup's DC resistance can correspond to these characteristics, but they are not necessarily a result of it. DC resistance is the measurement of the pickup's coil when not in use, or in other words, when the guitar isn't being played. When the pickup is being played, and the strings' vibrations are effecting the magnetic field, the coil is generating an AC signal, and its DC resistance changes as a result. Different pickups with approximately the same DC resistance react differently in use, so this measurement only takes you so far. Still, it has become a relative guideline to pickup strength, and often players aren't given much else to go on.

Other factors at play include magnet type and strength, the shape and positioning of the pickup's coil – whether, for example, it's tall or wide, close to the strings or further away – and the design as a whole. A pickup's AC impedance and its resultant inductance, measured in Henries, say more about how it sounds than its DC resistance, and the relationship between inductance and magnet strength is a prime factor. Also, resonant frequency can be of use in at least ball-parking a pickup's basic voice. When being used with the average guitar cord (lead), most guitar pickups have a resonant frequency in the 2,000Hz to 5,000Hz range. At the lower end of this range, pickups translate a darker sound, and at the higher end they can verge on sounding harsh and brittle. About midway between these extremes you get decent brightness combined with good body. There's also a lot of talk about alnico magnets versus ceramic magnets. Few tone hounds are happy with anything but the former, while plenty of heavy rockers use pickups employing the latter in 'high gain' and 'distortion' type designs.

Four different types of alnico are used for guitar pickup magnets, and they are designated with the Roman numerals II through V, differentiated according to their slightly different makeup, and thus their strength. The approximate composition is aluminum (10 per cent), nickel (18 per cent), cobalt (12 per cent), copper (6 per cent), and iron (54 per cent), but these figures vary slightly with each type, and some alnicos might also contain a little titanium and niobium, while you will often see cobalt content quoted as being up to 20 per cent with the other ingredients varying accordingly. Alnico II and V are by far the most common. The pickup made with alnico II is the weakest of these four, and has a slightly softer, sweeter sound, while the alnico V pickup is punchier and more aggressive. Alnico IV is still considered muscular, but with clear highs and less aggression than alnico V, while alnico III is rich and a little softer. Keep in mind that these comparisons are all relative, and they can also be extremely subtle – if detectable at all to some ears, depending upon other variables at play. Fender is most often quoted as having used alnico V poles in its legendary pickups of the 1950s and '60s, and these certainly don't sound 'aggressive' to many people, although they do possess a lot of clarity, punch, and twang. (I have also heard it said that Fender used alnico III early on, but I have no confirmation of that.) Gibson's original PAF humbuckers were spec'd for alnico V by their designer, Seth Lover, but, in fact, the company used whichever of the II through V stocks it could get its hands on in the early years of that component's history, so what we might think of as 'the sound of alnico X' might be coming from a differently proportioned alloy altogether. On top of this, there are a few pickup manufacturers who say they can make a pickup with either alnico II or alnico V and get it sounding virtually identical.

In the end, as you can see, statistics on paper won't tell you very much about how different pickups sound. You really have to listen to them, or to guitars in which they are installed, or talk to a reliable source who has done so.

Single-Coils > The single-coil pickup is the simplest and oldest of magnetic transducer designs, yet it continues to be the preferred choice of many guitarists today, and makers continue to develop new variations on many of the classic themes, plus some entirely fresh designs as well. This self-descriptive unit consists of a magnet or magnets (in the singular, a magnet in contact with separate steel polepieces or a 'blade' arrangement; in the plural, an integral magnet/polepiece for each string, also known as a 'rod magnet'), with a coil of thin wire wrapped around them that generates a small AC current when the magnetic field around the polepieces is disturbed by the vibration of the steel strings. All traditional single-coil pickup designs are susceptible to hum, generated from 60 cycle AC sources, fluorescent lights, computer and television monitors, and so forth.

If we want to categorize these components according to the major manufacturers with which they are most associated, we might generally think of single-coils as being the classic Fender pickups. But Gibson's single-coil P-90 pickup was in use on a hollowbody electric guitar for a full four years before the first Fender guitar hit the market, and has been in continuous production longer than any other guitar pickup. But the pickups that evolved into the Esquire/Broadcaster/Telecaster pickups were in use by Fender in the 1940s, too, on the young company's lap-steel guitars, so it's fair to say that both companies have a longstanding pedigree in the breed. Other companies such as DeArmond (on Gretsch and Guild guitars), Danelectro, and Rickenbacker also got in on the act pretty quickly, and have pickup designs still used today whose origins go back more than 50 years. First or not, however, Fender is still the name most associated with single-coils, so let's examine the basics of that company's classic designs first.

The Telecaster bridge pickup is a tone icon, and bears a large degree of responsibility for bringing guitarists to the front of the stage – and therefore helping to give birth to rock'n'roll and contemporary country music – when it arrived on the first successful production solidbody electric guitar in 1950. This pickup consists of six alnico V magnet polepieces – which were level on early examples, but later were staggered to account for differing string outputs – a coil of between about 7,800 and 9,000 turns of insulated 42-gauge wire, and a copper-coated tin base plate that is fixed to the bottom of the bobbin in contact with the polepieces.

Compared with a Stratocaster pickup, the Tele pickup has a relatively fat coil for a single-coil, and its magnetic window is a little wider. A pickup's magnetic window – that is, the width of the region in which its magnetic field is sensitive to string vibration – plays a big part in determining its voice; specifically, a narrower window means a brighter, sharper sound, and a wider window means a fuller, darker sound. The Tele pickup is therefore a little darker and warmer than the Strat pickup, but is still a bright, incisive unit. Its base plate has the effect of raising its induction and therefore increasing its output by about ten per cent over that of a similarly wound pickup without a base plate. As discussed in the section on bridges and tailpieces above, the mere fact of mounting this pickup as a hanging assembly in the semi-floating steel Tele bridge base plate also affects the pickup's response, adding a little more metallic twang to the overall sound. Even the steel springs used to mount the pickup contribute slightly to its zingy, snappy tone – although they can also increase the feedback and microphony to some units, and players occasionally replace them with rubber grommet-style spacers. Overall, it's a gutsy, muscular pickup that still retains clear, cutting highs, and it can even surprise some humbucker players who haven't had much experience with Telecasters.

Fender's 1950s and early '60s Tele pickups were generally hotter than those of the late 1960s and the '70s. Through the 1950s in particular, they had an average of around 9,000 turns of 42-gauge wire, for a DC resistance of about 7.5k and an inductance of 3.2H. Interestingly, the two different pickups on a Telecaster make a good lesson in how DC resistance isn't always an accurate measure of a pickup's power or, indeed, its sound. Given the neck pickup's size, Fender wound it with finer 43-gauge wire to achieve a DC resistance of around 7.75k from an average of about 8,000 turns, but the pickup's inductance is only around 2.2H, and – as any Tele player will tell you – it's a weaker pickup, but sounds bright, full, and warm in its neck-mounted position. By the 1970s Tele bridge pickups were down to a DC resistance of around 6.5k or less, and an inductance not much over 2H. Fender's own Vintage Reissue guitars of the past couple of decades, Custom Shop models, and the Tele-style pickups of other manufacturers usually replicate the specs of the desirable 1950s units.

Fender's Stratocaster pickup is even more legendary, and really has become the standard type of single-coil pickup mounted by the majority of other manufacturers on just about anything other than Tele or Gibson copies. During the development of the Stratocaster in the early 1950s, Fender also saw fit to develop a tailor-made pickup voiced for the new guitar. Brightness and clarity were important considerations of the day, and these were the characteristics with which the fledgling solidbody electrics were winning some players away from the boomier, woollier sounding hollowbody electrics. The Strat pickup was an important ingredient in Fender's attainment of that goal, and it has remained a revered component.

This pickup has a coil of 42-gauge wire wound around a slightly taller, narrower bobbin

Top to bottom > Gibson's wide P-90 pickup, Fender's Telecaster bridge pickup, and the Stratocaster pickup: the three most revered single-coils of all time

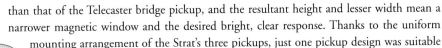

than that of the Telecaster bridge pickup, and the resultant height and lesser width mean a narrower magnetic window and the desired bright, clear response. Thanks to the uniform mounting arrangement of the Strat's three pickups, just one pickup design was suitable for all three positions. As with the Telecaster pickups, Strat pickups of the 1950s and early '60s tend to be a little stronger and warmer – averaging around 7,500 to 8,000 turns of wire for a DC resistance of around 6k and an inductance of about 2.2H – and those of the late 1960s and '70s tend to be weaker and thinner sounding. I've always thought that those too-bright Strat bridge pickups of the 1970s were a big inspiration to the whole hotrod replacement pickup market, which brought us early units like the DiMarzio SDS-1 high-output single-coil. It's worth noting that the Strat pickup's design results in a 'tall' and powerfully focused magnetic field at the top of the unit, and if positioned too close to the guitar's strings it can even pull them out of tune, introduce 'ghost notes' – a somewhat dissonant double-note effect – or generally deaden the sound of some strings.

When the Strat pickup was developed, loud, clean, clear sounds were a primary design goal, and makers didn't want guitars to overdrive amps. In the bridge position, a standard Strat pickup usually won't do so until you get a tube amp really cranked up, but because of its positioning – which introduces a fuller, warmer sound from the strings – the neck pickup yields a bigger, ballsier sound that will start to crunch up at the amp a little quicker, and it has become the real favorite of blues players seeking that warm-but-hot, edge-of-breakup sound. With the flick of a switch, the exact same pickup positioned near the bridge elicits extremes of snap, sparkle, and twang. As with Tele pickups, current reproductions either from Fender or other makers usually emulate the slightly more powerful, tonally superior pickups of the 1950s. They also frequently go to lengths to duplicate the Stratocaster pickup's staggered polepieces – a feature that was originally included as an improvement on the Telecaster's flat poles, and which soon followed on the Tele itself – and the beveling of the tops of the polepieces. Fender most likely ground the beveled edge into the tops of its magnet slugs to make it easier to insert them into the fiber bobbin, and it's inconceivable that the removal of a fraction of a gram of alnico from each of these polepieces would make a difference in tone, but vintage Strat fanatics wouldn't have their pickups made any other way.

There are other Fender pickups, but the Gibson P-90 deserves more prominent attention than any of these, thanks both to its status as the longest-serving single-coil design and its resurgent popularity in recent years. It appeared in 1946 on such guitars as the ES-300 and ES-150, and in 1949 on the more enduring ES-175. The P-90 is constructed with a relatively wide, flat coil of 42-gauge enamel-coated copper wire wound to approximately 10,000 turns around six adjustable, threaded steel fillister-head screw polepieces, beneath which are positioned two alnico bar magnets held in place by a bottom plate. P-90s come either with plastic or metal 'dog-ear' covers (which have triangular mounting tabs positioned at the ends of the covers) or 'soapbar' covers (which have holes between the A/D and G/B polepiece pairs for the insertion of mounting screws). The threaded polepieces allow some degree of minor adjustment for string balance, but are not designed to afford major increases in string output.

These are powerful pickups when compared with Fender single-coils, and – although we have already agreed that this isn't an absolute standard of pickup measurement – they often have an equal or greater DC resistance to vintage-style Gibson humbuckers (discussed below), with readings in the 7.5k to 8.2k range, with an inductance of around 7H. Their design yields a wide, low magnetic window, and therefore a fatter, warmer sound than that achieved by most taller, narrower single-coils. The combination of the adjustable steel polepieces and the magnets positioned at the bottom of the pickup assembly means that the P-90's magnetic field is relatively low, although wide, and these pickups can usually be positioned a little closer to a guitar's strings than can a Strat pickup – although with the dog-ear-style P-90s this requires plastic shims to raise the entire mounting apparatus.

The classic P-90 sound is full and aggressive, with pronounced mids, a thick bottom end, and slightly gritty highs. In the right application, and in all cases coupled with amplifiers with low-gain front ends, they can be very appealing jazz pickups, but most players find they sound their best cranking out raw, gnarly rock'n'roll. The original Gibson P-90 pickups were not potted – 'potting' involves dipping pickups into a melted paraffin mixture to seal and protect the coil and components – so they are prone to microphony and some mechanical as well as sonic feedback. To an extent, that edge-of-howl status lends a wired, alive feel to the sound, and is one of the ingredients of their slightly gnarly distortion sound. For some players, however, the microphony and howl are unacceptable in big-gig situations; they either get their old P-90s potted, or buy replacement units from makers who routinely pot their products.

Even before the P-90 was making much of a splash in rock'n'roll circles, the DeArmond 200 – also known as the Gretsch Dynasonic – as used on Gretsch hollow archtop and semi-solid guitars was setting a tonal standard in the new hormone-fired music of American youth of the 1950s. These pickups may look like mini-humbuckers, with one row of six slug polepieces and another row of irregularly spaced screws, but the latter are, in fact, the adjustment screws for the alnico poles. Very fine 44-gauge wire is used to wind the coils, for a relatively high DC resistance of around 8.5k and an inductance of approximately 3.5H. Its fat alnico slug polepieces, however – which are wider than those of Strat or Tele pickups – help to brighten what would otherwise be a dark pickup, and the overall tonal result is a unit with punchy mids and crisp, snappy highs. It can be surprising to discover how much twang and sparkle these pickups will elicit from a hollowbody guitar such as a Gretsch 6120, but they also deliver a pretty full-bodied sound overall, with a good deal of richness and warmth.

Opposite > Gibson's 'dog-ear' P-90s in an ES5 archtop
Above top to bottom > Gibson's less-often seen alnico V single-coil pickup; 'soapbar' P-90s in an early Gibson Les Paul

The newer DeArmond 2K pickups used on Fender/DeArmond guitars of the late 1990s and beyond look very much like Dynasonics at first glance, but they are constructed very differently, and sound different as a result. Despite their look, these pickups are very much like P-90s under the cover; their polepieces are steel slugs – not alnico magnets like the originals – which run through the bobbin to a pair of alnico V bar magnets. The coils are wound with 43-gauge wire, and the units have a DC resistance of about 7.5k and an inductance of about 6H. The result is a pickup that sounds pretty much like a P-90, too, although the 2Ks are perhaps a little brighter and not quite as thick in the mids.

Another bright pickup came in the form of the Rickenbacker 'toaster top' of the late 1950s and '60s. Although these, too, appear as if they might be humbuckers, thanks to the parallel rows of black inserts beneath their covers, they are also single-coils: lift the cover of one and you find a row of six alnico polepieces, around which is wound a coil of 44-gauge wire, although 42- and 43-gauge coils are also reported. These Ricky pickups can vary greatly, and early toaster-tops often had a DC resistance in the 5k range, while mid-1960s examples can run to anything in the 7k to 8.5k range. Their construction helps to keep them pretty bright in most instances – inductance usually seems to be around the 2.5H mark – but those with the higher resistances certainly tend to be beefier and barkier. These are a classic pickup for jangle and chime, but in the right guitar they are by no means thin or brittle sounding, and they can exhibit plenty of bite with a tube amp cranked up a little.

Before retracing our steps to look at some of Fender's B-list designs, the Danelectro Lipstick Tube pickup deserves consideration. These nifty little units – which perhaps came back into favor with some custom and repro-style guitar makers in the 1990s as much for their look as for their sound – are often ignored in the tone stakes, and they aren't powerful pickups by any means, but they can be sweet, silvery sounding units, and have contributed to some classic recordings over the years. As the name suggests and the look implies, these pickups use two genuine chromed metal lipstick-tube tops joined end-to-end, acquired by Danelectro in bulk at the time of the units' original development in the mid 1950s, to enclose an alnico bar magnet wound with a wire coil: simple, but effective.

The combination of the narrow magnetic window, the pickups' relatively low DC resistance – which is usually in the 4.25k to 4.75k range – and the alnico bar magnet give it a bright, snappy, twangy sound, but with velvety rather than harsh highs and a certain plummy richness, if not a lot of what we might technically refer to as 'balls.' As with Strat and Tele pickups, a lot of players have come to appreciate the fact that a relatively weak but balanced-sounding pickup pushing a good amplifier can yield plenty of sparkly, crunchy, harmonically saturated tones for blues and rock'n'roll playing, and good examples of lipstick-tube pickups can do all of that and more. Of course, the select compound fiber tonewoods of the guitars on which they usually appear – by which I mean the thin Masonite tops and poplar center blocks – add their own sonic variables, too.

Fender's Jazzmaster and Jaguar pickups deserve some consideration before we move on to humbuckers. The former has a wide, flattish coil of 42-gauge wire wound to about 8,500 turns around six alnico polepieces, for a DC resistance and inductance of approximately 8k and 4H respectively. They aren't as powerful as P-90s, despite the similar appearance, and aren't quite as fat and hot either, but offer a good blend of warmth – thanks in part to that wide magnetic window – and jangle. They have a roundness and a slight midrange accentuation that can push a cranked tube amp nicely, but when reigned back they offer smoother sounds.

The Jaguar pickup might look something like a Strat pickup with added steel 'claw' brackets either side, but, in fact, it was an entirely new design developed in the early 1960s for the guitar that was intended to be Fender's top-of-the-line model. These pickups used alnico polepieces, and their coils were wound with 42-gauge wire – as were all noteworthy Fender pickups other than the Telecaster neck pickup. The distinguishing brackets at the sides of the pickup covers were added to focus the magnetic field a little more tightly at the top of the pickup, and the extra steel also raises the pickup's inductance. As a result – and in spite of specs like a DC resistance of around 6.5k and an inductance of close to 3H – they are usually pretty bright, thin sounding pickups. They excel at tight, jangly tones, which was a big part of their objective.

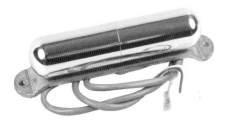

Two of Leo Fender's post-Fender developments from G&L also warrant a few words here. Having had a hand in producing half a dozen seminal pickup designs, Fender also churned out a couple more toneful and effective units for his final company. The G&L Magnetic Field Design (MFD) pickups are shaped a little like a P-90 soapbar-style pickup, but are actually made quite differently. These pickups use a ceramic magnet mounted below the coil to transfer magnetic force to six adjustable threaded steel polepieces. The strong ceramic magnets allowed Fender to design a single-coil pickup with a slightly higher output than his earlier Tele and Strat designs, but without overwinding the coil to create a dark, muddy sound. As a result, these pickups have a DC resistance of only around 4.8k to 5.3k and are bright, snappy, and full, and with relatively low noise for a single-coil thanks to their fairly high output – that is, their favorable signal-to-noise ratio. Overall, they are able to replicate closely the classic Telecaster twang – although, being pickguard mounted, they are somewhat different in nuance – but are also ballsier-sounding pickups.

G&L Z-Coils are genuine single-coil humbuckers that Leo Fender designed in the mold of his Fender Precision Bass pickups. Rather than having two side-by-side or stack coils, they are made by 'splitting' a single-coil, if you will, and winding the two small, three-pole bass and treble string coils in opposite polarity. These pickups' characteristic Z shape results from the necessity of offsetting the coils slightly to allow the windings to fit end-to-end. The Z-coils remain a true single-coil in the tonal sense, and retain the narrow magnetic window and resultant bright, harmonically rich sound of classic singles, but achieve extremely good hum rejection, too. Otherwise, they are made much like G&L MFD pickups, with ceramic magnets and threaded polepieces, and achieve a DC resistance of around 4.5k but are hotter than that reading might suggest. G&L also makes MFD-type designs to fit traditional Telecaster pickup positions for their ASAT Classic, and traditional Stratocaster positions for some Legacy models. In any case, both the soapbar and Z-coil-style MFD units prove that careful design can yield a tuneful pickup from the oft-derided ceramic magnets.

There are other single-coil designs that occasionally feature in tone history – Gibson's alnico V pickup that featured in the neck of pre-humbucker 1950s Les Paul Customs; the much-derided Gretsch HiLo'Tron; Burns Tri Sonics; Fender Mustang and Duo Sonic pickups; the budget Teisco pickups that some players, including Ry Cooder, are fond of; the fat P-90-like DeArmonds that appeared in some early Guilds – but the majority of units on the market today are based on those detailed above.

There are also a number of more powerful single-coil options available today, made with the stronger ceramic magnets and overwound coils. Through clean amps they can sound muddy and dark, but with a heavy dose of high-gain distortion, which is how they are generally intended to be used, they have all of the grind, bite, and sustain that many heavy-rock players seek. More often than not, however, hotrodded pickups using ceramic magnets will be found in the humbucking format.

Humbuckers > While the Fender single-coils and Gibson's own P-90 were successful from the start in tonal terms, the hum that these units picked up became an early annoyance to some players and designers alike. Gibson's legendary 'Patent Applied For' (PAF) humbucking pickup was developed by Seth Lover in 1955 to achieve hum elimination. The pickup doesn't, strictly speaking, eliminate hum so much as it partially cancels it out, by employing two similar but opposite-polarity coils side by side to create a reverse-phase relationship for any hum induced in the unit. When the two coils are summed – or joined together – in the coils' connection (they are usually wired in series, but can be switched to a parallel connection in some models), the two opposite-phase hum signals are canceled, but the AC signal generated by the guitar's string vibration remains, and it's the AC signal that carries the guitar sound to the amplifier.

The Gibson design – and most that followed it – doesn't totally cancel out electronic hum because the coils used in the pickup are not absolutely identical. Each produces a similar but slightly different signal – as measured in the laboratory, at least – and therefore the hum

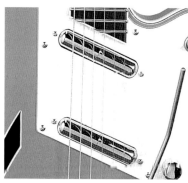

Opposite top to bottom > DeArmond 200 – AKA Gretsch Dynasonic – pickup; reissue DeArmond 2000 pickup; Danelectro 'lipstick tube' pickup
Above top to bottom > original Rickenbacker 'toaster top' single-coil pickup; Charvel pickup based on the Danelectro 'lipstick tube'

Top to bottom > Fender Jaguar single-coil pickup; Gretsch Filter'Tron humbucking pickup; Burns Tri-Sonic pickup on a Baldwin Double Six; funky single-coils on a Del Rey May Queen

signals are not a full 180 degrees out of phase. Identical coils would have the same exact sizes and types of polepieces – the PAF has adjustable steel screws in one side, and steel slugs in the other – and the exact same number of turns of wire in each coil, whereas many manufacturers' pickups of the 1950s were pretty unevenly wound. Even so, this pickup reduces hum significantly, and has been a major success since its introduction more than 50 years ago.

The wider magnetic window created by the two side-by-side coils of most humbucking pickups gives standard types an inherently fatter, thicker sound than the majority of single-coil pickups. Even when its specifications read similarly to those of a single-coil, the humbucker will generally sound bigger, warmer, and more powerful. It will also usually be less bright, too, and occasionally woollier and less tightly focused, because each of the two coils is sensing vibrations from a slightly different portion of the string, and this proximity results in the cancellation of some high harmonics within the pickpup. A player's choice of one type versus the other therefore comes down largely to tonal objectives, although most agree that less hum is desirable in any circumstance.

As mentioned above, the Gibson PAF is the granddaddy of all humbuckers, and still the standard by which all others are judged. This pickup has a rich, elegant voice with fluty mids, lacy highs, and round lows. It isn't an overly hot pickup by any means, but it is extremely fat sounding, thanks to its broad soundstage and the sonic depth and dimension presented by its wide magnetic window. Without being a high-gain pickup by any definition of the term, it is still able to drive a semi-cranked tube amp, and can offer excellent sustain in the right guitar.

The Gibson PAF and similarly styled pickups that followed, from Gibson and other makers, use a single alnico bar magnet placed at the bottom of the unit between the parallel rows of polepieces that ran through each of the two coils, one row of adjustable steel screws, the other of fixed steel slugs. Seth Lover originally specified alnico V for the magnet, but during the first few years of the humbucker's manufacture Gibson used whatever alnico bar magnets were already on hand for its P-90 single-coils – which, interestingly, used two magnets per pickup – and these could be anything from alnico II through alnico V. These variables, plus others involved in the inconsistencies of the winding process, meant that no two early PAFs tested side by side are likely to sound exactly the same. However their ingredients and construction might vary, most of them have a sonic character that's in the ballpark described above, and the fairly accurate PAF reproductions made today by Gibson and a number of other quality pickup makers follow suit.

Gibson wound each coil to a nominal 5,000 turns of 42-gauge plain enamel-coated wire, although different examples received between 5,000 and 6,000 turns. The results yielded average DC resistance for the two coils in series of around 7.5k and an inductance of 4H or a little more, but plenty of hotter PAFs exist, and some weaker ones, too. Gibson did not pot the original PAFs, so some can be susceptible to vibrational noise, squeals, and microphony – even while 'bucking hum' quite effectively – and some reproduction makers stick to the original blueprint on this matter, while others don't. Gibson itself, for example, currently pots its standard PAF reproductions, although Seymour-Duncan does not pot its Antiquity humbuckers. The nickel-silver covers on the original Gibson humbuckers raised the capacitance of the units slightly, and therefore made them sound just a little darker than they did without the covers attached, which is why many players in the 1960s and '70s removed them from their pickups. Good contemporary makers of PAF reproductions understand the big picture, however, and they wind their pickups to achieve an optimal capacitance – and, therefore, sound – once the covers were added, and you have to think that the pickup's inventor, Seth Lover, designed the unit with similar considerations in mind. Aside from issues of capacitance, the cover helps to shield the pickup from electrostatic noise, that induced by fluorescent lamps, for example, which is why Lover included them in the first place.

Gibson was finally granted its patent for the humbucking pickup in 1959, but it kept applying 'Patent Applied For' stickers to the bottoms of the units until 1962. By this point the pickups' specifications had become more consistent – alnico V was used exclusively, and the number of turns in the coil winding was standardized – and despite the change to patent number stickers in late 1962, these pickups continued to be made very much the same way for the best part of another year. The first of a handful of alterations that took Gibson humbuckers out of the hallowed PAF realm really came later in 1963, when a move from plain enamel-coated coil wire to polyurethane coated wire signaled a surprisingly noticeable change in tone. The different insulation material resulted in a different thickness, or 'build up,' as the coil was being wound, which changed the capacitance and therefore the sound of the newer pickups. This is a perfect example of what a difference the tiniest variables in construction can make in a guitar's sound: same magnet, same nominal manufacturing specs, same number of turns of 42-gauge copper wire per coil, but the difference between two different types of that extremely thin insulation could lead to a detectable difference in sound. Gibson didn't return to plain enamel-coated wire until 1990, when it designed its '57 Classic pickup.

Gibson's humbucker appeared first on steel guitars in 1956, and then on the Les Paul in 1957, by which time there was already a rival in the hum-free pickup race. At guitar legend Chet Atkins's urging, Gretsch adopted another humbucking design invented by Ray Butts as early as 1954 or '55 for its Filter'Tron pickups, introduced at the 1957 NAMM (National Association of Music Merchants) show in Chicago. (Note that this is the same Butts who built a limited number of EchoSonic amplifiers with built-in tape echo for players such as Atkins, Scotty Moore, and Carl Perkins.) The new Gretsch pickup carried a pair of side-by-side coils that were, in theory at least, more 'identical,' given that they both used a row of six adjustable threaded steel polepieces, although as ever back in the day, coil winding specs were somewhat inconsistent. The pickup carried an alnico V magnet between the bottoms of the two coils, each of which was wound with only about 3,000 turns of polyurethane coated 43-gauge copper wire for a combined DC resistance of only around 4k. Each of these two coils is narrower than those in Gibson's classic humbucker, and so is the pickup's magnetic window. As a result, in addition to being less powerful than a PAF the Filter'Tron also has sweeter highs. So, despite the move from DeArmond 200/Dynasonic pickups to the new Filter'Tron humbuckers, Gretsch guitars maintained a high twang factor with a little growl in there when played through a pushed tube amp.

Despite apparently having arrived at his humbucking pickup design along parallel but separate lines at around the same time, if not earlier, as Seth Lover had for Gibson, Ray Butts applied for his patent a little later, and was later in receiving it. Filter'Tron pickups carried no cover inscriptions in their first year, then bore the legend 'Pat. Applied For' for the following two years, and the actual patent number itself after 1960. Later in the 1970s and into the early '90s, Filter'Tron pickups were made with ceramic magnets, and while they were more powerful as a result, many Gretsch fans consider that this introduced a major departure from the classic sound of the component. In 1964 Gretsch also introduced the

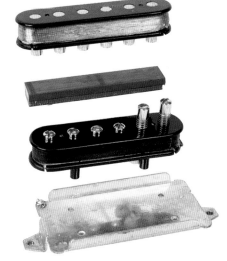

This exploded view of a Gibson PAF-style humbucker – as seen on the 1959 Les Paul Standard with factory-fitted Bigsby (top) – displays the similar, but not identical, dual-coil construction.

Super'Tron humbucker, which was a slightly more powerful version of the Filter'Tron. It was housed in a similar cover, but used a parallel pair of laminated 'blades' instead of individual polepieces, and had a DC resistance in the region of 4.5k to 5k. Super'Trons have their fans, too, but they never knocked the Filter'Tron off its throne as king of the Gretsch humbuckers.

After vanishing for much of the 1960s, the Gibson Les Paul returned first as the P-90-equipped gold-top model in 1968, then as the Deluxe in 1969, wearing Mini-Humbuckers borrowed from sibling company Epiphone. Gibson had acquired Epiphone in the late 1950s, and these small humbuckers had appeared on Epi models such as the Sheraton, Crestwood, Riviera, and Sorrento before arriving on Gibson's new Firebird line in 1963. Six years later they became the pickup of choice for the Les Paul Deluxe, which is probably the model with which they are most associated, and that for which they are most reviled. While plenty of players find them perfectly good-sounding little humbuckers, others in their thousands ripped them out of LP Deluxes to replace them with full-size PAF repros, converting their guitars into the 'LP Standards' that were absent from the Gibson catalog in the early years of the Deluxe.

These mini-humbuckers have a DC resistance in the ballpark of 6.5k to 7.5k, with an inductance of around 3H or a little over, and use the alnico bar magnets that were still in favor at Gibson in the 1960s and early '70s. Given their narrower dimensions and specs, they are a little brighter than full-size, PAF-style pickups, and plenty of players find this a good thing on a Les Paul or a Firebird, especially considering that the larger Gibson humbuckers were tending to be darker sounding by the late 1960s. Aside from their relative brightness, these pickups have a decent amount of midrange punch and bark, and tight, crisp lows. They don't drive an amp quite as hard as most full-size humbuckers – other than Gretsch's Filter'Tron, that is – but they have enough beef and body for cutting, high-gain playing with plenty of sustain.

Although the company is far and away best known for its single-coils, the Fender humbucker that was introduced on the updated Thinline model of 1971 as the 'Fender Wide Range Humbucking Pickup' is a unique design from PAF inventor Seth Lover, who had defected to Fender in 1967, and is a pretty nice-sounding humbucker in its own right. The pickup has roughly the same size and coil configuration as a PAF, but Lover used polepieces made from cunife magnets – a copper-nickel-iron alloy that is soft enough to be threaded – rather than steel poles with an alnico bar magnet beneath them. The Fender humbucker is distinguished visually by its opposing rows of three adjustable polepieces (the three bass poles being mounted in the forward coil, the three adjustable treble poles in the rearward, with the remaining six concealed beneath the cover). The unit has a DC resistance of around 10k and an inductance of 4.5H, and is therefore a pretty hot humbucker, but the cunife magnets help to maintain a distinctively Fender-esque brightness in the pickup.

Put concisely, Gibson's original humbucking pickup was so successful that – excluding modded and hotrodded pickup models – there are fewer all-original humbucking designs than there are single-coil designs because the vast majority of players and manufacturers alike want the humbuckers on their guitars either to sound like vintage PAFs or like hotrodded vintage PAFs. Other original designs have existed, of course, and some have sounded very good, but they are usually limited to use on the models offered by the maker who designed or commissioned the pickup, and haven't merged into wider usage on a wide range of guitars the way Seth Lover's original Gibson humbucker has. The Guild humbuckers used in upscale models since the early 1960s are fine-sounding units: they're not excessively powerful, but they are a little brighter and janglier than some other full-size humbuckers, and have a rich bite to them when you dig in. Hofner, Guyatone, Hagstrom, and others made some interesting, vintage-vibed humbuckers in the 1960s, but since that time it's hard to escape the fact that most makers have used pickups fitting the Gibson template.

Many guitar makers don't try to replicate great designs themselves but buy them in from noted pickup makers such as Seymour Duncan, DiMarzio, Paul Reed Smith – a guitar maker, but more and more popular as a pickup supplier, too – Lindy Fralin, and Kent Armstrong. The first two of these in particular really led the replacement-pickup boom, and offer an enormous range of pickups, from very close vintage reproductions to super-hot hotrod models. Some of their designs have achieved 'standard' status in their own right: DiMarzio's SDS-1 single-coil pickup was one of the first popular replacement units for Stratocasters, and lots of heavy rockers have fitted its humbucking sibling, the Super Distortion, to their Les Pauls and SGs from the 1970s on. Seymour Duncan models such as the single-coil alnico II Pro and Quarter Pounder, and the humbucking SH-1 '59, Pearly Gates, and Trembucker have also been enormous sellers.

Perhaps more significantly for our purposes here, we have these two pickup manufacturers largely to thank for the advent of single-coil-sized humbucking pickups, which represented a revolution for rock-minded Fender players in particular when they began to proliferate in the 1980s. Such pickups are split into two formats: stacked humbuckers, and side-by-side humbuckers.

As their names suggest, the former places one coil on top of the other to maintain an approximation of the ordinary single-coil's narrow magnetic window, while the latter places two very narrow coils in the traditional manner to fit within the usual space of the pickup that it's intended to replaced. Although the side-by-side humbuckers are the same size as, for example, a Fender Stratocaster pickup, the way their magnetic fields react around the tops of the two coils, and the fact that they use two rows of polepieces or two blades, mean that they still read a wider area of string vibration, and therefore present a sound that is fatter and more 'humbucking' in tone than the stacked designs. On the other hand, stacking coils also changes the way that both the coils and the magnetic field react when compared with those of a standard single-coil, so these don't achieve the goal of sounding identical to the single-coils they are intended to replace either. Nevertheless, such hum-resistant pseudo-single-coils have become extremely refined in recent years, and when I say they "don't sound exactly like standard single-coils" I'm splitting hairs to some extent.

Because of the inherently thinner or fatter characteristics of each of these two types, players seeking single-coil tonal accuracy will often select stacked humbuckers, whereas those seeking more power and sustain in a single-coil-sized pickup will usually go for side-by-side humbuckers. DiMarzio's Virtual Vintage range and Kinman's AVn line are the most popular examples of a newer breed of stacked pickups, which employ slightly dissimilar upper and lower coils and 'U' section metal shielding both to reduce hum and to maintain vintage-accurate tonal response. Among the plethora of side-by-side humbuckers available, Seymour Duncan's Hot Rails has probably been the most successful. In addition to the hotrodded, single-coil-sized humbuckers, there are, of course, as many hotrodded full-size humbuckers as there are single-coil pickups, and a wide range of high-output or otherwise modified humbuckers – using ceramic as well as alnico magnets – are available to suit all tastes.

Top to bottom > Gibson's mini-humbucker, which was actually borrowed from an Epiphone design; Fender's Wide Range Humbucking Pickup, designed by former Gibson man Seth Lover

Active pickups have also won over many supporters. The most famous brand of these is EMG, whose units function much as do traditional passive pickups, which is to say they rely on coils wound around magnetic elements, but also carry built-in preamps for increased power, further decreased noise, and a low impedance output. EMG makes a wide range of pickups so it's impossible to generalize with any accuracy, but active pickups as a breed do tend to sound quite precise and hi-fidelity when compared with traditional passive pickups. For some players, that's a very good thing: EMGs have won fans among many heavy rock and shred players, as well as a number of jazzers, country players, and guitarists of other genres. They seem to be less favored in blues circles, but that's a famously traditional crowd to begin with.

Pickup Positioning

I have looked at the designs and characteristics of pickups in some detail, but whatever pickup a guitar carries, its positioning along the length of the string is a crucial factor in determining the sound that it converts into a signal. We discussed harmonics and nodes in the section on scale length, and learned that the character of these is determined partly by the length of the vibrating string. It follows that the exact point at which a pickup is positioned will determine the harmonic content of the vibrations it picks up at the body portion of the moving string.

As the vibrating string is divided into second, third, fourth, and further harmonics, the corresponding nodes that appear between the point where the harmonics sound on the open string – the nodes being the dead spots discussed earlier – represent a place where that harmonic will not be heard by the pickup. These nodes are the same places where you rest your finger gently to produce a plucked harmonic on the guitar; we usually think of them as being the 12th, seventh, and fifth frets – to produce the second, third, and fourth harmonics respectively – but they are just as effectively the 12th, 19th, and 24th frets, so you can see that these nodes run all the way to the body portion of the string, too.

In short, place a pickup directly under a node for the fourth harmonic, for example, and it won't sense that harmonic – it will appear to filter it out, and its signal will be a clearer representation of the sound of the string minus that harmonic, but carrying others. Since a pickup placed near the bridge is not in proximity to any of the nodes corresponding to the lower notes of the upper harmonic range, it presents a bright, harmonically rich signal. In addition, its signal is also somewhat weaker, given pickups of the exact same type and specs, than a pickup placed more towards the center of the vibrating string, because there is less vibrational energy to sense here near the anchor point of the bridge saddle. Many guitars' neck pickups, on the other hand, are placed very near one of the nodes for the fourth harmonic, which is at the 24th fret, if one exists. The front edge of a Stratocaster's neck pickup, for example, is under the node for this harmonic, and as a result, the fourth harmonic is removed to a degree from that pickup's signal, which is part of what gives a Strat neck pickup its warm, deep character. Of course, the string's wider movement here during vibration – this pickup's location being further toward the center of the moving string – gives this pickup more output and a fatter sound. To compensate for this disparity in volume introduced by pickup position alone, by the way, many makers either use a slightly more powerful, overwound pickup in the bridge position than in the neck, or simply lower the neck pickup into the body more and, consequently, further away from the strings. In any case, pickup positioning is something to which any careful designer will give a lot of thought, as it plays a major part in shaping the voice of any electric guitar. This is just a brief look at a complex subject, but it goes some way toward showing you the importance of this variable.

Pick Positioning

As an addendum to pickup positioning, let's briefly consider the sonic effect of plucking a guitar string at different points along its length, which is to say, in most cases, along the portion of its length that runs across the body. This isn't a 'component' of guitar construction, but it is still a considerable tonal ingredient.

Say you'd just landed from Mars, and the first question you wanted to ask about life on Earth was, "What do pickups sound like in different positions on an electric guitar – 1½″ from the bridge, 3¾″ from the bridge, and 6″ from the bridge?" I would hand you my acoustic guitar and a pick and say, "There you go. Pick a string in those positions and find out." You see, most guitarists know this already, even if they don't think about it much. Strum a guitar – acoustic or unplugged electric – close to the bridge and the resultant timbre sounds relatively like the timbre presented by a pickup in the bridge position, which is to say it is bright and silvery, and perhaps a little thin. Strum at the neck end of the body, and it sounds similar to a pickup in the neck position, dark and full. The act of picking the strings in a particular position – and the effect is more pronounced with a pick than with the fingers – is creating a different relationship between the nodes and antinodes that make up the harmonic series on the guitar, and is therefore predetermining the harmonic content, or voice, of that guitar's sound. Pick positioning and pickup positioning may seem like very different things, but the resultant sound of each is greatly affected by any node at or near its position, and by the harmonics it accentuates or negates as a result.

SWITCHES, CONTROLS, AND WIRING

The jobs of these components might primarily be to select and regulate the various sounds offered by different pickup positions, but their values, quality, and the ways in which they are configured all play a part in shaping the sound of an electric guitar's output. Most switches perform obvious functions, with the most common by far being, on a two-pickup guitar, to select either the bridge pickup or neck pickup, or both together. Some guitars' switches add more subtle variations to this, such as the five-way selector on later Stratocasters. Positions two and four on this switch select a pair of pickups together – either neck and middle or bridge and middle – a wiring format which in itself introduces considerations such as phase canceling between pairs of pickups located in different positions. Although frequently referred to as the 'out of phase' position, these two-pickup selections are actually in phase, but their thin, hollow sound results from the blending of harmonics sampled at two different points along the strings. Other guitars have added switches actually to flip pickups out of phase, or to configure humbuckers for series or parallel outputs. I don't intend to outline all the variables here – we'll see some more in the following chapters that cover specific types of guitars – but it's important to note that a guitar's switching arrangement will raise further variables for the designer, manufacturer, or player to consider.

Potentiometers themselves contribute to the sound of the pickups mounted on the guitar. A potentiometer is a variable resistor, which imposes a resistance on the signal according to

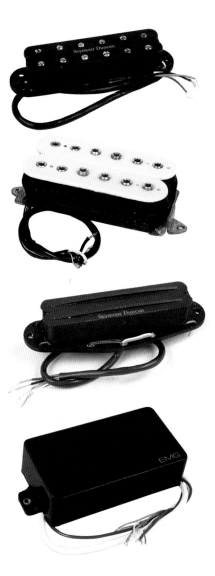

Top to bottom > specialty humbuckers: Seymour Duncan Li'l '59; DiMarzio Super Distortion; Seymour Duncan Hot Rails; EMG active humbucker

where the wiper is positioned along its track, in other words, the point to which you turn the knob. Any resistor in line with a guitar's signal will have an effect on its treble content; the higher the value of the potentiometer, the greater the high-frequency response of the guitar. Fenders with bright single-coils have traditionally used 250k potentiometers because these guitars have the desirable amount of treble in their sound with this value in place. Gibsons and many others using darker-sounding humbuckers use 500k pots to give their highs a little lift. Tone controls also have an obvious effect on a guitar's sound – namely, again, its treble content – but the degree to which a tone control rolls off highs is determined by the value of the capacitor linked between the pot and ground (earth). The lower this capacitor's value, the lower the frequency at which it 'shelves' the signal, that is, the level above which it removes highs from the signal. With some guitar-and-pickup combinations a change from a .02 microfarad (µF) tone cap to a .01µF cap will result in less muddiness when the tone control is rolled down a little, although cutting the cap's value in half again down to .0047µF might take things too far and render the control ineffectual. (Of course .0047µF isn't exactly half of .01µF, but these are the values most commonly manufactured, so they are traditionally considered 'half the value' of .01µF. As it happens, the 'half value' cap for a .0047µF is usually a .0022µF, not a .00235µF.)

While many guitars follow the classic templates for switching and volume and tone controls, and are therefore largely simple affairs, there are many, many ways a guitar maker can wire the pickups to the output jack. If desired, he can provide for many sonic variables along the route.

THE 'CONSUMABLES'

The following two categories of components don't apply as ingredients of choice specific to any particular design of guitar, and instead can be used equally on any guitar as a matter of player choice according to tastes and styles. They are both still critical ingredients in the sonic stew, however, and deserve a little consideration here for that reason.

Strings > I have known plenty of players who have undertaken a quest for a major tonal shift, only to ignore the component where the sound begins: their strings. Perhaps they seek a warmer, rounder sound from their late-era Stratocaster – it might even be just a subtle change, but one that is considerable to their ears – so they install a different type of vintage-voice pickup, change the bridge's inertia block from Mazac to an original steel type, and perform a dozen other tweaks, without ever considering to try something other than their ultra-bright chromed steel-wound strings.

It can be too easy to forget that your tone all starts at the string, and the gauge, condition, and makeup of that string obviously has a major impact on what comes out of it. A lot of players give some thought to the feel of their strings and select them according to gauge but, aside from a simple awareness of the fact that new strings sound a little brighter than older strings, don't consider how different metals used in string manufacturing can elicit different sounds, as indeed can different shapes of 'winds,' the wraps of finer wire wound around the cores of low E, A, and D strings, and sometimes G strings on heavier gauges or older styles of strings.

For much of the modern era, strings wrapped with nickel-plated plain steel have been the standard, while guitarists have also been sold on the improved brightness, power, and longevity available from stainless steel and chrome-wound strings. These certainly do accentuate highs, and their harder materials can make them longer wearing, too. But other guitarists seeking tones closer to the classic vintage sounds forged in the 1950s and '60s have also gone in the opposite direction: toward softer strings and warmer sounds. Prior to 1970, when the cost of nickel skyrocketed, strings were wound almost exclusively in pure nickel wraps around a plain steel core. These pure nickel strings are a little softer to the touch than nickel-plated plain steel, chrome, or stainless-steel-wrapped strings, and their tone is slightly softer and a little richer as well. They wear better than nickel-plated strings, and are easier on frets than hard chromed or stainless-steel strings, which are harder than most frets themselves, the majority of which, as we have seen, are made from an alloy containing nickel-silver. One trade off is a lower output from pure-nickel strings, because their lower steel content offers less interaction with the pickup's magnetic field, but for many players this is just part of the magic, and they find tonal benefits in making up the gain at the amp anyway. Then again, many players find the increased highs and extra power of other string types really helps their sound to cut through, and for them the nickel-plated steel, stainless steel, or chromed alternatives are the better choice. The important point here is that players should at least be aware of the alternatives, and understand that any efforts at tone-template shaping can and should begin right with the string.

Part of that, of course, has to do with string gauge, and even the shape of the wrap, too. Assuming you play hard enough to get the heavier strings moving, a change from .009″ to .010″ or .011″ will give you a bigger, heavier tone with a firmer fundamental – but the player's touch is critical, and the added tension of heavier strings, coupled with a too-light attack, can often just result in a dull, choked sound. The result, for some players, can be a thinner sound and a loss of shimmer and jangle, too, that goes with any move to heavier strings. Rather than just equating heavy strings with heavy sounds, it's a matter of matching playing touch to string gauge, and with the right marriage of the two, different players can

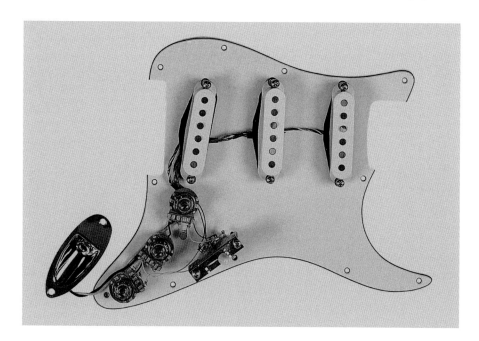

A Fender Stratocaster 'wiring harness' with related pickups and electronics laid out in corrrect relative positions above the pickguard

often achieve equally heavy tones. Players who want to experiment with the potentially greater power of a heavier string gauge but who find the change tough on the fingers, can try down-tuning half a step to ease the tension a bit. Moving from .009″ to .010″ while simultaneously dropping from standard tuning to a half-step down (E flat) keeps the string tension – that is, the ease of fretting and bending – feeling very nearly the same.

A lot has been made of the notion that Stevie Ray Vaughan achieved his legendary big tone thanks in part to the use of .012″-gauge strings, but SRV also tuned down a semitone to ease the tension a little. Jimi Hendrix commonly used .010″-gauge strings, and very often tuned down to E flat also, which would have resulted in a pretty soft playing feel close to that of a set of .009″ in standard tuning. Was Hendrix some kind of wimp, or what? No. The gauge, and the tuning change, just suited his touch, and the resulting tone was undeniably gargantuan.

Another easily forgotten factoid is that most rock and pop hits prior to the mid 1960s were recorded with flatwound strings. The classics of early rock'n'roll, the early Beatles recordings, and the great surf instrumentals were all recorded with flatwound pure-nickel-wrapped strings. Between them, they display an impressive range of jangle and twang sounds – characteristics few players today would associate with flatwound strings – and with bags of depth and dimension in those outstanding old recordings, too. Few players today other than some jazzers choose to play flatwound strings, and, of course, they are a little harder to come by, too, but they offer another exciting variable in both sound and feel. A change even from pure-nickel roundwounds to pure-nickel flatwounds will not only add both a smoother feel and sound, but will bring a little more solidity to your tone as well, along with a subtle silky sizzle that can be really appealing in certain styles. They can be addictive to the fingers, too, and make standard roundwounds feel positively abrasive after a while; however, flatwounds don't bend in quite the same way, and they do lack some of the brightness of roundwounds, and many players will no doubt want to retain the status quo in their strings as regards these characteristics. In any case: variety… spice… life… etc.

Picks > Otherwise known as plectrums, guitar picks come in an extremely wide variety of shapes, thicknesses, and materials, and the balance of these characteristics can – you guessed it – affect your sounds considerably. This is another 'not part of the guitar' category, but every guitar makes its sound thanks to the initial contact of pick or fingertip upon string, so I wasn't entirely truthful a few paragraphs above when I said, "Your tone all starts at the string." It starts with the confluence of string and pick, and the role of the latter is crucial. (Let's agree to ignore the relatively rare instances of EBow or Gizmotron usage for our purposes here.) A brief look at the sonic effect of the pick is warranted, but let's do so with the full awareness that – as with strings – this isn't an integral ingredient in any one type of guitar, so you are gloriously free to use pick choice to adapt the tone of any instrument you choose.

Much of the tonal characteristic imparted by any particular pick has to do with how easily it bends when attacking the strings. Or, in other words, the proportion of energy it transfers into the strings themselves versus how much it absorbs itself. Thin, flexible picks are sometimes preferred by players who have a light touch, or by those seeking a jangly, percussive sound for rhythm playing. Thinner picks also elicit a brighter tone from the strings. They can, however, have a difficult time getting heavier gauges of strings going, and

Above top to bottom > Fender three-way and five-way switches are virtually identical, although the latter is notched to provide two extra 'in-between' positions
Opposite top to bottom > standard guitar potentiometer; potentiometer with push-pull switch attached for pickup-coil splitting and other functions

absorb a relatively high amount of energy. Heavy picks absorb less energy, and therefore transfer more of it into the strings themselves, for a louder, fuller sound. This also results in a slightly darker sound, however, and an attack that might overwhelm some light gauges of strings. It behoves most players to try a range of pick gauges to learn which ones are best for their own playing style and string gauges.

The material from which a pick is made is to some extent a component that functions hand in hand with thickness, although it has its own influence, too. As with any transference of energy, the relative degrees of hardness or softness of a material will play a part in determining how much energy is passed on from object A to object B, and how much is merely absorbed by object A itself. A pick's willingness to bend – or not – occurs at the molecular level. Consider the example of being whacked in the head with a plank as against being whacked in the head with a steel pipe. Neither object bends noticeably on impact, but the plank does a little less damage because wood gives more than steel – which is to say, in fact, that it 'takes'. For the same reasons, a vinyl pick and a tortoiseshell pick of the same gauge will elicit a slightly different attack, the latter being firmer, with less give.

The shape of the portion of the pick that attacks the strings also plays a big part in the sound it elicits, as does the angle at which it strikes the strings. When any pick strikes a string, it bends it briefly and ever so minutely at the point of impact. A pointed, angular tip bends the string(s) sharply and at a tightly focused point, eliciting tight note definition, considerable treble content, and a high degree of harmonic sparkle. A rounded attacking edge induces a rounder, broader bend where it contacts the string, and elicits a rounder, slightly warmer sound as a result. Warmer and rounder still is the bare thumb or fingertip, while the fingertip with a bit of nail thrown in gives a smooth sound with an edge of snappy attack.

Along with your experimentations with different gauges of picks, try as many different shapes and compositions as you can get your hands on. It's even worth keeping a variety of pick types on hand to help you achieve different sounds, particularly when recording. If you've been in a rut of using just one type for an extended period of time and suddenly find yourself in need of a firmer/brighter/warmer sound – fill in your own adjective as appropriate – try a different pick before going to the trouble of swapping pickups or retubing your amp. It might just do the trick.

Now let's look at some *whole* guitars.

2

Bolt-Neck
Solidbodies

Hollowbody archtop guitars with magnetic pickups were being amplified for many years before solidbodies became widely available, but the solidbody has taken the crown for 'most popular electric format.' Certainly Rickenbacker had produced some solidbody electrics with bolt-on necks, mostly with bakelite bodies, as early as 1935, but these were never taken up by a large number of players. Given that Fender's groundbreaking screwed-on neck design was the first successful mass-production solidbody – and has remained a popular template for the style to this day – this is the ideal place to begin our analysis of specific makes and models.

For Fender, the bolt-on neck – which, in fact, was attached with long screws, not bolts, and almost always still is today – was a purely utilitarian piece of design. It simplified production and made both repair and total replacement of a guitar's neck much easier and less expensive. Leo Fender reasoned that a totally solid guitar could be made in an entirely new way, and didn't require the labor-intensive glued-in, dovetailed neck joint of a guitar with acoustic roots, considering the main intention was to amplify the sound captured by a magnetic pickup anyway. Alongside the considerable design elements that went into making the instrument easy both to produce and repair, however, a new feel and tonality were introduced.

The revolutionary Fender guitar arrived in the summer of 1950, first in the form of a few one- and two-pickup Esquires, then in larger quantities as the two-pickup Broadcaster, which finally took the longstanding Telecaster name in mid 1951, following a brief 'model-less' period of production that has become known as the 'Nocaster era'. I have talked a lot about the bolt-on neck mainly because that's the most obvious characteristic distinguishing Fender guitars and those of its ilk from the glued-in-neck Gibson topology that would follow, but the Telecaster's solid body is really what got it noticed. Although it was jeered at and derided by many players and guitar makers alike as a 'plank'

or a 'canoe paddle,' both camps came to accept – gradually at first, then pretty darn quickly – that this instrument was primed to set new standards in amplified popular music.

Leo Fender built on his experience in a relatively few years of lap-steel guitar design and manufacturing to bring all of the advantages that steel players in country-and-western swing bands were enjoying from their solidbodied instruments to the benefit of the Spanish-electric player. The thinking was very much along the lines of, "If we're going to amplify these guitars, let's *just* amplify them." Building a guitar along acoustic lines and adding a pickup did perhaps yield an instrument that could be strummed unplugged for practice, but it severely compromised its performance for many styles of playing, resulting in an amplified tone that was often somewhat muddy, ill-defined, and prone to howling with unwanted feedback.

Despite its plank-like simplicity, Fender's new guitar was conceived very much as a professional instrument, designed for the hard-working, road-weary musicians who had already become Fender's repair and amp customers in such large numbers. The new solidbody guitar was feedback-resistant to high volume, had a bright, ringing sound that could cut through even a large band with horns, and it had excellent sustain and dynamics – all characteristics that were prime designer criteria during Fender's development of the

⌃ Early-1960s Fender Telecaster

> **Body:** custom-color Telecasters (that is, anything not in blond) now had bodies made from alder
> **Neck:** in mid 1959 Fender changed to a glued-on rosewood fingerboard, which it stayed with exclusively until 1967
> **Electronics:** Telecaster pickups grew progressively weaker from the mid 1960s into the '70s
Sound: much as the 1950s Telecaster, but with a slightly smoother, warmer edge from the alder and rosewood elements

⌄ Mid-1950s Fender Telecaster

> **Body:** solid swamp-ash body (usually two-piece) with single deep cutaway for good access to the 21st fret; thin, semi-transparent blonde nitrocellulose lacquer finish standard
> **Neck:** bolt-on, one-piece maple neck and integral maple fingerboard with 7¼" fingerboard radius, 21 nickel-silver frets, and 1⅝" nut width; 25½" scale length
> **Headstock:** asymmetrical headstock with six-in-line Kluson tuners, bone nut; single round, steel string tree (later stamped steel 'butterfly' tree)
> **Bridge:** through-body stringing; semi-suspended bridge with three adjustable brass saddles (later steel)
> **Electronics:** single-coil bridge pickup with six individual alnico pole magnets; DC resistance of 7k to 7.5k, with a steel base plate to aid shielding and raise inductance; single-coil neck pickup with six individual alnico pole magnets; DC resistance of approximately 7.75k; three-way switch and two 250k potentiometers for volume and blend, to select: (models built 1950–52) 1) neck pickup with bassy sound and no tone control, 2) neck pickup straight to volume control, 3) neck and bridge pickups with former blended in by second rotary control; (models built 1953–67) 1) same as above, 2) neck pickup through tone and volume controls, 3) bridge pickup alone through tone and volume controls; after 1967, altered for standard neck, both, and bridge switching
> **Sound:** bright, snappy, cutting, harmonically rich, and – dare I say – twangy, but with a nicely balanced voice, good midrange grunt, and ringing sustain

guitar. New pickup designs that accentuated brightness and improved individual string definition, the resonant and sustainal through-body stringing, and the combination of bright, hard maple and ringing, open ash all worked together toward a common goal.

Despite looking very unlike a musical instrument to many of the early doubters, it proved to be an extremely expressive guitar indeed when amped up. Many musicians quickly discovered it was a surprisingly playable instrument, too. Although some early 1950s Tele necks are considered pretty 'clubby' by contemporary standards, they felt slicker, faster, and more comfortable in the hand than the guitar necks a lot of players had wrestled with before that time. The bolt-on neck left only a minimal heel to contend with, so upper-fret access was also better than a lot of players had experienced previously. Given the solidity of the bridge and the straight, in-line run of the strings from the nut to the tuners, tuning stability was also good. Finally, the Tele offered better intonation adjustment than ever before seen on a production guitar.

Leo Fender had always worked closely with professional musicians in the Southern California area where he established his business, and the local and touring country-and-western swing artists in particular really took to the solidbody Telecaster. For many, it was the first opportunity of staking an equal claim with the steel-guitar player to the band's solo spotlight, and it enabled such great pairings as Speedy West (steel) and Jimmy Bryant (Tele), who recorded a number of groundbreaking sides for Capitol Records. The guitar has remained the modern-day country standard, and virtually defines 'twang,' but it has been taken up by a wide range of blues, rock, and even jazz players. A young B.B. King was pictured with a Telecaster, and Eric Clapton, Muddy Waters, Mike Bloomfield, and Albert King all played one, too, at one time or another. And although they are primarily known for playing other models, both Jimmy Page and Jimi Hendrix gave credence to the Tele's heavy rock potential. Page used one for the solo to 'Stairway To Heaven' and elsewhere on the first two Zep albums; Hendrix donned a Tele for 'Purple Haze' and 'Hey Joe,' among other tracks. Even today, plenty of players who think of a Fender Telecaster as 'the country twang guitar' are surprised by its punching power when they plug in a good one for the first time.

Fender's own Stratocaster stormed on to the scene before another maker of any significance had much of a chance to compete in the slab-styled, solid wood, bolt-neck market. Gibson's Les Paul was making waves, although surprisingly gentle ones, and even the budget-model Gibson electrics would stick with the company's longstanding tradition of set-neck construction. The Telecaster had already embodied

⊗ Early-1960s Fender Stratocaster

> **Body:** much as per the 1950s Stratocaster, but with alder body other than blond examples

> **Neck:** in mid 1959 Fender changed to a glued-on rosewood fingerboard, which it stayed with exclusively until 1967

> **Electronics:** Strat pickups grew progressively weaker from the mid 1960s into the '70s, sliding from around 6k to around 5.7k or less; five-way switch became standard in 1977, offering the two popular between-pickup selections

> **Sound:** similar to 1950s Stratocaster, but a fraction less snappy while a little warmer

⊗ Mid-1950s Fender Stratocaster

> **Body:** from 1954–56 solid swamp-ash body (usually two-piece) with dual asymmetrical cutaways for good upper fret access; thin, semi-transparent two-tone sunburst nitrocellulose lacquer finish standard; after 1956 alder is standard body wood, with ash used only for blond-finished guitars

> **Neck:** bolt-on, one-piece maple neck and integral maple fingerboard with 7¼" fingerboard radius, 21 nickel-silver frets, and 1⅝" nut width (approximately); 25½" scale length

> **Headstock:** asymmetrical headstock with six-in-line Kluson tuners; bone nut; single round steel string tree (later stamped steel 'butterfly' tree)

> **Bridge:** Fender Synchronized Tremolo (vibrato) standard; six individual stamped steel saddles, fully adjustable for height and intonation; steel base plate; steel inertia bar (trem block) for string ball-end anchoring

> **Electronics:** three identical single-coil pickups, each with six individual alnico pole magnets; DC resistance of approximately 6k; three 250k potentiometers for master volume, neck pickup tone, and middle pickup tone, and three-way switch to select each pickup individually only (could be carefully balanced between positions to select neck-plus-middle or bridge-plus-middle)

> **Sound:** snappy and slightly springing, with a bright, cutting character overall and lots of harmonic sparkle, but good roundness, depth, and warmth from the neck pickup; an element of soft compression at all settings

a total rethink of the guitar as an electric instrument, stripping down the template and retaining only the bare bones of the form. When it hit the scene in 1954 the Stratocaster represented just as much of a geometric progression of the solidbody as a refined, versatile instrument. Its newly developed pickups, although roughly similar to those of the Tele – but lacking the Tele bridge pickup's base plate – achieved even more of the highly desirable brightness, and the use of three of them tapped a wider range of tones from the guitar. The inclusion of a highly engineered, extremely efficient, tailor-made vibrato tailpiece offered more dramatic manual effects than had ever before been available, and the guitar's deep contours in the ribcage and right-forearm regions of the solid wood body made it the most comfortable and form-fitting guitar manufactured.

Aside from the shape and the new pickups, the Stratocaster's spring-loaded vibrato bridge helped to make it a very different-sounding electric from the Telecaster, as discussed in much more detail in Chapter 1 under 'Bridge And Tailpiece' and 'Vibrato Bridge-Tailpiece.' (I am referring you backward to the preceding chapter here to start a pattern, but since the intention of the tonal primer in Chapter One is that it be used as a cross-reference to provide more in-depth analysis of the ingredients of specific models covered here and in the following chapters, I won't always point you back to the start of the book after this reminder.)

In addition to the sound of the guitar, its playing feel represented a change from that of the Tele. Part of this might have been an unintentional side effect, but that same spring-loaded vibrato bridge that lent the Stratocaster a slightly softer, rounder, more self-compressing sound also gave it a softer playing feel and made the strings easier to bend than the same gauge loaded on a Tele. This is because a traditional Strat bridge, the springs in particular, allows more give to the strings when they are strummed or picked hard; also, the assembly pulls forward slightly when a string is bent by the player, which makes it easier to push that string with the fingertip, but also leads to slight detuning inaccuracies with styles that involve bending one or two strings while holding

the pitch of others. The latter happens to be a popular technique of 'faux-pedal-steel' country bends and, what do you know, the Telecaster remains the more popular guitar for these styles. Heavy-bending blues players have by and large – although not entirely – preferred the easier-bending Stratocaster.

Which is not to say, by any means, that country players have rejected the Stratocaster. In the earlier part of the model's lifetime, the efficient tremolo provided a means of bending the heavy strings of the day that took real muscle to bend on a Telecaster; indeed the Strat was developed with considerable input from country-and-western artist Bill Carson, and Carson's early endorsement certainly helped the model's popularity in the country community. Today, however, any attempt to produce even a partial list of 'famous Strat players' seems rather pointless. The model is arguably played by more major-name artists than any other electric guitar: from Buddy Holly, to Dick Dale, to Hank Marvin, to Jimi Hendrix, to Buddy Guy, to Jeff Beck, to Eric Clapton, to Ritchie Blackmore, to Yngwie Malmsteen, to David Gilmour, even the skeleton of such a list covers a broad territory. Flesh it out further – as any guitar fan can easily do for themselves – and the names still represent a range of players with diverse and distinct sounds, a testament to the Stratocaster's versatility.

Few makers even attempted to compete with Fender's style for the first 15 or 20 years of the company's existence, and the majority of bolt-on solidbody models that might be seen as rivals according to their specs on paper were really just cheap beginner's models or imports that weren't yet even worthy of the label 'copy.' There were a few exceptions to this, of course, and these have proved to be some of the more enduring of the early bolt-on solidbody electrics. Danelectro and Silvertone guitars were 'cheap' compared with the Fenders, Gibsons, and Gretsches of their day, but they were far from copies. Of course, the real classics of these models weren't actually solidbodies, either, but were, in fact, of a semi-solid construction, but they were clearly intended to appeal to young or thin-walleted players eager to pick up on the solidbody craze, so we might as well include them in that company.

Nathan I. 'Nat' Daniel made guitar amplifiers for a number of companies way back in the 1930s, and began supplying major catalog companies Montgomery Ward and Sears in the late 1940s, shortly after founding his Danelectro brand. He diversified into manufacturing solidbody electric guitars for Sears under the Silvertone name in 1954, and introduced the first of his most classic models in both the

> **◀ Late-1950s Danelectro U 2**

> **Body:** solid poplar core and side frames (sometimes pine, and later plywood) with ⅛" Masonite top and back; side joints covered with stick-on wallpaper tape
> **Neck:** bolt-on, one-piece poplar neck and rosewood fingerboard with approximately 9½" radius, 21 nickel-silver frets, and 1⅝" nut width; 25" scale length
> **Headstock:** three-per-side Kluson tuners; aluminum nut
> **Bridge:** height-adjustable steel bridge plate with one-piece, non-adjustable rosewood saddle
> **Electronics:** two identical single-coil 'lipstick tube' pickups, each with single alnico bar magnet and a DC resistance of approximately 4.25k to 4.75k; one stacked double potentiometer with 1M and 100k for volume and tone for each pickup; three-way switch to select each pickup individually or both in series for a hotter output (standard both-pickups wiring is in parallel)
> **Sound:** fairly light and bright, but with a sweet blend of sparkle and depth, and a gently percussive attack

Danelectro and Silvertone brands in 1956 in the form of the U-1 and U-2 guitars, costing $75 and $100 respectively at the time for the single- and double-pickup models. These single-cutaway models were joined by the three-pickup U-3 in 1957, but segued into the Standard and Deluxe 'short-horn' double-cutaway models in the course of 1958, which were manufactured in Danelectro's New Jersey plant until it closed in 1969.

The fact that the Danelectro body – made from front and back faces of ⅜″ Masonite (hardboard) attached to poplar wood center block and side wings – is totally out of the realm of what we generally consider 'tone woods' means it merits some tonal consideration in itself. These guitars were more resonant than you might think, and while they didn't possess outstanding amounts of sustain, they sang a little longer than some other guitars on the shelves. In a sense, they embodied similar thinking to that which had gone into Gibson's laminated-top ES-175 only a few years before: why put a tone wood valued for its acoustic properties into a guitar that was intended as an amplified instrument? So, while technically a 'semi-solid' design, Danelectros were not designed as such with any particular goals of heightened acoustic resonance in mind. The design primarily offered a simple, cost-effective way to manufacture a guitar that looked like the popular new solidbody electrics, and had the bonus of being light. Of course, other major brands such as Gretsch and Guild offered semi-solid electrics with the appearances of solidbodies, but these makers evolved from a tradition of hollowbody guitar building, so we'll consider their instruments in that light.

Plugged in, a Danelectro U-2 had a crystalline chime, percussive attack, and bright cutting edge that made it a very effective guitar for a lot of styles. Plenty of players also found its slim poplar neck with Brazilian rosewood fingerboard and 25″ scale length very playable, and the template has therefore endured as a surprisingly pro-friendly example of budget-guitar design.

Despite their associations with vintage Gibson Les Pauls, or Fender Strats and Teles, such legendary players as Eric Clapton, Jimi Hendrix, Stevie Ray Vaughan and Jimmy Page all selected Danelectros or Silvertones at one time or another, the latter even making a double-cutaway Danelectro Standard his mainstay for slide work well into Led Zeppelin's heyday. Link Wray played a Danelectro Longhorn for a time in his post-'Rumble' period, and Dano six-string basses – known in Nashville studio circles as 'tic tac' basses – and 12-string electrics were popular with many session players.

With what's available to the player today – as new designs, old classics, accurate reproductions of old classics, and 'retro' twists on vintage styles – we don't really have to limit ourselves to a chronological trawl through electric guitars, and

> **1958 Supro Dual Tone**

> **Body:** plastic-covered solid body constructed from a softer hardwood; single cutaway
> **Neck:** bolt-on maple neck with rosewood fingerboard, 20 nickel-silver frets, and 1⅝" nut width; 24¾" scale length
> **Headstock:** three-per-side Kluson tuners; plastic nut
> **Bridge:** height-adjustable floating two-piece rosewood bridge; stairstep trapeze tailpiece
> **Electronics:** two identical single-coil pickups, each with single side-on alnico bar magnet and threaded steel polepieces; three-way switch to select each pickup individually or bridge pickup with preset bright sound; individual volume and tone controls for each pickup
> **Sound:** fat, clanky, and bright, with a slightly gritty edge

> **1964 National Newport 84**

Valco also made National guitars in fantastic shapes from molded 'Res-O-Glas' – such as the one pictured here resembling a map of the U.S.A. – which shared many of the same electronics as their more traditionally constructed stablemates.

Danelectro makes a good case in point. The original Korean-made Danelectro reissues of the late 1990s were largely pretty accurate versions of the 1950s and '60s Danos, with the weak but twangy alnico lipstick-tube pickups, concentric volume and tone controls, and crude rosewood bridge saddle all retained in the construction. The more recent Korean reissues of 2005 have slightly hotter alnico pickups and improved bridges and tuners, but still retain the gist of the Dano vibe. Purists will usually argue for the originals of just about anything, and there's no doubt that the majority of 40-plus-year-old guitars have a certain patina and played-in feel that is often unavailable from newly manufactured instruments. But, given the churn-'em-out cheap credo of the originals, both the original 2001 U-2 reissues and the 2005 56 Pro reissues come

a lot closer to the originals than do many of the sub-custom-shop repros of other classic makes and models on the market. Other U.S.-made guitars from Jerry Jones and Reverend bear constructional similarities to the Danelectro-Silvertone template, with even more attention to detail (in the case of the former) and some variations in hardware and pickups (in the case of the latter).

As Fender's bolt-on designs ascended into the hierarchy of electric guitardom, many others following the format were resolutely downmarket – an opinion of all solidbody electrics held by many of the old-school guitar makers right into the late 1950s and early '60s. Among the better respected and more collectable of this bunch were the Supro and National guitars made by Valco in the mid to late 1950s and 1960s.

These were high-end guitars in catalog terms – a Supro Dual Tone sold for $149.50 in 1956 – but weren't on a par pricewise or in terms of quality with the upper-range Fender, Gibson, Gretsch, or Guild models. Supro's first solidbody electrics arrived in 1952 in the form of the very basic Ozark and Ozark Cut-Away Jet (an Ozark was Hendrix's first guitar), but by the mid 1950s the more impressive Dual Tone and Belmont models had evolved. These guitars had solid wood bodies that were 'shrink-wrapped' in a plastic covering, which at first was often just a plain color such as the ivory of the Dual Tone featured here, but later incorporated fancier pearloid textures. Their necks were attached with two bolts that were covered with chrome caps, and they carried either one or two metal-covered pickups that appear outwardly to be humbuckers, but are, in fact, single-coil units.

In the early 1960s Valco changed from wood Supros to making guitars with bodies of molded fiberglass – a material that the company promoted as 'Res-O-Glas' – which is how the best-known of its more exotic National solidbody electrics also appeared. These shared the same pickups, but were molded in far more futuristic shapes that often resembled an outline of the map of the U.S.A. Both National and Supro guitars occasionally carried Valco's forward-looking but largely under-appreciated 'contact' pickup, which was built into the floating archtop-style rosewood bridge and produced a sound similar to the piezo-loaded bridge saddles that have become more popular recently on hybrid electric-acoustic solidbodies. Quirk factor aside, these wild-looking Valco productions have been responsible for some groundbreaking sounds in the hands of a diverse spectrum of players from Link Wray (a Supro Dual Tone) to Jack White of the White Stripes (an Airline-branded version of the National).

Semie Moseley's Mosrite guitars aimed squarely at the higher end of the solidbody market, and were generally well made instruments, but their persistently left-field nature kept them from ever reaching the mainstream. Most players will be aware of Mosrites from one of two camps, those of Nokie Edwards of surf instrumentalists The Ventures, or of Johnny Ramone of punk-popsters The Ramones. But Mosrites have also been played by Buck Owens (chief proponent of the 'Bakersfield sound,' named for the

California town where Mosrite was once based), Merle Haggard, Kurt Cobain, and others. Funk, soul, and R&B fans might even recognize the distinctive Mosrite shape from the black Joe Maphis double-neck often played by Leroy 'Sugar' Bonner of the Ohio Players. Then, of course, there was Joe Maphis himself, the country and gospel guitarist who was an important early endorser of Mosrite.

Although early Mosrites were made with set necks – including the first few official Ventures Models of around 1963 – the majority of these and other Mosrites were bolt-neck guitars from 1964 onward. The classic Mosrite body profile roughly reflects that of an upside-down Stratocaster, but Moseley's creations have always been highly original. Their necks in particular feel quite like no others, the classic Mosrite profile being both narrow and slim – that is, diminutive in both width and depth – with low-profile 'speed frets' and a zero fret. Moseley even designed his own vibrato units, which look a little like a Bigsby, and similarly gain their tension from a single, short, vertical spring mounted below the arm joint, but have a lighter touch and a smoother ride at the bridge, thanks to Moseley's unique bridge with six individual roller saddles.

Such was Moseley's propensity for invention and hands-on manufacturing, in fact, that throughout their heyday in the 1960s, the Kluson tuners used on Mosrite guitars were the only component not made in-house by Mosrite themselves. Mosrites have a fat, well-defined sound with plenty of poke when required, as exhibited by Johnny Ramone through a Marshall stack, but enough brightness to

achieve good cutting power and the seminal twang factor required for surf or even country guitar, as found in The Ventures' music. While they have never been widely accepted in rock circles, they have become an extremely popular brand with some collectors, and more recent reissues made both in the U.S.A. and Japan have met with some interest. The brand has always enjoyed an elevated popularity in Japan, thanks in part to The Ventures' own popularity in that country.

Of course, many of the most popular alternatives in bolt-neck solidbody designs throughout the formative years of the electric guitar were other models made by Fender. The Jazzmaster was introduced in 1958 as Fender's top-of-the-range model, which sold for $329 at the time, compared with $274.50 for a Stratocaster. Four years later Fender awarded the Jaguar top-dog status when it came out, and it was more expensive still, but neither guitar ever lived up to its billing and, while they sold in pretty good numbers, the Telecaster and Stratocaster remained the flagship Fender six-strings in the eyes of most players.

The Mustang, on the other hand, introduced in 1964, knew its place from the start, attained it swiftly, and stayed

> ◀ 1966 Mosrite Ventures MkI

> **Body:** double-cutaway body of solid alder with a 'German carve' beveled edge and offset horns
> **Neck:** bolt-on maple neck with bound rosewood fingerboard, 22 narrow nickel-silver frets, and $1^{7}\!/_{32}$" nut width; $25\!/_2$" scale length
> **Headstock:** three-per-side Kluson tuners; chromed brass nut and zero fret
> **Bridge:** Moseley vibrato tailpiece with roller bridge; bridge has six individual saddles adjustable for intonation and overall height
> **Electronics:** two identical single-coil pickups, each with an alnico bar magnet beneath and six adjustable threaded polepieces, made with a wide coil wound to 10,000 turns for a DC resistance of 10k to 12k; toggle switch for each pickup individually or both together; controls for volume and tone
> **Sound:** bright and thick, with enough sparkle and attack for good cutting power but also enough gain to get crunchy through a cranked amp

there for a decade and a half. This student-grade model was an excellent introduction to Fender quality for its price, and even proved to be a great sounding instrument in the hands of many professionals. Despite its shorter scale length of 24″ and simplified vibrato system, a lot of players will tell you the Mustang retains more of the seminal Fender vibe than the upscale, overly complex Jaguar, which shares its scale.

The Jazzmaster represented Fender's first effort to branch out from its bright sound and to reach another market beyond the country players and rock'n'rollers who had taken to Stratocasters and Telecasters in growing numbers through the course of the 1950s. The guitar was aimed at those players that its name clearly suggests, in an effort to win some jazzers over from the firm grip that Gibson, Guild, Gretsch, and Epiphone archtops had in that genre. As such, the Jazzmaster was the first Fender to carry a more traditional glued-on rosewood fingerboard, and its pickups were designed for a slightly mellower, thicker sound. A smooth offset-waist body shape made it look a little less radical than the Strat, while a new floating tremolo and wiring for switchable preset lead and rhythm sounds were among features that Fender hoped many professional players would appreciate.

A clever design in many ways, it has nevertheless taken the Jazzmaster a lot longer to fight its way on to the list of solidbody classics. The sum of the parts was still too radical to lure many big-name jazz players for long, and many existing Fender fans found they still preferred the bright, cutting twang of the Tele or the Strat's elegant blend of simplicity and versatility. The Jazzmaster did take hold with players in the burgeoning surf crowd, however, who enjoyed its smooth tremolo and somewhat thick but cutting sound. Having remained a rather outré Fender throughout its days, the Jazzmaster became the weapon of choice for many guitarists in the punk and new wave scenes a decade and a half after surf fizzled, finding its way into the hands of such artists as Tom Verlaine of Television and Elvis Costello.

The Jaguar was aimed more squarely at the surf

🔵 1963 Fender Jazzmaster

> **Body:** double-cutaway, offset-waist body of solid alder
> **Neck:** bolt-on maple neck with unbound rosewood fingerboard with 7¼" radius, 21 narrow nickel-silver frets, 1⅝" nut width; 25½" scale length
> **Headstock:** asymmetrical six-in-line Kluson tuners; single 'butterfly' stamped steel string retainer on B and E strings
> **Bridge:** Fender floating tremolo vibrato system, with rocking bridge and 'trem-loc' button, bridge has six individual saddles, adjustable for intonation and for overall height
> **Electronics:** two identical single-coil pickups, each with six non-adjustable alnico slug polepieces; DC resistance of approximately 8k; lower control section has toggle switch for each pickup individually or both together; controls for volume and tone; upper 'rhythm tone' control section has slider switch to select preset rhythm (neck pickup) sound with its own roller pots for volume and tone in this mode
> **Sound:** snappy but slightly sizzly, and thicker than other Fenders to date, with a certain amount of grunt and grind, but still some ability to twang when set to bridge pickup

🔼 1962 Fender Jaguar

> **Body:** body and headstock similar to Jazzmaster
> **Neck:** bolt-on maple neck with unbound rosewood fingerboard with 7¼" radius, 22 narrow nickel-silver frets; 24" scale length
> **Bridge:** same 'floating tremolo' vibrato system as on Jazzmaster, with the addition of a switchable automatic string mute
> **Electronics:** two single-coil pickups with U-shaped metal brackets to shield the sides of the coils, six individual non-adjustable alnico slug pole pieces; DC resistance of approximately 6.5k; switching features the same selectable preset rhythm section on the upper horn as the Jazzmaster, but lead circuit comprises slider switches for tone selection and on/off for each pickup, along with master volume and tone controls
> **Sound:** bright and light overall, but with a roundness and a blurrier edge to the harmonic content, thanks to the 24" scale length; less midrange thump than a Jazzmaster

instrumentalists that Fender had unintentionally courted with the Jazzmaster, and is another of the classic guitars of that sound. But while it had some success with that crowd during the initial excitement surrounding its release, it has fared less well down the years than the Jazzmaster that preceded it. Overly complex switching, a less-preferred 24″ scale length, intricately designed new pickups that merely ended up sounding rather thin, and the tonal constraints of the floating vibrato unit – the same used on the Jazzmaster – all combined to mar its appeal. As a result, the vintage Jag that sat at the top of Fender's price list at $379.50 in 1962 fetches considerably less than an original Jazzmaster in today's vintage market, and far, far less than a pre-CBS Stratocaster or Telecaster.

While trying to inch its way upmarket with the Jazzmaster and Jaguar, Fender also recognized the need to court beginners and students once its flagship models had taken hold. The 22½″-scale Musicmaster and Duo-Sonic – with one and two pickups respectively – were introduced in 1956 and fit the bill well, but Fender best fulfilled its intentions with the Mustang, released in 1964. This guitar was a great halfway house between a cheap Musicmaster and a full-grown Strat; its price was at about half that of the Jaguar, and for many players it offered a comparable, if not better, sound and greater functionality. With its more basic

appointments and smaller, non-contoured, slab-style body, the Mustang was always considered a B-list Fender, as vintage prices continue to reflect, but its vibrato tailpiece worked well despite its minimal travel, and its pickups offered a sound that was a little more Strat-like than those of the Jazzmaster or Jaguar.

The no-frills stylings of the Mustang, along with its bargain prices on the used market, made it a favorite of many alternative, grunge, underground, and alternative artists in the 1980s and '90s. Steve Turner of Mudhoney, Kurt Cobain of Nirvana, and Thurston Moore of Sonic Youth have all made a big sound with this semi-diminutive Fender at one time or another, and it can certainly be argued that the Mustang boasts a simplicity that determinedly fails to get in the way of your technique. For today's collector the Mustang is often viewed as an avenue to vintage Fender wood and wires – and occasionally a tasty custom-color finish – at prices far, far south of those commanded by Strats, Teles, and even Jazzmasters.

Many other bolt-neck solidbodies worth examining have also grown from the Fender template, and two of them have direct lines to Fender itself. The Music Man company was set up in the early 1970s by Leo Fender and former Fender employees Forrest White and Tom Walker, and it released its first guitar in 1976 in the form of the StingRay,

which was followed two years later by the Sabre. The bolt-on maple necks and slightly Strat-ish bodylines of these guitars clearly reflected their Fender lineage, but they carried the humbucking pickups that Fender himself saw as the way forward, along with revised switching and hardtail-only tailpieces. They were well-made guitars, but never jibed with the demands of the day: as ever, most Fender players still wanted Fenders – even though these were relatively poorly made at the time – and most Gibson players wanted Gibsons. Far more successful were the revitalized designs introduced in the mid 1980s after string-and-accessories manufacturer Ernie Ball acquired the Music Man company. Leo Fender had already departed in 1979 to set up his own G&L company, along with former Fender colleague George Fullerton, but, if anything, many new Music Man models proved to be even more Fender-like than the StingRay and Sabre.

The Silhouette, introduced in 1987, was the first Music Man guitar to attain anything like 'modern classic' status. It was designed by Dudley Gimpel with input from country session ace Albert Lee, and embodied elements culled from Fender's two most popular models, with – in its most archetypal form – its shrunken-Strat outline, three narrow single-coil pickups, and fixed, strung-through-body bridge. It was also designed to be a modern workhorse, and in its original incarnation had a great deal of built-in versatility. A single large central 'swimming-pool' body rout and Molex-clip wiring harness connections allowed players to quickly swap different pickguard and pickup assemblies to change to H/S/S or H/S/H formats without any modifications or soldering,

and there was an option for a double-locking vibrato system for divebombers.

Smoothly contoured and extremely ergonomic body styling made the Silhouette a very intimate-feeling instrument in the player's grasp, and the Music Man neck – as featured on the Axis (formerly the EVH), Silhouette Special, and others – is another of these guitars' main talking points. It employs an irregular profile in cross section that is fatter on the bass-string side than the treble-string side, in order to fit more closely the natural curvature of the hand. In addition, necks with maple fingerboards have the truss-rods inserted by slicing the fingerboard from one piece of maple, then reattaching the piece with a seam so slight as to often be virtually undetectable.

The original version of the Silhouette model carried a 24-fret fingerboard, which cramped the pickup positioning somewhat. In 1995 Music Man released the Silhouette Special, which had a 22-fret fingerboard that allowed the neck pickup to be positioned closer to the Strat's tonally seminal position near the harmonic where the 24th fret would exist. An optional non-locking tremolo – at first a Wilkinson unit, later one of Music Man's own making – also made this a more vintage-leaning design.

A growing roster of professionals who endorse the brand

has also helped the contemporary Music Man line to fly. The twin-humbucker Axis – known from 1990–95 as the Edward Van Halen signature model – the Steve Lukather signature Luke, the Albert Lee, John Petrucci, and Steve Morse models have all included specs determined with the close cooperation of their namesakes, while also being set up for the working guitarist.

Leo Fender's creations during the first years of G&L's existence bore some resemblance to his Music Man designs, as well as to the Fender templates from which both companies sprang. Rather than recreate his all-time classics, however – which would probably have proved an extremely popular move given the continuing decline in the quality of Fender guitars in the late 1970s and into the early '80s – Leo Fender expanded upon many of his own latter-era design innovations at Music Man. Early G&L models such as the F-100, S-500, Cavalier, Broadcaster (later ASAT), and Comanche had the bullet headstock truss-rod adjustment and a much improved version of the three-bolt, micro-tilt neck joint that had become somewhat infamous as telltale signs of the less-popular 1970s Stratocasters – which sported a more poorly executed version of this three-bolt neck fixture – along with un-Fenderish humbucking pickups on many models, and often deluxe switching and control options, too.

> **1988 Music Man Silhouette**

> **Body:** solid alder with dual asymmetrical cutaways; polyurethane finish (all blue with eagle graphic, built for 1988 NAMM show)
> **Neck:** five-screw bolt-on maple neck with glued-on maple fingerboard with 10" fingerboard radius (rosewood optional), 24 nickel-silver frets, and 1⅝" nut width; 25½" scale length
> **Headstock:** asymmetrical headstock with four-plus-two Schaller tuners aligned for short but straight string pull from nut to tuner post; string clamp separate from nut
> **Bridge:** Music Man two-post locking Floyd Rose-style vibrato system
> **Electronics:** DiMarzio humbucking pickup in the bridge position and DiMarzio single-coil Strat-style pickups in middle and neck; five-way switch and two 500k potentiometers for volume and tone
> **Sound:** hot and punchy in the bridge position, round and open but with some high-end bite in the neck position

And Leo Fender's own Saddle Lock Bridge design, as seen primarily on the ASAT model, is one of the first departures from the classic Telecaster bridge that is widely acknowledged as capturing that gutsy, sustaining Tele tone.

Pickups have been another of G&L's major points of departure. Aside from the Strat- and Tele-like vintage-style alnico pickups included on some of the more recent Legacy and ASAT classic models, G&L's magnetics have included a broad range of original designs. The Legacy-sized, ASAT-sized, and narrow-soapbar-sized Magnetic Field Design pickups (MFDs) are all ballsy yet bright, and prove that sensitive, musical pickups can indeed be made with ceramic magnets. The distinctive, offset-coil Z-Coil units are wound with each half of the coil at opposite polarity to create a degree of hum rejection, but with a bright, snappy, and high-output single-coil sound. These are available with various combinations of features, including semi-hollow construction with or without an f-hole, different neck widths and radii, and an optional Bigsby on the Special and Z-3 models only.

Following Leo Fender's death in March 1991, control of G&L passed to BBE Sound, which continued production of many of the co-founder's newer designs, along with a number of guitars that were closer in spec and sound to Fender's early Telecaster and Stratocaster models in the form of the ASAT Classic and Legacy series. The Tele-shaped ASAT has been a particular favorite of new-country players, and comes in three major flavors: Classic (with vintage-Tele-like appointments), Special (MFD pickups), and Z-3 (three Z-coils).

To a great extent the full G&L line has become recognized as offering excellent American-made quality, but the basic versions of these models in particular are frequently praised for being good value for money. In 1997 G&L started a gradual move to a four-bolt neck joint, even though the three-bolt joint has always been praised for its solidity,

1992 Music Man EVH

> **Body:** single-cutaway body of solid basswood with quilted maple top; bound top
> **Neck:** five-screw bolt-on maple neck with maple fingerboard with 10" fingerboard radius (rosewood optional), 22 nickel-silver frets, and 1⅝" nut width; 25½" scale length
> **Headstock:** asymmetrical headstock with four-plus-two locking Schaller M6LA tuners with pearloid buttons; locking nut with string-tension bar
> **Bridge:** Music Man Floyd Rose-licensed locking tremolo with individually adjustable saddles; fine-tuners for each saddle
> **Electronics:** two custom-wound DiMarzio humbuckers; three-way toggle switch to select pickups individually or together; single 500k potentiometer for volume (knob labeled 'Tone' rather than 'Volume,' just as on EVH's original-parts guitar)
> **Sound:** fat, hot, and singing; good note definition and snappy attack, with plenty of midrange growl

and the company has also phased out the bullet headstock truss-rod adjustment. While the Fender company manufactures its guitars mostly in Corona, California, Scottsdale, Arizona, and Mexico, G&L has achieved a subtle bit of one-upmanship by locating its factory on Fender Avenue in Fullerton, California.

The Paul Reed Smith company (PRS) is best known for its set-neck guitars such as the Artist, Custom, and Santana models, which blend Gibson-esque features with functional and contemporary twists. But the bolt-neck CE model introduced in 1988 has remained popular, thanks in part no doubt to its utilitarian blend of full-bore PRS workmanship at a more affordable price. The earliest PRS production models blended Gibson and Fender to some extent, given their hybrid 25″ scale length and 10″ fingerboard radius, mix of carved maple tops and humbucking pickups with coil-tap switching options, and a vibrato tailpiece that was clearly Fender-inspired. But, given the set neck and frequently stunning figured maple 'Ten Tops' under sunburst and other translucent finishes, their look and playing feel always leaned a little more to the Big G. With its maple neck and fingerboard and alder body, the early CE was initially a way of reaching out to more Fender fans, but the later availability of rosewood fingerboards and some nice maple-capped mahogany bodies a little later made it into more of a bolt-on PRS for the masses, and that is the image it has retained.

Other PRS models will be examined in the following chapter, but the fact that the CE shared so many of the top models' clever features – including a smooth and efficient vibrato, a slick graphite-like nut, and proprietary tuners that all combined to minimize tuning hassles even during extensive vibrato use – made it a real bargain. As originally intended, with the bolt-on neck and, particularly, the maple fingerboard-alder body option, the guitar really did provide one of the better means of obtaining bright, snappy twang – in coil-tapped switch positions – or thick, warm, meaty lead sounds from one and the same guitar. In the early 1990s PRS also released the even more affordable

1998 PRS CE 22

> **Body:** double-cutaway solid alder body with arched figured maple top

> **Neck:** bolt-on maple neck and unbound rosewood fingerboard with 10" radius, 22 medium-jumbo nickel-silver frets, and 1¹¹⁄₁₆" nut width; 25" scale length

> **Headstock:** back-angled headstock with three-a-side sealed PRS locking tuners; friction-reducing nut

> **Bridge:** PRS 'stay in tune' vibrato tailpiece with individual saddles adjustable for both height and intonation

> **Electronics:** one HFS Treble (neck) pickup and one Vintage Bass (neck) pickup, both humbuckers; the former – which stands for 'hot, fat, and screams' – is wound hot with an alnico magnet and intended to excel at lead sounds through a cranked amp; the latter is an alnico-magnet pickup designed in the mold of the famous Gibson PAF; master volume and tone controls, and five-way rotary pickup selector giving: 1) treble pickup alone, 2) outer coils of each pickup in parallel, 3) inner coils of each pickup in series ('fat-Strat' sound), 4) Strat-like 'out of phase' (between bridge/middle) sound, 5) bass pickup alone

> **Sound:** wide-ranging, from hot humbucking bridge-pickup grind – although a little muddy and dark played clean – to warm, smooth neck-bucker tones, with plenty of snap and definition, and reasonable Fender impersonations in split-coil settings

2005 G&L ASAT Z-3

> **Body:** single-cutaway solid alder slab body

> **Neck:** bolt-on, one-piece maple neck and rosewood fingerboard with 12" radius, 22 medium-jumbo nickel-silver frets, and 1⅝" nut width; 25½" scale length

> **Headstock:** asymmetrical headstock with six-in-line sealed G&L tuners; bone nut; single friction-reducing string tree

> **Bridge:** Tune-o-matic-style bridge with Bigsby B-5 vibrato tailpiece, both partially routed into the body to increase break angle, and therefore tone and sustain

> **Electronics:** three G&L Z-Coil single-coil pickups, made with two individual 'half-length' coils wound to opposite polarity for hum rejection; ceramic magnets with adjustable threaded steel polepieces; DC resistance approximately 4.5k, although output is deceptively high, given the unusual design; five-way selector switch to give each pickup individually plus bridge-and-middle, neck-and-middle; 250k potentiometers for volume and tone

> **Sound:** snappy, cutting, and well-defined, with a full, round voice and relatively high output for a single-coil guitar; good hum rejection

bolt-neck EG series, some models of which were even more Fender-like than the early CEs, with three single-coil pickups and five-way blade switches rather than the traditional PRS rotary switch. It seems, however, that these didn't quite float with players as legit PRS guitars – despite being of good workmanship and value – and the line was discontinued in 1995.

Ibanez was probably better known early on in the copy era of the 1970s and early '80s for its semi-accurate renditions of Gibson models, but the company has evolved into one of the prime makers of superstrat-style instruments – that is, guitars with the approximate styling of a Fender Stratocaster, but with updated and hotrodded features – and has used bolt-neck construction in plenty of other models as well. Its Roadster series, launched in 1979 and popular

through the '80s, carried distinctly Fender-inspired models with a few twists, and offered playable, well-made guitars for the money.

While other Gibson-inspired models continued to proliferate from the Japanese company, however, the late 1980s and early '90s saw Ibanez shifting in a big way toward producing hotrod heavy-rock instruments for riff monsters. These were vaguely Strat-inspired, in that they carried some semblance of the seminal Fender's offset double-cutaway body styling and six-in-line headstock, but wide-thin neck profiles, dual humbuckers – or sometimes H/S/H setups – and dual-locking vibrato systems made them very different beasts indeed.

With the opening of a U.S. Custom Shop in 1988 along with endorsements from top heavy-rock players such as

Steve Vai (the JEM scrics), Joe Satriani (Radius models and later the JS series), John Petrucci (JPM100), and Frank Gambale (the FMG series), Ibanez staked a claim as pre-eminent rock-guitar manufacturer, a claim that the company has largely hung on to ever since. Meanwhile, other bolt-ons such as the discontinued Talman and more recent Jet King lines adopted retro looks and quirky appointments that helped them appeal to players in the indie and alternative fringes. Ibanez is another Japanese maker that has earned a lot of respect in the U.S.A. and Europe, and has become a big rival to the home-grown brands throughout a broad price range.

The Ibanez JS carries many of the features that have become standard fare on Satriani signature guitars, such as the twin humbuckers, double-locking vibrato system, slightly scalloped back, and the deluxe 'Chrome Boy' finish as used on many of the rock virtuoso's own guitars. In fact, by gaining the endorsements of both Satriani and fellow shredmeister Steve Vai, Ibanez has achieved a real coup in the progressive heavy rock market, and set itself up as the maker to beat.

Back when Japanese makers were still turning out cheaply made sub-copy-grade instruments from which even

1998 Ibanez JS 10th Anniversary

> **Body:** double-cutaway, chrome-covered synthetic luthite with slightly scalloped back (standard JS Series models usually have bodies of solid basswood, sometimes covered in a thin aluminum skin that is chromed)

> **Neck:** bolt-on maple neck with rosewood fingerboard, with 9½" fingerboard radius, 22 nickel-silver frets, thin 'JS' profile, and 1¹¹/₁₆" nut width; 25½" scale length

> **Headstock:** asymmetrical headstock with six-in-line Schaller tuners; steel locking nut and full string retainer

> **Bridge:** locking Edge Pro vibrato system

> **Electronics:** dual DiMarzio custom model humbucking pickups; two 500k potentiometers for master volume and tone controls; standard three-way switching

> **Sound:** hot and lithe, with a firm emphasis on performance through high-gain amplification; good sustain and easy harmonic feedback

beginners dreamed of moving on pretty quickly, some European manufacturers were making top-quality instruments. Although some of them look pretty funky – or, well, simply out of it – next to the Detroit-inspired Fenders and Gretsches and meticulously crafted Gibsons being made in the U.S.A. at the same time, companies such as Burns in Britain, Framus and Hofner in Germany, and Hagstrom (also known as Goya) in Sweden turned out many well-crafted and surprisingly playable models in their upmarket lines.

Some of these did carry touches of inspiration from the popular – and expensive – U.S. brands, but most also incorporated twists and innovations of their own. Many such makers had been building acoustic guitars for years before electrics boomed in the rock'n'roll craze of the 1950s and '60s – Hagstrom had been founded in 1921, for example, and Framus in 1946 – and their craft was well-honed by the time they turned to electrics in the 1960s to take advantage of the rage that was sweeping through Europe's teenagers.

Jim Burns founded the Ormston Burns Company in 1960, and for a time made some of the most distinctive

guitars to come out of Britain, or just about anywhere. The company's original high-end model, the Bison, debuted with four pickups and a set-neck. By 1962 the Bison had become a three-pickup, bolt-neck guitar, but was still an elaborate, very well-made instrument, and was the choice of many British players when U.S.-made Fenders and Gibsons were still expensive and hard to come by.

Burns's greatest achievement in the PR department came in 1964, when the company convinced Shadows guitarist Hank Marvin to put down his Fender Stratocaster in favor of the Burns Marvin model. As regards body shape, scale length, and electronics, the Marvin was very much in the shadow of the Strat nonetheless, although its multisegmented pickguard, scrolled headstock, and Rezo-tube vibrato system set it apart. The latter was a pretty complex piece of engineering, which used a knife-edged fulcrum point intended to reduce the friction encountered at the pivoting edge of the classic vintage Stratocaster vibrato, and six individual tubes for string anchoring rather than the single steel inertia block of the Strat. The tube part of the Rezo-tube system has also been used in non-vibrato

The Electric Guitar Sourcebook

Burns models, in the belief that these anchoring tubes increase the resonance of individual strings at the body end of the guitar.

The Burns company has had its ups and downs over the years: it was sold to the Baldwin Piano & Organ Company in 1965 – which also acquired Gretsch in 1967 – and subsequent London-based offshoots started by Jim Burns himself have come and gone, and Burns himself died in 1998. Since 1991 Burns London has produced a number of reissue and new models, manufactured both in the U.K. and overseas. Some are just Burns-flavored takes on timeless electric guitar styles, while others go to greater lengths to capture the genuine Burns quirks of old. Baldwin-era Bisons were more like the Burns Marvin than their original template; Baldwin ceased production of Burns-style guitars in 1970, after which time the company's fortunes have fluctuated.

A number of Hagstrom models found there way to the U.S.A., and became semi-successful mid-level alternatives despite competition from the big U.S. brands and cheaper imports. The most commonly seen of these were probably the models with distinctly Strat-like body lines and headstock shapes. Many had the central plastic fascia with slide-switch pickup and tone selectors, and some also had entire top overlays of plastic, too.

Players who picked up one of these models from the early 1960s often remember them for their thin necks; they could be pretty good instruments to play, if your hands took to that shape, and had a distinctive, bright, cutting sound that hinted at the twang and shimmer of many models from the Big F, but generally didn't capture the same woody resonance, sustain, or overall refinement. Other Hagstrom models have occasionally attained popularity, such as the Swede model that has proved a Les Paul alternative for some players – and which became the host guitar for Ampeg's short-lived Patch 2000 guitar synth system – or the diner-on-acid-styled P46 Deluxe, with sparkle-finish body and pearloid fingerboard.

A great many independent guitar makers today are designing and building original electrics to some of the highest standards ever achieved in the industry. Others are turning out studiously detailed and beautifully rendered versions of past classics, occasionally with subtle modifications and improvements intended to address the needs of modern players. Makers such as Don Grosh, Tom Anderson, John Suhr, Michael DeTemple, Rick Turner,

◁ 1964 Burns Marvin

> **Body:** Body: offset double-cutaway body of solid alder, with ribcage and forearm contours
> **Neck:** bolt-on maple neck with unbound rosewood fingerboard; with 7¼" fingerboard radius, 21 nickel-silver frets, 1⅝" nut width; 25½" scale length
> **Headstock:** symmetrical scroll-topped headstock with three-a-side tuners; zero fret
> **Bridge:** Burns Rezo-tube vibrato system
> **Electronics:** three Burns Rez-o-matik single-coil pickups with six individual alnico slug polepieces; DC resistance approximately 6k; three-way switch to select each pickup individually, with three 250k potentiometers for master volume and tone controls for neck and middle pickups
> **Sound:** bright and cutting, with a certain openness and depth at its core

Gerard Melancon, and many others in the U.S.A., and their British colleagues such as Patrick Eggle, Hugh Manson, and the late Sid Poole have achieved new heights in look, tone, and playability. Many of the great electric guitar makers of the 1950s and '60s benefited from having access to well-aged supplies of good, light timber, and the fact that so many vintage guitars contain great tone wood can be chalked up partly to good fortune and, simply, what was available at the time. High-end contemporary makers are arguably putting even more thought into their woods than did Fender, Gibson, Guild, and others in the past, and are offering single-wood types and combinations that are both thoughtful and adventurous. Today's makers also have access to countless advancements in hardware and pickup manufacturing that vastly broaden the tonal palette available to them.

Grosh Guitars, for example, offers both original designs and updated partial-reproductions of vintage classics. Even when doing the latter, this luthier adds subtle touches that make these guitars their own, and simultaneously more appealing to those of today's players who appreciate hand-honed playability and other tonal and functional advantages that a custom-made guitar can often have over even the finest vintage examples. John Suhr Guitars likewise does a Classic range, that includes guitars that are in many ways close reproductions of vintage Fender Stratocasters and Telecasters but with subtle updates and improvements; but

❯ 2002 John Suhr Standard

> **Body:** double-cutaway solid basswood body with highly figured maple top; smoothly sculpted body-neck joint
> **Neck:** bolt-on maple neck with pau ferro fingerboard with compound 11" to 14" radius and 1¹¹⁄₁₆" nut width, with slim 'C' profile, 22 nickel-silver frets; 25½" scale length
> **Headstock:** asymmetrical headstock with six-in-line staggered Sperzel locking tuners; Buzz Feiten Tuning System (compensated nut)
> **Bridge:** Gotoh 1099 vibrato bridge, with cast-steel saddles and two-post fulcrum pivot
> **Electronics:** Suhr-made JST humbucking pickup in the bridge position (alnico bar magnet, steel polepieces), and Suhr-made V60 single-coil pickups in the middle and neck positions (made with alnico slug magnets); five-way pickup selector, and master volume and tone controls
> **Sound:** full, responsive, and dynamic, with good sustain and considerable punch; from throaty and round in the neck position, to thick and wailing with some midrange emphasis in the bridge position

◀ 1963 Hagstrom Kent PG24G

> **Body:** alder with screwed-on plastic facing; offset double-cutaway design
> **Neck:** bolt-on maple neck with rosewood fingerboard and distinctively narrow-thin profile, 22 nickel-silver frets; 25½" scale length
> **Headstock:** asymmetrical headstock with six-in-line no-name tuners; black plastic nut and full-width retaining bar
> **Bridge:** one-piece rosewood bridge with plastic saddle; Hagstrom vibrato system
> **Electronics:** two single-coil Hagstrom pickups with medium-low output; potentiometer for volume control; slide switches for individual pickup on/off, preset tone selections, and mute
> **Sound:** bright and light, with a certain graininess when pushed

the 'classic' Suhr style in itself is probably the superstrat shape – which Suhr calls the Standard – with a highly figured maple top on a body of alder, ash, or basswood, a humbucker in the bridge position, and other clever design points to make the instruments versatile tools for the modern musician.

John Suhr was the luthier behind the Pensa-Suhr guitars offered with partner Rudy Pensa at Rudy's Music in New York in the 1980s, as played by Mark Knopfler, Lou Reed, Eric Clapton, and others. Suhr later worked as a Senior Master Builder at the Fender Custom Shop, then set up his own shop in the late 1990s. While the Suhr flagship line has been called the Standard, the guitars in this range are anything but, and, in fact, they vary widely according to customer's desires or the maker's fancies: carved or flat tops;

chambered or solid bodies; rosewood, ebony, or pau ferro fingerboards; and many other variables are encompassed in the line.

Suhr Guitars uses a blend of hand-building and state-of-the-art technology. Modern CNC routers are used to carve bodies and necks, but each guitar is made and completed by a single builder, and a great amount of attention to detail goes into the process. Suhr guitars also blends other elements of old and new, using vintage-style single truss-rods for tonal considerations, but carving necks to a range of compound radii – that is, a fingerboard radius that gradually widens from the nut to the upper frets, for example from 11" to 14" or 9" to 12". Ultimately, this is a guitar maker that shows that it might still be difficult to escape the classic molds entirely, but you can go a long way by trying.

3

Set-Neck Solidbodies

With Fender's Telecaster proving it was no flash in the pan, other manufacturers who had avoided jumping on the solidbody bandwagon soon realized they might miss the hayride altogether if they didn't adjust their conservative thinking. Many of these were long-established makers with deep roots in guitar tradition, and they weren't about to abandon their established design formats entirely in order to turn out plank-bodied electrics. Many of them, therefore, blended elements of more labor-intensive craftsmanship with the new solidbody ethos.

Foremost among these companies was Gibson, the biggest name to take the solidbody plunge. Gibson had built up an enormous roster of players who endorsed its hollowbody archtop electrics long before it ever considered 'stooping' to solidbody electric-guitar construction. Orville Gibson had invented the archtop guitar in the 19th century, and the company had introduced the first widely available and truly successful electric guitar in 1936 in the form of the ES-150, so a great weight of heritage underpinned its fledgling efforts to market a solidbody electric.

Jazz- and pop-guitar star Les Paul had been trying for some years to convince Gibson to make a solid guitar, and with upstart Fender fast gaining a monopoly in the new market, company execs finally decided it would be good to put together Paul's ideas with those of their own designers to see what they could come up with. The result, the Gibson Les Paul of 1952, was, therefore, far more a blend of existing guitar-making tradition and slab-body-style thinking than the Telecaster had been, or even most of the experiments and prototypes that other makers had worked with up to that time. It had a bound, carved maple top, a glued dovetail neck joint, a separate bound rosewood fingerboard, and a back-angled headstock, all in hollowbody archtop tradition, and all married to the solid slab of mahogany that constituted the body, and this made this guitar something truly new. One element from archtop tradition that Gibson should have kept on the original Les Paul, but didn't, was the

fully back-angled (pitched) neck, and this was the model's great failing. A relatively flat neck angle resulted in a very low string height across the face of the guitar to the bridge, and required Gibson makers to wrap the strings under rather than over the stop-bar of the integral trapeze bridge-tailpiece. The guitar still played, but not as well as it should, and edge-of-hand string muting while picking was all but impossible.

Gibson corrected the design at Les Paul's own urging, but only some 4,000 guitars down the production line. Even in its flawed state the Les Paul had been making some waves; with a corrected neck pitch and improved wrapover tailpiece, it gained further followers, and was a much more toneful and playable instrument, too. Now Gibson had a sturdy, resonant, long-sustaining solidbody on its hands, with a core voice that blended excellent warmth and balance from the mahogany neck and body, along with plenty of

◄ 1959 Gibson Les Paul

> **Body:** solid mahogany body with carved, arched maple top (usually two-piece); top binding; single cutaway; semi-transparent cherry-to-amber sunburst finish in nitrocellulose lacquer

> **Neck:** glued-in, one-piece mahogany neck with rosewood fingerboard with 12" fingerboard radius, 22 jumbo nickel-silver frets, and 1¹¹⁄₁₆" nut width; 25⅝" scale length (in 1958 and '59 neck profile was chunky, but became much thinner in 1960)

> **Headstock:** symmetrical 17-degree back-angled headstock with three-a-side tulip-button Kluson tuners; bone nut

> **Bridge:** adjustable Tune-o-matic bridge and stop-bar tailpiece

> **Electronics:** dual humbucking pickups constructed of single alnico bar magnet beneath, six fixed steel-slug polepieces in one coil and six threaded adjustable polepieces in the other; DC resistance of 7.5k to 8k; nickel-plated steel cover; three-way toggle switch to select either pickup alone or both together; four 500k potentiometers for individual volume and tone for each pickup

> **Sound:** thick, warm, fluty, and vocal from the neck pickup, punchy and cutting from the bridge; muscular punch and singing sustain; good hum rejection

⌃ 1953 Les Paul Gold-top

> **Body:** same construction as 1959 Les Paul, with gold nitrocellulose finish

> **Bridge:** steel wrapover bar bridge-tailpiece with stud mounting

> **Electronics:** two identical P-90 pickups, constructed with a pair of alnico bar magnets and six threaded, adjustable steel polepieces each; DC resistance of approximately 7.25k to 8.25k; same switching and controls as 1959 Les Paul

> **Sound:** roughly as per 1959 Les Paul with humbuckers, but with a grittier and slightly more raw tone in both positions; a little more snap and twang from the bridge selection, and more noise and potential microphonics

sparkle and definition from the maple top. Most importantly it had the far sharper attack, considerably less woolly sound, and excellent avoidance of feedback compared with similarly attired Gibson hollowbody electrics. The hot P-90 pickups, set neck, more complex 'wood-sandwich' construction, and 24¾" scale length all combined to make it a fatter sounding guitar than the Fender Telecaster or the Stratocaster that was soon to arrive, all of which combined to make it an effective instrument for the player seeking to cut through the mud in a big-band context. This suited some players well, and, indeed, helped carry the Les Paul over to a few forward-looking jazz players who had habitually played earlier Gibson models, but others wanted brighter sounds and a less willing distortion, so this now-legendary guitar wasn't quite the success early on that we might expect it to have been.

Still, Gibson forged on with improvements almost yearly through the course of the 1950s. One of Gibson's crowning achievements, the Tune-o-matic bridge, appeared on the black-finished Les Paul Custom in 1954 and on the standard model late in the following year, bringing individual string intonation adjustment to Gibson guitars for the first time. The bridge made it a more effective instrument for many players, and increased its sustain as well, although some still swear by the solid tones and easy bending afforded by the wrapover bridge that followed the rather abysmal 'wrapunder' trapeze design, despite the all-or-nothing intonation capabilities of the single-bar unit. But in 1957 the Les Paul really secured its status as one of the top tone-classics of all time with the introduction of Gibson's humbucking pickup, developed by Seth Lover. A year later, when a sunburst finish was applied to the guitar's maple top, the package was complete. Other changes included the use of wider frets from 1959 onward, and a slimmer neck in 1960.

Gibson's new humbucker, as discussed in detail in the opening chapter, proved the optimum pickup for capturing the Les Paul's potential. It emphasized the guitar's warmth while still projecting enough high-end sizzle to cut through the band, and finally made the most of the instrument's potential for singing sustain, helped by the solid string anchoring of the Tune-o-matic bridge and stop-tail combination at the body end and the steeply back-angled

headstock at the other, which created good resonance-enhancing string pressure in the nut slots. Oddly enough, the guitar's full potential wasn't even realized until after the model's demise in 1960, when it was replaced by the SG-shaped Les Paul model, known simply as the SG after Paul's endorsement deal ended a couple years later. While the humbucker-loaded Les Paul of 1957–60 was a fine design for jazz and rock'n'roll, it really came into its own when married with a cranked amp, as British blues-rock players in particular began to discover in the mid 1960s. The American guitar and a British Marshall amplifier proved unrivaled partners, and Eric Clapton, Peter Green, Jimmy Page, Paul Kossoff, Mick Taylor, and many others have proved the potency of that combination ever since. This sturdy instrument's fat-sounding pickups both drive an amp hard, and do a good job of igniting the kind of relatively hum-free, harmonic feedback cycle that elicits a really wailing tone and potentially endless sustain. While the original 1957–60 model is the epitome of the form, plenty of great rock has been played on later models. When fitted with good pickups and set up right, they still capture the essence of the seminal set-neck, solidbody, maple-mahogany, humbucker-fired sound that has forever been associated in rock circles with the Les Paul name.

None of this is entirely what Mr Paul himself envisaged back in the late 1940s and early '50s while experimenting

1961 Rickenbacker 460

> **Body:** solid maple body with flat face; top binding; deep double cutaways with easy access to the top fret; semi-transparent cherry sunburst finish in nitrocellulose lacquer
> **Neck:** maple through-neck (integral neck and central body block cut from one piece of wood), with rosewood fingerboard, 10" fingerboard radius, 21 nickel-silver frets, and 1⅝" nut width; 24¾" scale length
> **Headstock:** back-angled asymmetrical headstock, with three-a-side Kluson tuners; synthetic nut
> **Bridge:** strings top-anchored in rear lip of sheet-steel base plate, forming bridge base-tailpiece unit; one-piece die-cast compensated aluminum bridge, adjustable for height only (bridge derives from the design of the floating bridge of the Bigsby vibrato)
> **Electronics:** dual single-coil pickups; early 'toaster tops' had quite low DC resistance readings in the 5k to 6k range, while those of the mid 1960s ranged widely between 7k and 8.5k; three-way toggle switch to select either pickup alone or both together; two 250k potentiometers for individual volume and two 500k pots for individual tone for each pickup; 500k pot for blend control, which can add a little of the non-selected pickup to the sound of the one selected by the switch, or emphasize more of either pickup in the middle switch position
> **Sound:** generally bright, chiming, and cutting, with a good blend of sparkle and tightness, and just a little sizzle; a classic rhythm guitar for British invasion or West Coast jangle sounds

with his solid-timber-centered 'log' guitar, Gibson's rendering of which took so many revisions – and involved so many compromises – that the man whose name it bore was never entirely happy with production models anyway. But talk to plenty of players today who crave that sweet, vocal, singing rock lead tone, and they'll tell you a Les Paul is the first choice for the job. Of course, some of the changes over the years are not looked favorably upon. Gibson changed headstock angles from 17 degrees to a shallower 14 degrees between 1966 and 1973 in order to reduce the likelihood of breakage. The change also lessened the tone in the opinion of some players. Les Pauls weren't being made during the earlier part of that run, but the first reintroduced Les Paul Standard models of 1968 and the Deluxes that followed had this lesser headstock angle. The mini-humbuckers of the Les Paul Deluxe model are decent enough pickups in themselves, but they still don't do the full-size humbucker thing, and many, many players have swapped them out over the years. Also, wood combinations in later Les Pauls were not always faithful to the original formula. Many Deluxes had a different body construction, with a mahogany-maple-mahogany body sandwich with maple top, a three-piece or all-maple neck, and so forth.

Some later, more affordable opaque-finished versions of the Les Paul were also made with solid mahogany bodies, without the maple top at all. Buyers should check specific models when shopping for a guitar, and not assume that all Les Pauls were created equal. Later reissues of the Les Paul Standard are sometimes more faithful to the original design and sound than mid-period versions of the model.

Rickenbacker had experimented with solidbody electric guitar designs well before Fender and Gibson

entered the game. The company had offered both lap-steel and Spanish-style instruments in wood and bakelite way back in the mid 1930s, but units never approached anything like mass production until the 1950s. Even with what should have been a considerable head start, Rickenbacker was relatively slow to evolve solidbody electric styles that would have any staying power, and it wasn't until the latter part of the rock'n'roll decade that the company introduced any instruments whose legacies remain with us today.

Rickenbacker Combo models of the mid 1950s had

either tulip-shaped bodies or the long, pointy, slightly offset horns that would become more familiar a few years later on the semi-hollow 325 – the so-called 'John Lennon model' – and carried either toaster-top pickups or the large horseshoe pickup familiar from their earlier lap-steels, or both. All are distinctive guitars, and have their place in history, but the point of this book is to assess specs and sounds that are, by and large, within reach of players today, so it makes more sense to look at a model from the 400 series or the similar 600 series. These, for the most part, had full-scale necks, solid maple bodies in the 'cresting-wave' cutaway style, and a pair of toaster-top pickups.

The 400 models, introduced in 1958, were the more affordable of Rickenbacker's full-size guitars, with single-level scratchplates and simpler adornment. By marrying hard, bright woods and single-coil pickups with set-neck construction and a 24¾" scale length they could be considered as blending the Fender and Gibson sound and feel to some extent. In fact, the necks on many of these Rickenbacker models was more than just 'set,' it ran all the way through the body in an integral neck and center-block unit carved from a single piece of wood. (Note how the cream binding stops at the point where this center block arrives at the tail end of the body in the 460 in the main photo.) As might be expected, such through-neck designs offer even greater transference of vibrational energy between neck and body, since, in fact, they are one and the same. The tonal results of this are not necessarily that much different from those of a well-constructed glued-neck guitar, but subtle variations might be

detectable in some examples, showing up as elements such as a firm response and good sustain.

In any case, given their maple-on-maple construction – plus, in most cases, a rosewood fingerboard – and snappy single-coil pickups, these Rickenbackers leaned more toward the jangly, twangy, and shimmery sides of the tonal spectrum, although their voice was indeed rounded out some by the denser and slightly more blurred harmonic content of the 24¾" scale length. Given their snappy attack, propensity to brightness, and slightly sizzling undercurrent, such guitars can still drive an old tube amp pretty well, however, and they generally offer good dynamics and a surprising degree of versatility. Early Rickenbacker bridges, however, weren't quite as solid or resonance-inducing as any of the major Gibson or Fender designs, and this piece of hardware served to lighten the guitars' tone somewhat.

A Catch-22-like combination of the Rickenbacker's sonic signature and the playing styles of the majority of name artists who have used them has resulted in a reputation that pins the model down as a rhythm-guitar-only design. Indeed, the classic Rickenbacker sound is neither bluesy nor heavy, and the players who do use them to solo with more often do so in the context of short, melodic breaks rather than extended, wailing solos slathered in heavy distortion. The likes of Roger McGuinn, George Harrison, Peter Buck, Tom Petty, and Mike Campbell exhibit the classic jangle and chime of which these guitars are capable – although very often on other, semi-hollow models, which will be discussed later in the book – while Pete Townshend in his early years and Paul Weller of

◄ 1962 Gretsch Corvette Princess

> **Body:** solid mahogany body with beveled edges and dual equal-depth cutaways with pointed, non-concentric horns; finished in ivory nitrocellulose lacquer
> **Neck:** one-piece mahogany neck with rosewood fingerboard, 21 nickel-silver frets, and $1^{23}/_{32}$" nut width; $24^{1}/_{2}$" scale length
> **Headstock:** back-angled symmetrical headstock, with three-a-side tuners; headstock-end truss-rod adjustment
> **Bridge:** slotted bar bridge adjustable for height only; trapeze tailpiece; optional clip-on vibrato unit
> **Electronics:** single HiLo'Tron single-coil pickup; DC resistance averaging around 3.5k; two 250k potentiometers for individual volume and tone
> **Sound:** bright, tight, and well defined, with a little roundness and warmth from the all-mahogany construction

⌄ 1961 Gretsch Corvette

> **Body:** slab-style solid mahogany body with dual asymmetrical cutaways
> **Neck:** similar to 1962 Corvette above, but with body end truss-rod adjustment

The Jam display the Rickenbacker's potential as a more powerful rhythm and chordal-lead instrument.

Gretsch had competed with Gibson through much of the jazz age, even though the New York maker's big archtops were not quite as well made as those of the Kalamazoo originator of the breed. But when rock'n'roll burst on the scene, Gretsch put a lot more emphasis on its electric models, and gave Gibson a good run for its money throughout much of the 1950s and '60s. All of the classic, higher-end instruments in the line, however, were semi-solid or hollowbody models, and will be discussed in later chapters. Gretsch's genuine set-neck solidbodies were mid-level instruments aimed at the Michigan competition's Les Paul – later SG – Special and Junior models,

and were pretty simple affairs compared with the elaborate, even complex brand leaders such as the 6120, the Country Gent, and the Duo Jet. Although these downmarket Gretsch guitars never attained anything like classic status, they still make a good case study in the resultant sound and performance of their collected parts and design criteria.

While the big U.S. makers, Fender, Gibson, Gretsch, and Rickenbacker, largely avoided copying each other through the early days of their head-to-head competition, Gretsch appears to have thrown aside this point of pride around 1960 as regards its budget-range guitars. The first solidbodied Corvette models looked very similar to a double-cutaway Gibson Les Paul Special or Junior – albeit

with different pickguards and hardware, and a slightly withered treble-side horn – and models that followed in the mid 1960s paralleled the pointier SG shape to an equally asymmetrical degree. The original Corvette had a slab-style mahogany body with mahogany neck joined at the very end of the 21-fret rosewood fingerboard. One HiLo'Tron pickup and standard controls was all you got for electronics, while the bridge was Gretsch's most basic slotted-bar design coupled with a foreshortened trapeze tailpiece.

The HiLo'Tron pickups are much maligned units, partly because they don't achieve sounds anything like the long-worshiped DeArmond or Filter'Tron units that upmarket Gretsch models carried, but they are effective enough as bright, low-output single-coils go. On the plus side, they offer good string definition and a high twang factor, which is what a lot of players seek in a Gretsch guitar in the first place. On the down side, their low output – usually between 3k and 4k, give or take a few hundred ohms – doesn't give these lower-priced guitars the ability to rock that, for example, a Gibson P-90 gives a Les Paul or an SG Junior. Even so, they have a similar no-frills, ready to rock – or at least roll – appeal to Gibson's basic models, and, with a good booster pedal in the chain, they are good guitars for raw rock'n'roll or driving punk styles. Also, many examples have round, clubby necks, which can be appealing to some players, although off-putting to others, and many of the later SG-like versions are delightfully light guitars, weighing in at around 6¼ to 6¾ pounds.

The Corvette's details evolved over the course of the 1960s, taking on the beveled-edge body styling in 1962 and a two-pickup option a year later. In 1965 the body adopted a notched recess at the tail end where the strap button was located, along with a two-and-four tuner array on the headstock. For a brief period, between 1962 and '63, custom-dress Princess and Twist variations were available, in pastel and peppermint-red paint jobs respectively – the latter with a candy-striped pickguard to boot – and special gold sparkle or silver sparkle Gold Duke and Silver Duke versions were offered in 1966. Of all Corvettes, these are the only ones to have attained truly collectable status so for. Throughout its run, the Corvette offered a number of different vibrato options: first the highly ineffectual clip-on vibrato handle that clasped the strings between the bridge and the trapeze tailpiece, and later a Bigsby vibrato or Burns vibrato. (As we have seen the British Burns guitar company had been bought by the Baldwin Piano & Organ Company in 1965, which subsequently courted Gretsch, and closed the deal on the New York guitar and drum maker in 1967.)

Aside from their fun, utilitarian vibe, the likes of the Gretsch Corvette offer slimmer-walleted players a chance to grasp a little vintage wood and wire without selling the farm. At the time of writing, standard-finish, single-pickup versions could still be had for well under $1,000. The Corvette is also a good generic example of the single-coil, set-neck, slab-bodied type of instrument, the qualities of

which can be applied to a large number of lower- and mid-priced models that have been produced over the years. Adjust for variables in pickups and wood types, conduct a little sonic extrapolation, and you can largely determine the similarities between a great number of outwardly different-looking guitars.

Just as Fender dominated the ranks of quality bolt-neck electrics in the 1950s and '60s, Gibson's presence accounted for far more than just the Les Paul Standard in the set-necks camp. At the mid-priced level – or what you might call the entry level of the professional market – the Les Paul Special and Junior models really were the guitars to gun for, as mentioned in the above analysis of the Gretsch Corvette. They offered slab-bodied simplicity and retained their simpler, noisier single-coil P-90 pickups long after the humbucker was invented, yet they were Gibson all the way, and they won over a huge number of followers.

When the Les Paul Junior was first introduced in 1954 there was a little less to differentiate it from its big brother than there would be a few years down the road – given that the full-priced Les Paul still carried P-90 pickups and a

ⓦ 1957 Gibson Les Paul Special

> **Body:** solid mahogany slab body with single cutaway; pale 'limed' finish in nitrocellulose lacquer, no binding
> **Neck:** one-piece mahogany neck with bound rosewood fingerboard, joining upper bout at the 16th fret, 22 nickel-silver frets, 1¹¹⁄₁₆" nut width and 12" fingerboard radius; 24⅝" scale length; chunky, rounded neck profiles in the mid to late 1950s, and slimmer from around 1960 onward
> **Headstock:** back-angled symmetrical headstock, with three-a-side Kluson tuners; headstock-end truss-rod adjustment
> **Bridge:** wrapover bridge-tailpiece
> **Electronics:** two single-coil P-90 pickups with dual alnico bar magnets mounted beneath, and six threaded steel polepieces; DC resistance approximately 7.5k to 8.2k; three-way toggle switch for either pickup independently or both together; individual volume and tone controls
> **Sound:** warm, round, and full, with plenty of power and a pronounced midrange honk for rock leads

ⓥ 1961 Gibson SG/Les Paul Junior

> **Body:** slab-style solid mahogany body with pointed horns and beveled edges; finished in translucent cherry nitrocellulose lacquer
> **Neck:** slim neck profile, unbound rosewood fingerboard, joins body at the 22nd fret; otherwise similar in materials and proportions to the Les Paul Special in the main photo
> **Electronics:** single dog-ear P-90 pickup with volume and tone controls
> **Sound:** open, ringing, and bright, with an edge of grit and some midrange emphasis

wrapover bridge – but it was clearly a more basic model. Its solid, flat-topped mahogany body lacked the flagship model's carved maple cap, and was unbound like its neck. The neck shape and scale were similar, although the neck-body joint was cruder and more squared-off, and the fingerboard carried simple abalone dot position markers rather than the dressier crown inlays. Still, the single-cutaway body lines were much the same – if a little less elegant in the black-to-amber sunburst finish rather than the gold – and if you preferred the bridge pickup selection anyway you weren't getting a wildly different sound, either.

The two-pickup Special, introduced in 1955, brought you even closer to the big boy, with a bound neck and a full array of controls; but, of course, either guitar, when compared with a carved-top Les Paul gold-top, provides a lesson in a wood's contribution to any instrument's tonal palette. The all-mahogany Junior and Special lack a little of the maple-capped Standard's attack and definition, and come off sounding just a shade woollier as a result. Just a shade, mind you, and they remain outstanding, no-nonsense rockers in a slightly raw vein. The P-90 pickup and a slab of mahogany go well together, and the partnership emphasizes these models' full, round voices with an edge of grainy texture that helps the sound cut through. The basic

wrapover bridge makes them solidly resonant and affords easy bending at the same time. Whereas the carved-top Les Paul with humbuckers is your stadium-rock guitar, the Junior and Special are your choice for the sweaty stage of a heaving punk club.

The Les Paul Junior and Special received the pale 'limed' finish of the very collectable TV model in 1957. The former adopted double-cutaway body styling in 1958, and the latter followed in '59. The pale TV-finished version of the Junior became the SG TV later in 1959, while the standard-finished versions remained the Les Paul Junior; at the same time the Les Paul Special became the SG Special. In 1961 both guitars adopted the thinner, beveled, pointy horned SG body styling.

With pickups and hardware staying pretty consistent, these changes to body styles didn't affect the sound of the guitars greatly, although the sound of the Les Paul/SG Junior and Special did evolve somewhat. The move to a double-cutaway body took a chunk out of the neck-body coupling and opened up the sound somewhat, creating a difference between the two models that some players like and others don't. The further move to the SG shape robbed a little more mass from the body, and consequently lightened the tone just slightly. In truth, there is often so

⌃ 1961 Gibson Les Paul/SG

> **Body:** solid mahogany double-cutaway body with 'almost concentric' pointed horns, beveled edges, no binding; nitrocellulose finish

> **Neck:** one-piece mahogany neck with bound rosewood fingerboard, 22 nickel-silver frets, 1¹¹⁄₁₆" nut width, and 12" fingerboard radius; 24⅝" scale length; slim, flattish neck profiles in the early 1960s, and a little chunkier later in the decade

> **Headstock:** back-angled symmetrical headstock, with three-a-side Kluson tuners; headstock-end truss-rod adjustment

> **Bridge:** Tune-o-matic bridge and Maestro Vibrola tailpiece

> **Electronics:** two PAF humbucking pickups with single alnico bar magnets mounted beneath one coil with six steel-slug polepieces and one with six adjustable threaded steel polepieces; DC resistance approximately 7.5k; three-way toggle switch for either pickup independently or both together; individual volume and tone controls

> **Sound:** warm, chunky, and largely very well balanced, with a characteristic sizzle; decent sustain and good power for rock soloing

much variation between such guitars, even of the same year and model, that players who are shopping for 'the ultimate Junior' – or the ultimate anything, vintage guitars in particular – need to A/B as many as possible to discern the differences – or indeed to A/B/C/D/E… The important thing to be aware of is that the differences do exist, and that the slight changes made over these years affected the guitars in ways that are often discernible to the player.

A more easily detectable consequence of these changes is the weakening of the neck-body joint in the move to the double-cutaway models. When the extra wood was removed from the upper bout, it left the neck hanging on to the body by nothing but the tenon – the block at the end of the neck that extends into the body pocket – which resulted in a far less stable structure overall. The two-pickup Specials in

particular suffered from a distressing number of neck breaks, because of the even thinner coupling resulting from the necessity of routing out more wood for a neck pickup, and Gibson later moved the neck pickup further into the body in an effort to correct this weakness. Throughout the 1960s similar changes were made to SG Specials in an effort to strengthen the neck-body joint, but it remained something of an Achilles heel for Gibson. Even when actual breakage isn't an issue, these double-cutaway guitars can have their own form of built-in vibrato thanks to the flimsier joint: strum an SG Special and give the neck a shake, and the pitch wobbles considerably. Some players have made good use of the effect, while others have found that this weakness just leads to problems staying in tune.

Both the SG and Les Paul variants of the Junior and Special

1959 Gibson Flying V

> **Body:** slab-style solid korina body (usually two-piece)

> **Neck:** chunky korina neck with unbound rosewood fingerboard, joins body at the 22nd fret

> **Headstock:** arrow-shaped headstock with three-a-side Kluson tuners

> **Electronics:** dual PAF humbucking pickups; three-way toggle switch for each pickup individually or both together; three 500k potentiometers for individual volume and master tone

> **Sound:** round, rich, and resonant, with good power and excellent sustain

have remained popular throughout Gibson's run. A number of good, workmanlike models have been made available in more recent years, some of which have carried the newer stacked-coil P-100 humbuckers. To some players' ears these pickups don't quite replicate the authentic single-coil P-90 sound, but good, well-made P-90 replacements are available from both Gibson and after-market replacement pickup makers.

Having also briefly passed on the Les Paul Standard and Custom names to the SG body style in the early 1960s, Gibson created a taste among some guitarists for the thinner, lighter, pointy-horned electric that stayed even after the return of the single-cutaway, carved-top model. The SG has always been seen as somewhat of a more raw, rebellious rocker compared with the Les Paul, maybe because it was often the choice of heavy players: Tony Iommi, *Live At Leeds*-era Pete Townshend, and AC/DC's Angus Young, for example. In truth, it's another pretty versatile Gibson, capable of excelling at anything from blues to jazz to alt-rock, but it does somehow seem a down'n'dirty rocker at heart.

Comparing an SG with a Les Paul makes another good exercise in the tonal changes wrought by tweaking just a few variables on otherwise similar guitars. A 1959 Les Paul and a 1969 SG Standard – with stop-bar tailpiece rather than Vibrola unit – both possess two humbucking pickups, a body in which mahogany is the main proportional ingredient, glued-in 22-fret mahogany necks with rosewood fingerboards, and 1¹¹⁄₁₆″ nut widths, and the Tune-o-matic bridge and stop-tail pairing. Tonally, they are both within the ballpark of 'warm, powerful, humbucking guitars,' but if you listen closely there are discernible differences within that

framework. The SG's tone is certainly big, but is often a little lighter or less dimensional than the Les Paul's; it is less refined overall, and also usually has a little less string-to-string definition, but can sometimes sound a little snappier at the same time. Of course, depending upon your amp and other variables within your rig, you might pluck one SG and one Les Paul out of runs of thousands, and find they sound almost identical. As a species, however, these subtle differences in sound tend to hold true. Of course, a late 1960s or early '70s SG would have that slightly shallower headstock pitch of 14 degrees, but so would any single-cutaway Les Paul from the same era.

The SG's thinner mahogany body and lack of a dense maple top also makes it a lighter guitar, and this alone was enough to win over many fans, especially in the 1970s when Gibson was turning out some real dead-weight Les Pauls. The pointed, almost demonic horns of the double-cutaway design also give the model a more radical, more 'let's rawk' look than the gentle Les Paul's elegantly arched sunburst top, which aped the hollowbody jazz-guitar designs that had already been around for a couple of decades when it was launched. Indeed, the SG was surprisingly modern looking for the conservative Gibson company of 1960, if slightly less so than another pair of radical upstarts that never made it far out of the blocks. Clearly aware that Fender was leaving them behind in the hotrod-visuals department, and hence earning greater appeal to the booming rock'n'roll market, Gibson pulled out all the space-aged stops in 1958 and came up with the two-model Modernistic series: the Flying V and the Explorer. These carried mostly standard Gibson humbucking pickups and hardware, and surprisingly staid translucent amber finishes on their korina wood bodies, but the shapes of those bodies were out of this world: the Flying V, obviously, taking a fat, swept-wing V-shape, and the Explorer an angular, wedge-like concoction of transversal points.

Gibson either went too far for public taste with the Modernistics, or simply didn't give the new designs time to find their market. Slightly fewer than 100 Flying Vs and fewer than a quarter of that number of Explorers were made in the late 1950s, with a couple of dozen more of each assembled in the early 1960s out of leftover parts. But their later adoption by a number of major players – Jimi Hendrix, Eric Clapton, and Michael Schenker among them – has posthumously raised them to classic status, and the two have proliferated in the forms of reissued and updated models, both from Gibson and from rival makers.

Original and good reissue examples of the Flying V and Explorer are distinguished not only by their radical shapes, but by the korina wood from which they are made. At the risk of sounding like a broken record, these models toss yet another variable into the set-neck-and-humbuckers stew that allows otherwise similarly outfitted guitars to sound somewhat different, as seen in our Les Paul and SG comparison. Korina is an African hardwood that is not dissimilar to mahogany, but is often a little lighter and highly resonant, and imparts excellent sustain. It isn't widely imported to the U.S.A., and therefore hasn't been seen in a great number of guitars, but has been used by other makers, as seen in the Ibanez Destroyer and Rocket Roll models – Explorer and Flying V copies respectively – or the Hamer Artist Korina. The unusual shapes of these guitars also impart their own tonalities that, combined with the korina's

⊙ 1981 Ibanez Artist 2618

> **Body:** solid mahogany body with carved maple top; double-cutaway body with concentric horns; top binding; polyurethane finish

> **Neck:** three-ply maple neck (birch on some models) with bound rosewood fingerboard, 22 nickel-silver frets, 1¹¹⁄₁₆″ nut width, and 12″ fingerboard radius; 24¾″ scale length

> **Headstock:** back-angled symmetrical headstock, with three-a-side Velve-Tune Ibanez tuners; headstock-end truss-rod adjustment

> **Bridge:** Ibanez Gibralter bridge (adjustable Tune-o-matic derivative); Quick Change tailpiece with plate

> **Electronics:** two humbucking Super 70 pickups with no covers, alnico magnets (possibly alnico VIII) and adjustable polepieces; three-way toggle switch for either pickup independently or both together; individual volume and tone controls

> **Sound:** this Artist model, which is similar to the later AR100 series, is obviously very Les Paul-ish – fat, full, and ringing, with decent cut and excellent sustain

resonance, makes each model a unique prospect in the sound stakes. Beyond the subtleties, however, given the dual humbuckers, sturdy hardware, and thick slabs of quality hardwood, these are generally powerful, singing, and open yet punchy instruments, classic heavy-rock stuff in both sound and look – although players such as Lonnie Mack and Albert King have used a Flying V for their countrified blues and, well, bluesified blues.

In addition to that the very good copies the company turned out in the 1970s, Ibanez started making some more original guitars in the late 1970s and 1980s – prompted partly by a lawsuit from Gibson – soon proving the big Japanese brand could stand on its own two feet design-wise. Early beveled-edge, ash-bodied Artist and Professional models won some followers, although the styles appear somewhat dated today. Slightly later AR series guitars are a more timeless in style, and are generally double-cutaway variations on the Les Paul theme. The general format for these includes the solid mahogany back and carved maple top; mahogany or maple necks with rosewood fingerboard – ebony on deluxe models – 22 or 24 frets and 24 3/4_ scale; two humbuckers, four controls, and three-way toggle, plus added coil splitting or series-parallel switching, and sometimes active EQ on deluxe models.

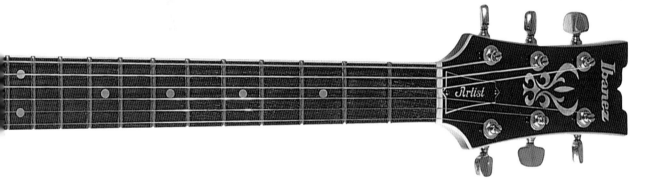

By the mid to late 1970s players had come to see that Japanese makers could turn out fine guitars, but these still had a reputation – in many cases – for using inferior tone woods and underpowered or just generally mediocre pickups. In moving to well-crafted original designs, Ibanez began to secure a reputation as a quality maker capable of producing instruments that were impressive from all angles, but were nevertheless still more affordable than big U.S. brands like Gibson and Fender. In doing so the company also helped to consolidate the reputation of Japanese guitar making as a whole. Serious weekend-warrior-style amateurs, pros on a budget, and even a few big name artists latched on to Ibanez instruments, along with those of other rising Japanese brands. As a consequence, U.S. guitar manufacturers' hold on the 'Serious Pro Electrics' crown diminished considerably – also thanks, in part, to the decline in quality in some big U.S. guitar factories in the late 1970s and early '80s.

By the mid 1980s the world had seen Bob Weir, George Benson, Steve Miller, Randy Rhoads, Paul Stanley, and Phil Collen wielding Ibanez electrics in the Gibson mold; by the 1990s, two of the top instrumental rock icons, Steve Vai and Joe Satriani, would further cement the brand's image by endorsing superstrat-style Ibanez models, as discussed in the previous chapter.

Ibanez's move into more original territory was successful in that it still accomplished the main tasks of producing

good copy guitars: most models still sounded rather like classics from the past, but achieved this goal for a lot less money than the real thing. The move from slavish copying of long-established designs also enabled the taking of certain desirable liberties, such as providing a double-cutaway body in a Les Paul-ish mold that was so popular at the onset of the 1980s, for example, or adding deluxe switching and hardware that was functionally upgraded.

Working alongside Ibanez at the top of the Japanese guitar tree in the late 1970s, Yamaha produced high-end models that were simultaneously more esthetically conservative while being more adventurous as regards structural design. The company was founded in the 1880s as a manufacturer of reed organs, started building acoustic guitars in 1946, and moved into solidbody electrics in the mid 1960s. Early models followed the slightly oddball pseudo-modern designs that are seen in many of the more 'original' Japanese designs of the 1960s, but in 1976 Yamaha really hit one out of the park with the launch of the SG2000. Carlos Santana adopted a customized version of the model as his main guitar for many years, and numerous other pros also picked up on the instrument, which was truly the Les Paul-beater of its day.

Outwardly, the SG2000 looks like a somewhat modified double-cutaway homage to the Les Paul, but with the SG's pointier horns. Its hardware, electronics, and

Late-1970s Yamaha SG2000

> **Body:** double-cutaway body made from mahogany back and arched maple top, with mahogany-maple-mahogany center core; five-ply binding; polyurethane finish
> **Neck:** three-piece mahogany-maple-mahogany through-neck with bound ebony fingerboard; 22 nickel-silver frets, 1¹¹/₁₆″ nut width, and 12″ fingerboard radius; 24¾″ scale length; full and chunky neck profile
> **Headstock:** back-angled symmetrical headstock, with three-a-side Yamaha tuners; headstock-end truss-rod adjustment
> **Bridge:** Yamaha Tune-o-matic-style bridge and stop-bar tailpiece
> **Electronics:** two Yamaha alnico humbucking pickups, each with one coil with six steel-slug polepieces and one with six adjustable threaded steel polepieces; three-way toggle switch for either pickup independently or both together; individual volume and tone controls; early models had no coil tapping facility, but from the early 1980s spring-loaded push-push switching tone controls provided coil tapping for each pickup
> **Sound:** thick, round, slightly dark, with excellent sustain; excels at rock and fusion styles

headstock shape all vary only slightly from the classic template. But if you run the guitar's body through a bandsaw – which I hope you won't – you will discover considerable deviations from the mahogany back-maple top construction of the classic Gibson. The Yamaha SG2000 – later SBG2000 after Gibson's objection to the use of the SG tag – was a neck-through-body design, made with a three-piece mahogany-maple-mahogany neck and body core, filled out by a mahogany back and arched maple top at the body end and topped by an ebony fingerboard at the neck end. Unlike the square-backed Les Paul, Yamaha very cleverly added a ribcage contour to the upper waist at the back of the guitar for improved playing comfort. Although the bridge and tailpiece were modifications of the standard Tune-o-matic-plus-stop-bar format, the SG2000's bridge was mounted into a brass sustain plate set into the body for improved sustain. The device seems to have worked pretty well: these guitars are noted for their singing, sustaining tone, which Santana himself made great use of – with a little help from Mesa/Boogie.

The new Yamaha model's quality of design, construction, and finish was acknowledged from the start, and the SG2000 had little difficulty finding a market. Again, with Gibson's quality control flagging in the late 1970s, plenty of players were primed to appreciate even an offshore attack on the Les Paul's supremacy in the set-neck-and-dual-humbuckers stakes, and little touches such as immaculately applied five-ply body binding, gold-plated parts, elegant abalone position markers, high-ratio tuners, and the easy high-fret access afforded by a double-cutaway body and smoothly tapered heel created a lot of converts. In the eyes of most players and gear historians, the Yamaha SG2000 even tops the broad Ibanez Artist range as the

guitar that first earned due respect for the quality achieved by Japanese guitar makers in the late 1970s. Yamaha has continued to be recognized as a maker of good professional-grade instruments as well as a supplier of many more affordable yet playable guitars for beginners, but no other single model has had quite the impact of the SG2000.

At about the same time that Yamaha and Ibanez were proving how many players were willing to accept Japanese alternatives to Gibson's erstwhile domination of the big humbucker-driven sound, U.S. maker Hamer started launching their own very acceptable versions of format. Hamer's first serious offering in the mid 1970s was the Explorer-shaped Standard, as played by Rick Nielsen of Cheap Trick. The more conservative Sunburst and Special models followed, which offered another twist on the double-cutaway Les Paul theme. Original twists from Hamer included an elegant three-knob in-line control layout with

the toggle switch placed back behind the bridge, out of the way of enthusiastic strumming, and through-body stringing with a fixed bridge that was more Fender than Gibson in design. From the mahogany back-carved maple top construction to the smooth, playable necks, everything about these new Hamers spoke of quality. They often employed DiMarzio pickups as standard, eliminating the need for the upgrade to DiMarzios that many other players were routinely making, their finishes were beautifully applied, and they easily rivaled the products of the 'Big G' for sound and feel.

For all their achievements, however, these Les Paul-beaters – whatever their origin – largely serve to prove the immense and enduring popularity of the original concept. Which is to say that most of them still want to be the thing that the 1958 Gibson Les Paul finally achieved for the electric guitar, and has still achieved best in the minds of most players: the archetypal solid, fat-sounding, set-neck electric with singing humbucking performance. Some players choose

an alternative to Gibson because of price; others have done so – and did so in the late 1970s and early 1980s in particular – because the quality had slipped at Gibson. Others still have selected rival models because these have been freer to offer the slight modifications and upgrades that a seminal maker is hesitant to impose on a classic model. Meanwhile, many guitarists find it hard even to consider trying to attain that Les Paul sound with anything that doesn't say Gibson on the headstock. Gibson itself has capitalized on the desire for the sound that the company established nearly 50 years ago, but with a few modifications. For example, the Les Paul Classic M-III and Les Paul DC Standard brought hotrod electrics and double-cutaway styling respectively to the format. Despite everything, guitars such as the Historic Series Les Paul reissues from the Custom Shop still seem to garner the most attention.

Hamer has perhaps always remained somewhat under-recognized, given the all-round quality and bang-for-buck the company offers, but plenty of players in the know have

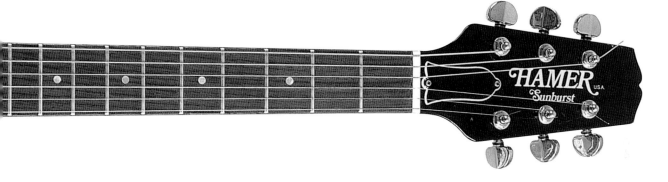

1979 Hamer Sunburst

> **Body:** double-cutaway body made from solid mahogany back and bookmatched arched maple top; single-ply top binding

> **Neck:** glued-in mahogany neck with unbound rosewood fingerboard, 22 medium nickel-silver frets, 1¹¹⁄₁₆" nut width, and 12" fingerboard radius; 24¾" scale length

> **Headstock:** back-angled symmetrical headstock, with three-a-side Schaller tuners; headstock-end truss-rod adjustment

> **Bridge:** through-body stringing into fixed-bridge base plate with six individual saddles adjustable for both height and intonation; string ball-ends set in individual ferrules in back of guitar

> **Electronics:** two custom-wound DiMarzio humbucking pickups of the Gibson PAF format, each with one coil with six steel-slug polepieces and one with six adjustable threaded steel polepieces; three-way toggle switch for either pickup independently or both together; individual volume controls and master tone

> **Sound:** warm and rich, but with good cut and definition as well as excellent sustain

enjoyed the Hamer Les Paul-alternatives in particular. For a time in the late 1980s and early '90s Hamer deviated from its Gibson-inspired roots – after the departure of co-founder Paul Hamer and the buy-out by Ovation parent company Kaman that followed it – and concentrated on even more hotrodded, often superstrat-like designs for the heavy-rock crowd. These attained some success, but the original double-cut Les Paul-like format bubbled along under the surface in the minds of players and Hamer co-founder and designer Jol Dantzig alike, and eventually resurfaced around 1990 and has remained popular ever since.

Although for many players the styles of the ultimate dream guitars today have come full circle back to the originals from Fender, Gibson, Gretsch, and other makes that originated in the 1950s – either in vintage, new reissue, or new and updated forms – a pioneering spirit that wholly embraced the 'we can make this better' line of guitar design goes right back at least to the 1960s. Alembic embodied the electric luthier's drive to take the format to the next level, with neck-through-body construction, intricate active electronics, exotic woods, upgraded proprietary hardware, and so forth. Alembic has become a byword for active electronics, and the company was the first to introduce active preamp and EQ modifications to musicians, even before it offered its first guitars.

The Alembic company was formed in 1969 in the San Francisco Bay Area with the notion of improving the recording and music electronics operations surrounding The Grateful Dead. By the early 1970s this endeavor had branched out to include custom guitar making, and eventually to releasing production-model guitars and basses. By this time the Alembic approach embodied the boutique ethos writ large: they were expensive guitars, hand-crafted to what were considered state-of-the-art standards, and aimed unashamedly at professional musicians.

Given their solid neck-body wood couplings, sensitive active electronics, and stable hardware, Alembic guitars are exceedingly responsive instruments. Many players find they have a feel and playability that is best described as 'hot-wired' or 'electrified' in a more intense sense than that projected by the standard, magnetic-pickup guitar. Proprietary Alembic pickups are very sensitive to string vibration, and they have a very full-frequency sonic character as well. Coupled with the active EQ and tone-sculpting switching options – not to mention the snappy, sustainful acoustic response from all that dense walnut, maple, mahogany and brass – it makes for a guitar with a lot more sound on tap than the average player might be used to.

The company's basses have been even more popular than its guitars, thanks in no small measure to the endorsement of one Stanley Clarke and a host of other major players, but also, perhaps, partly because of the rather mixed image the brand has attained for six-strings. From the outset, Alembic guitars appealed particularly to guitarists in the fusion and jam-band scenes of the day, but for some players they have always been anathema to all things rock'n'roll – that is, very different beasts from the plankish blond Tele, the battered Strat, or the faded Les Paul. Of course, as with any significant advancement in the hardware, certain prejudices come into play: we as players are often a pretty conservative bunch, and we don't always want the gear that sounds and plays best by some universal standard. Often we want the slab of archaic technology that best mimics the sounds that our heroes made decades ago. For some, the beautifully polished layers of purpleheart, walnut, cherry, flame maple, vermilion, and coco bolo are just too exotic to rock. Alembic continues to make both guitars and basses in Santa Rosa, California.

Despite the fact that plenty of fusty old rock'n'rollers

carried on with their inactive guitars, apparently oblivious that Alembic was shining a beacon on the way forward for all-powerful active electronics, the high-end maker's success was still enough to launch something of a battery powered revolution. Many makers added active preamps and/or EQ stages to their otherwise standard instruments, while some came out with rather close copies of the Alembic template, aping not only the electronics but the multiwood construction as well.

At first glance, players today might view a guitar like the Aria Pro II Rev-Sound RS-850 as an early superstrat, given the six-a-side headstock and vaguely Fender-ish body lines. But if you read the previous entry here, you already know it's an Alembic copy – even down to the brass hardware, five-layer through-neck, central dummy-coil pickup (to facilitate hum rejection with single-coil pickups), and oddball pointed rotary selector. Aria was another of the big Japanese companies of the copy era of the 1970s – and, in fact, played a major part in kicking off the whole game with its bolt-neck Les Paul copy of 1969 – and like others, Ibanez in particular, its 'homages' ranged further than just the big-selling Gibson and Fender models. By the late 1970s and early '80s Ibanez and Yamaha had branched out into more original territory, and were gaining respect for having done so. Aria gradually made the move to original designs, too, but also hung on to a strategy of copying more exotic U.S. brands

throughout much of the early 1980s, turning out guitars that owed stylistic debts to the likes of B.C. Rich, Dean, and Alembic, as seen in the example overleaf. Meanwhile, the company also made its mark with such models as the PE1000, a vaguely Les Paul-shaped guitar with enough twists to qualify as original, or at least about as original as rivals like the Ibanez Artist or Yamaha SG2000.

Copies or not, these Aria Pro IIs were very well-made guitars, and they further paved the Japanese makers' inroads into the professional market. In 1983 Aria changed the Rev-Sound series' lines from Alembic-like to Strat-ish, and, indeed, the line did gradually veer toward superstrat territory. Meanwhile, however, the Aria company continued to grow, and its guitar catalog seemed to broaden exponentially. A short run of U.S.-made Custom Series guitars offered in 1987 notwithstanding, Aria production has largely been in Korea since the late 1980s, although some upmarket models are still made in Japan. For this

◀ 1978 Alembic Series I

> **Body:** double cutaway body made from mahogany back and walnut top
> **Neck:** neck-through-body construction with five-piece maple and purpleheart neck-body core with unbound rosewood fingerboard, 24 medium nickel-silver frets, 1$^{11}\!/_{32}$" nut width (approximately), and 12" fingerboard radius; 24¾" scale length
> **Headstock:** back-angled symmetrical headstock, with three-a-side Schaller tuners; brass nut
> **Bridge:** proprietary brass bridge with individual brass saddles, adjustable for intonation and overall height by screws at either end of bridge unit; slotted top-loading tailpiece
> **Electronics:** two single-coil pickups with dummy coil between them for hum canceling; two volume controls, two active EQ controls, one three-position Q Switch for each pickup (a pickup frequency range switch), three-way pickup selector switch for pickups individually or together; standard ¼" mono output and 5-pin stereo output
> **Sound:** full-frequencied, with tight lows and sparkling highs; powerful and versatile tone-shaping from active electronics

◉ 1981 Aria Pro II Rev-Sound RS-850

> **Body**: double-offset-cutaway body made from walnut-stained ash with walnut stripes

> **Neck**: neck-through-body construction with five-piece maple and walnut neck-body core with unbound rosewood fingerboard, 24 medium nickel-silver frets, 1⅝" nut width (approximately), and 12" fingerboard radius; 25½" scale length

> **Headstock**: back-angled asymmetrical headstock, with six-in-line tuners; brass nut

> **Bridge**: roughly Tune-o-matic style brass bridge with individual brass saddles, adjustable for intonation and

overall height; slotted top-loading Aria Quick-Hook tailpiece

> **Electronics**: two single-coil pickups with dummy coil between them for hum canceling; one volume control, two active EQ controls, one three-position Q Selector for each pickup (a pickup frequency-range switch such as used by Alembic), three-way pickup selector switch for pickups individually or together; ¼" output

> **Sound**: responsive, bright, and full-frequencied; versatile tone-shaping from active electronics

reason, the earlier Japanese guitars of the late 1970s and early to mid '80s are seen by many players as good-value alternatives, whether copies or not. As for this Aria Pro II Rev-Sound RS-850, it's a real player, with a comfortable neck, good resonance, and versatile electronics.

Not that active electronics were the only developments touted as the way forward in the 1970s. Through-neck guitars had already come from such lofty heights as Gibson in the 1960s, as featured in the original 'reverse body' Firebird range, but they really took off a decade later, when the thinking was briefly pervasive in some circles that any serious instrument needed to have its neck and body core carved from a single plank or laminate of planks. We know better now, of course, and part of this book's purpose is to

celebrate the diversity of electric guitar building, while along the way recognizing that plenty of sweet and very useful tones are produced by a wide range of different designs. Back in the day, however, the through-neck was one of the signs of high-end achievement, and a lot of players thought you needed to add active electronics to that plank really to be taken seriously.

Many of B.C. Rich's pointy, demonic creations had both, and the blend of radical angles, solid build quality, and heavy sounds won the brand a lot of followers among rock players from the mid 1970s onward. Former flamenco guitarist and Los Angeles acoustic guitar maker Bernardo Chavez Rico first branched into electrics with deluxe Gibson copies in the late 1960s, but the radical lines and sharp

points began to appear through the early part of the following decade. Two B.C. Rich classics, the Mockingbird, and the ten-string Bich – the latter promoted with a memorable, if good-taste-challenged advertising campaign – first saw the light of day in 1976, while the very goth Warlock followed in 1981. Over the past couple of decades B.C. Rich guitars have been manufactured both in the U.S.A. and Japan, with more affordable models in the Rave and Platinum series today being built in Korea, although they were made in Japan between 1984 and '86. Since Rico's death in 1999 the company has been headed by his son Bernie Junior, who continues both to import more affordable B.C. Rich models from overseas and to manufacture high-end versions in Hesperia, California, the majority of which still appeal to the heaviest sectors of the rock market.

For all its radical points and blade-like contours, the Mockingbird is an extremely solid and well-made instrument under the surface. B.C. Rich has used a range of exotic woods over the years, although maple is the main ingredient in this example, and it's a sharp, ringing, well-defined instrument as a result. The company has mostly abandoned the extremely complex active electronics and switching array as seen on this model – few guitarists find they really need all that many different sound options on a

1979 B.C. Rich Mockingbird Standard

> **Body:** radical dual-offset-cutaway body made from maple with mahogany stripes, maple neck-body core
> **Neck:** neck-through-body construction with maple neck-body core with unbound rosewood fingerboard, 24 jumbo nickel-silver frets, 1¹¹⁄₁₆" nut width (approximately), and 12" fingerboard radius; 25½" scale length
> **Headstock:** back-angled headstock, with three-a-side Grover Imperial tuners; bone nut
> **Bridge:** Leo Quan Badass Bridge (modified wrapover style) with six individually adjustable saddles
> **Electronics:** two DiMarzio humbucking pickups; controls for master volume, preamp volume, and master tone; large three-way toggle switch for selection of pickups individually or together; mini toggle switches for preamp on/off, pickup phase, and Dual Sound selections for each pickup; six-position rotary control (chickenhead knob) for Gibson Varitone-style tonal presets
> **Sound:** bright, stinging, and hot at its core, with a broad range of passive and active variables

single guitar – but in the late 1970s an array of mini switches was the stuff of many rock players' dreams. Also, while many current U.S.-made models continue with the neck-through-body format that B.C. Rich helped to popularize, plenty of others use bolt-on necks.

Having ventured to the radical extremes of B.C. Rich, Dean, and a few other radical, 'rocktastic' makers, the guitar industry has accepted that the vast majority of players still want instruments that don't stray too far from the Gibson and Fender templates – although plenty certainly want elements of sound and playability that neither of those quite deliver. The most popular Les Paul-beaters of all have been the guitars of the Paul Reed Smith (PRS) company, and they've done it largely by being considerably less like Gibson than so many of their predecessors.

After a number of years of model evolution and development in the late 1970s and early '80s, PRS eventually settled on a fairly standard template that incorporated a set neck and humbucking pickups, along with plenty of variables. The company went a long way toward merging the feel of great Gibson and Fender models, while adding plenty of original touches. As we already explored to some extent in the previous chapter, most PRS guitars are made to a 25″ scale length, and the body shape of almost all but the Singlecut model – which, in fact, inspired Gibson to release the lawyers – has been more Strat-ish than Les Paul-ish. At the same time, the PRS vibrato system was clearly inspired by the vintage Fender vibrato. That said, the

majority of higher-end PRS guitars use a multiwood construction of mahogany and carved maple top that descends from the Gibson template, and the elegant figured-maple 'Ten Tops' on many of these – which employed the choicest bookmatched cuts of highly figured wood – is certainly a legacy of the rare flame-topped sunburst Les Paul of the late 1950s.

PRS guitars were the first guitars after Gibson and Fender – and perhaps Gretsch, Rickenbacker, and Guild – to be manufactured to consistent standards and in quantities that would give thye company 'U.S. classic' status, which is entirely a testament to their quality, playability, and insightful design. A single PRS guitar of the higher-end variety – such as the early Standard or Signature models, or the slightly later Artist, as seen here – covers a wide range of sounds and playing styles, from the thick, full, warm humbucker wail of a Les Paul to the bright twang of a Strat or a Tele (with switching set to split-coil positions), to the hot grind and divebombing antics of a superstrat. Some players might tell you it doesn't capture any of these moods exactly, but it comes impressively close on most counts, while also having a vibe that is all its own. This combination of talents has won PRS many, many fans, and a roster of pro players that rivals any of the longer-established big-name makers.

Having become known for its impressive blend of Fender and Gibson tonalities, PRS moved further toward the latter with its McCarty Model of 1994. The guitar was

◁ 1991 PRS Artist I

> **Body:** double-cutaway body with offset horns, made from carved flamed maple 'Ten-Plus Top' with mahogany back, thin nitrocellulose finish

> **Neck:** set-neck construction, wide-fat mahogany neck with unbound Brazilian rosewood fingerboard with bird inlays, 24 medium nickel-silver frets, 10" fingerboard radius; 25" scale length

> **Headstock:** back-angled headstock, with three-a-side PRS locking tuners; friction-reducing nut

> **Bridge:** PRS Stay In Tune vibrato system with back-loading strings in modified steel inertia block and six individually adjustable saddles

> **Electronics:** uncovered alnico Artist Treble (bridge) and Artist Bass (neck) humbuckers; controls for master volume, master tone; five-way rotary pickup selector for: 1) treble pickup alone, 2) outer coils of each pickup in parallel, 3) inner coils of each pickup in series ('fat-Strat' sound), 4) Strat-like 'out of phase' (between bridge-middle) sound, 5) bass pickup alone

> **Sound:** wide-ranging, from hot humbucking bridge-pickup grind to warm, smooth neck-bucker tones, with rounder, snappier single-coil-like sounds available

⌃ 1999 PRS McCarty Soapbar

> **Body:** double-cutaway body with offset horns, made from solid mahogany with a carved top; nitrocellulose finish

> **Neck:** set-neck of solid mahogany with unbound rosewood fingerboard, wide-fat profile, and elongated heel block, 22 medium nickel-silver frets, 10" fingerboard radius; 25" scale length

> **Headstock:** thinner and more steeply back-angled headstock than PRS Artist; three-a-side

lightweight Kluson-repro tuners

> **Bridge:** stud-mounted PRS wrapover-style bridge

> **Electronics:** two PRS P-90-style single-coil pickups; three-way toggle switch for either pickup alone or both in parallel; master volume, master tone

> **Sound:** full and round, with pronounced midrange emphasis and a slightly gritty-yet-snappy edge to higher-gain tones

inspired by former Gibson president Ted McCarty – who had overseen watershed moments such as the design of the Les Paul, the Tune-o-matic bridge, the ES-335 and more – and although it still carried the classic PRS body shape, it embodied the company's effort to capture the classic Les Paul sound. To this end, compared to a PRS Artist, Custom, CE or similar, the McCarty Model has a longer neck heel, a wider and fatter neck, a thinner headstock with lighter Kluson-style tuners and a deeper back-angle, a PRS wrapover bridge, simpler three-way switching, and two alnico humbuckers with nickel covers. As a result, the McCarty sounded somewhat fatter, sweeter, warmer, and more vocal than the typical PRS before it; in short, more like a Gibson Les Paul. PRS moved even closer to Les Paul territory, visually at least,

with the release of the Singlecut in 2000, but the fate of that decision is still being batted back and forth in court between the Gibson and PRS legal teams at the time of writing.

While PRS had emerged as the most significant 'independent' maker of the 1980s, its production levels have steadily grown to attain mass-manufacturer status, especially with the arrival of the budget-level offshore SE models in 2001. In the past couple of decades, however, a wealth of small-shop makers have sprung up, particularly in the U.S.A. and U.K., to offer custom-order and limited-run production models built largely by hand and to extremely high standards.

Don Grosh Custom Guitars was founded in 1993, and relocated its workshop from California to Colorado

> **2004 Don Grosh Set Neck**

> **Body:** solid mahogany back and highly figured carved maple top, deep-set single cutaway for ease of upper-fret access; translucent nitrocellulose lacquer finish
> **Neck:** set-neck construction, mahogany neck with unbound Brazilian rosewood fingerboard with 12" radius, 22 jumbo nickel-silver frets; 1¹¹⁄₁₆" nut width; 24¾" scale length
> **Headstock:** 17-degree back-angled headstock with three-a-side locking Magnum tuners, ebony headstock facing
> **Bridge:** Gotoh wraparound bridge with adjustable A/D and G/B string section
> **Electronics:** Lindy Fralin humbucking pickups made in the classic PAF style, with alnico bar magnets, six fixed steel-slug polepieces and six adjustable threaded polepieces; DC resistance approximately 8k neck, 9k bridge
> **Sound:** thick, throaty, and vocal, with more edge and midrange honk from the bridge position, more fluty warmth in the neck; excellent sustain

in 2005, where a small team of master-builders continues to hand-build guitars to order. Grosh is probably best known for his adaptations of bolt-neck classics, but he has also put a lot of research and development into improving the tone and feel of the set-neck guitar, mainly with the goal of attaining that hollowed 1958–60 Les Paul sound, but with a little more playing comfort. The result is the model that he calls, simply, the Set Neck. This guitar carries the classic wood combinations for the format of mahogany back with carved maple top and mahogany neck with rosewood fingerboard, and a shape that echoes the Les Paul without aping it, but the design incorporates several subtle nuances that help to fine-tune its performance.

The Set Neck is made with an elongated neck tenon in the neck-body joint, and has the tonally superior 17-degree headstock pitch, but has a slightly shallower overall neck pitch to make the left-hand playing position more comfortable. Also, the body shape has been tweaked to give the guitar better balance when played both standing and sitting. Grosh uses a double-action truss-rod in the neck because he believes it improves both tone and functionality, and also reinforces the area where the headstock extends from the end of the neck with a volute (an additional protrusion of wood), which he says also adds to the resonant character of that part of the guitar.

Instruments like the Grosh Set Neck are fascinating because, aside from being excellent guitars in their own right, they show how a slightly adapted approach to a seminal design can succeed both in capturing classic, vintage-voiced tones and in producing a guitar that offers the utmost in playability to today's artist.

Just as the active-electronics and neck-through-body brigade had its sights set on a higher plane in the 1970s, some makers working in more recent times have similarly refused to be bound by the conventional passive-magnetics-and-carved-wood concept of the electric guitar. Parker has been at the forefront of the hybrid-guitar concept since the mid 1990s, when it introduced radical new designs that carried both traditional magnetic pickups and piezo-pickup-loaded bridges capable of producing acoustic-like sounds. In fairness, the term hybrid doesn't do justice to the Parker designs: their flagship models are capable of performing as versatile fully magnetic electrics in the traditional style, or solidbodied piezo-acoustics, or a player-determined blend of both.

Models such as the Parker Fly Artist took the electric

guitar back to the drawing board to strip it down as thoroughly in the 1990s as Fender did in designing the Telecaster at the end of the 1940s. Fly models were made with a thin carved body of choice tone wood, such as mahogany, poplar, spruce, or maple, reinforced with a glass and carbon-fiber epoxy exoskeleton. Necks were similarly constructed, with a wooden core and epoxy outer covering that also formed the fingerboard, which carried glued-on stainless-steel frets. The result was an instrument that was extremely light, usually around five pounds, but also very resonant. From this template, features such as the newly designed, cast aluminum, flat-spring Parker vibrato system with Fishman piezo saddles, magnetic humbucking, or single-coil pickups – often supplied by DiMarzio – and Fishman-developed switching to blend the two sounds, all worked together to make the Parker guitars the radical creations they undoubtedly are.

As usually happens with any genuine left-turn in guitar

making, many players turned a cold shoulder to Parker's developments. This was largely because they just didn't look or feel like the guitars that Buddy Holly, Jimi Hendrix, Eric Clapton, or Jimmy Page had used to make those sounds that so many players have continued to chase. Ignore the electro-acoustic capabilities of a Fly, however, and the guitar does produce very traditional, albeit versatile and broad-voiced, electric guitar tones, with an extremely useable, stable vibrato system to boot. Dabble with the piezo capabilities, or blend the two voices, and you can explore entirely new sonic avenues.

Unsurprisingly, Parker's artists' roster has included a number of more eclectic, even 'out there' players, such as Dave Isaacs, Phil Keaggy, Reeves Gabrels, and Amir Derakh. But the brand has also won over a number of more traditional guitarists of a more broad-minded disposition, with Dann Huff, Joe Walsh, Joni Mitchell, and even Merle Haggard among them.

1997 Parker Fly Artist

> **Body:** thin, full-width core of solid carved spruce with non-concentric double cutaways; glass and carbon-fiber epoxy outer shell; polyurethane finish

> **Neck:** set-neck construction, poplar core with shell and fingerboard formed from glass and carbon-fiber; 24 medium glued-on hardened stainless-steel frets, 1¹¹⁄₁₆" nut width; compound (conical) fingerboard radius that gradually broadens from 10" at the nut to 13" toward the upper frets

> **Headstock:** recessed narrow-profile headstock with six-in-line Sperzel locking tuners

> **Bridge:** Parker flat-spring vibrato system with action-tension adjustment wheel

> **Electronics:** two DiMarzio passive magnetic humbucking pickups, six-element Fishman piezo system in bridge saddles; three-way selector plus master volume and master tone for magnetic pickups; master volume and master tone for electro-acoustic (piezo) pickups, plus three-way selector for magnetic/both/piezo operation

> **Sound:** full-throated traditional humbucking sounds with broad, open, resonant voice, or bright, snappy electro-acoustic tones, as well as a blend of the two

4

Semi-Acoustics

You would be forgiven for thinking that the semi-acoustic electric guitar represents an evolutionary halfway house between the hollowbody archtops with which players made their first forays into amplification, and the mass-production solidbodies that arrived with the Fender Broadcaster in 1950. In form, at least, the 'semi' represents a step between the two: a hollowbody guitar, usually with an arched top, to which some wood has been added to enhance stability, sustain and feedback resistance.

Taken chronologically, however, you could argue for the semi-acoustic as a solidbody from which some wood has been taken away. Other than a few one-offs, experiments, and prototypes (of which Les Paul's famous 'log guitar' was one), all of the more timeless semis arrived after Fender's groundbreaking, bolt-neck solidbody revolutionized the

⌃ 1955 Gretsch Duo Jet

> **Body:** single-cutaway mahogany body with routed chambers, pressed arched maple ply top with black plastic covering; top binding

> **Neck:** glued-in, one-piece mahogany neck with bound ebony fingerboard with 12" radius, 22 narrow-gauge nickel-silver frets, and 1¹¹⁄₁₆" nut width; 24⅝" scale length

> **Headstock:** symmetrical back-angled headstock with three-a-side Grover tuners

> **Bridge:** Melita bridge with six individual saddles adjustable for intonation, mounted in floating ebony base; thumb-wheels at either end for overall height adjustment; Gretsch trapeze bridge

> **Electronics:** two single-coil DeArmond 200 pickups (also known as Gretsch Dynasonics), with individually adjustable alnico slug polepieces; DC resistance of approximately 8.5k; three-way toggle switch to select either pickup alone or both together; controls for individual pickup volumes, master tone, and master volume

> **Sound:** snappy, bright, round, and gritty, with plenty of bite and edge

The Gretsch Duo Jet is a classic example of a semi-solid guitar. It was released in 1953 as direct competition both to Fender's Telecaster and Gibson's Les Paul, but was made with hollow chambers in the body. Few players of the day probably realized this or even cared, and these pockets of air aren't enough to greatly affect the Duo Jet's acoustic character, but they do affect it slightly, as any considerable alteration to a solid hunk of wood will. Of course, a Duo Jet is different from a Tele or a Les Paul in many other ways: like any guitar – and perhaps more so (as is the case with so many of those quirky Gretsches) – its tone is the result of the mix of many ingredients.

Most of these vintage semi-solid Gretsch models with DeArmond single-coil pickups – which include the Duo Jet, Sparkle Jet, Silver Jet, Jet Fire Bird and so on, all really just distinguished by the color of their plastic-coated or painted tops – sound bright and snappy, are somewhat thin on resonance but high on snarl, and have a kind of round, percussive bite that's hard to find in other guitars. With the Filter'Tron humbuckers they sound a little fatter and crunchier, but are still pretty bright and snappy. Gretsch bridges and tailpieces – which often include a Bigsby vibrato – don't do these guitars' resonance any great favors, and the pressed plywood top coated in synthetic sparkle drum covering doesn't rival many tone woods, but again, the sum of the parts still results in a highly desired Gretsch sound,

and players who want exactly that forgive the little failings of individual ingredients that go into the stew.

To be fair, the Melita bridge on our main example is a pretty solid and versatile piece of hardware, and one which predated the Gibson Tune-o-matic by a couple years. But the solid bar bridge that many other models carried, those with Bigsbys in particular, is a cruder device, and the floating wooden bridge piece into which both are set has been left by the wayside by most makers since the 1960s. To risk stating the obvious, such bridge pieces add a certain woodiness to the tone, and promote a round, almost hollow-sounding core that lends more of a hollowbody tonality to the sound of a solidbody or semi-solid electric, but this isn't always appropriate on an instrument that will be used for rock'n'roll or heavy rock. That said, the better Gretsch models do what they do well, and there's a certain magic in there, for all the little flaws and oddities.

Unlike the hollowed-out Gretsch Duo Jet, the Gibson ES-335 was constructed more as a traditional thinline hollowbody archtop, with the addition of a solid maple block that ran the length of the body's center and a little wider than the pickups and bridge studs. This feature considerably hampered its acoustic performance when

⊙ 1960 Gretsch Jet Fire Bird

> **Body:** same construction as 1955 Duo Jet, with red-painted finish
> **Neck:** same construction and proportions as 1955 Duo Jet, but with 'half moon' or 'thumb' position-marker inlays and a zero fret before the nut
> **Bridge:** Gretsch 'Space-Control' roller bridge adjustable for string spacing and overall height only, mounted in floating ebony base; Bigsby vibrato tailpiece

> **Electronics:** two Filter'Tron humbucking pickups; DC resistance of approximately 4k; three-way toggle switch to select either pickup alone or both together; three-way master tone switch; controls for individual pickup volumes and master volume
> **Sound:** similar core tonality to the 1955 Duo Jet, but a little fatter and thicker; the addition of a Bigsby often lightens the resonance and sustain slightly, too

compared with a fully hollow, deep-bodied acoustic, but reined in the potential howling feedback of the traditional jazz guitar as well. Gibson had already begun wooing players to the notion of a thinner-bodied archtop with the ES-350T and Byrdland models released in 1955. The ES-335 was a calculated step to take trad-minded players a step closer to the benefits of a solidbody, without asking them to broaden their thinking to accept a fully solid guitar like the Les Paul.

In fact, while Gibson's flagship solid was only ever a moderate seller throughout the 1950s, the ES-335 was an immediate success. The semi has remained in the Gibson catalog in one form or another since its introduction, while, as we've seen, the Les Paul was famously pulled from production for the best part of the 1960s. The success of the ES-335 is a testament to how well Gibson succeeded in designing the model: it is indeed far more feedback resistant than a fully hollow guitar of similar proportions, has greater sustain, offers a broad and powerful voice thanks to those twin humbuckers, and captures a little more of the woody resonance of a traditional archtop than a solidbody such as a Les Paul. That said, the acoustic energy of the ES-335's top is far less than a similar model that lacks the solid center

block. Compare an ES-335 with an ES-330 if you get the chance – or listen to the comparisons on the CD included with this book – and you will hear a lot more acoustic volume in the latter guitar. The ES-330 also feeds back more easily, too, so the tradeoff speaks for itself.

The first version 'dot-neck' ES-335s – so called because of the use of dot position markers on the fingerboard rather than blocks, made between 1958 and the middle of 1962 – are the models that collectors really lust over. This is partly because the dot position markers indicate the first few years of the model but also because in these years the ES-335 carried highly desirable PAF pickups. Although the pickups changed gradually through the 1960s, 'block-neck' ES-335s remained much the same as the dots that had come before them until the temporary change to 1⅝" nut widths between 1965 and '68, then the shallower headstock back-angle of 1966 to '73. During much of the 1970s Gibson also used a shorter center block in the ES-335 to reduce weight, and partnered it with a trapeze tailpiece rather than the stop-bar of earlier models. (This shorter block ran from the neck to the bridge, and there was therefore no solid wood to anchor adequately the studs of a stop-bar tailpiece.)

◀ 1959 Gibson ES-335

> **Body:** semi-acoustic construction with back, sides, and top of laminated maple, with a pressed arch on the top and solid maple center block; top and back binding; double-cutaway with 20th-fret neck-body joint; sunburst finish in nitrocellulose lacquer
> **Neck:** glued-in, one-piece mahogany neck with bound rosewood fingerboard with 12" fingerboard radius, 22 medium nickel-silver frets, and 1¹¹⁄₁₆" nut width; 24⅝" scale length; in 1958 and '59 neck profile was chunky, but became much thinner in 1960
> **Headstock:** symmetrical 17-degree back-angled headstock with three-a-side tulip-button Kluson tuners; bone nut
> **Bridge:** adjustable Tune-o-matic bridge and stop-bar tailpiece
> **Electronics:** dual humbucking pickups constructed of single alnico bar magnet beneath, six fixed steel-slug polepieces in one coil and six threaded adjustable polepieces in the other; DC resistance of 7.5k to 8k; nickel-plated steel cover; three-way toggle switch to select either pickup alone or both together; four 500k potentiometers for individual volume and tone for each pickup
> **Sound:** thick, rich, and vocal from the neck pickup, punchy and cutting from the bridge, with a slightly airy, woody resonance in all positions; good sustain; good hum rejection

▼ 1970s Gibson ES-335

This 1970s model of the ES-335 has block markers on the neck and a trapeze tailpiece.

Even so, plenty of versions of the model made through the years capture the essential ES-335 vibe, as do many good reissues from Gibson and copies or near-copies from other makers. Not many players can afford an original PAF-loaded dot-neck, but that classic semi vibe can be captured in a number of forms, and at a wide range of prices.

After Gibson purchased Epiphone and moved the company from its former New York home to Kalamazoo, Michigan, this former rival became mainly a support brand offering models that were either more affordable or slightly modified alternatives to those branded with the Gibson name. Many Epiphone electrics of this era are therefore nearly identical in appearance to some classic Gibson designs – but the key word here is 'nearly.'

The Sheraton, introduced in 1959, is one such guitar. While it looks very much like the Gibson ES-335 that appeared a year before it, and indeed was made to the same basic construction specifications, the Sheraton has a few twists that make it feel and sound very different. It has the ES-335's rounded-double-cutaway, semi-acoustic body with maple center block, and, of course, the same glued-in neck, and the controls are the same, but the Sheraton departs most notably in the pickups. This is another of our looks at Epiphone's mini-humbucking pickup, which would become even better known about a decade later when it graced the Gibson Les Paul Deluxe. Other details include seven-ply body binding and a multi-ply ebony fingerboard, gold-plated hardware, more elaborate inlays such as the Epiphone vine headstock inlay and V-block position markers, and a Frequensator trapeze tailpiece. The latter was a split-anchor design that allowed for longer string length behind the bridge for the three bass strings than for the three treble strings, with the

intention of better balancing the tension of the different gauge strings.

Naturally, the smaller humbuckers made a difference to the guitar's sound, being brighter and lighter but still fairly full-frequencied pickups. The Frequensator trapeze tailpiece also loosened up the guitar's tone a little, and made a Sheraton just a hair tougher to bend than a similarly strung and set-up ES-335 with a stop-bar tailpiece. Finally, the ebony fingerboard contributed a brighter, snappier, and more defined attack to the sound.

Shortly after CMI's sale of Gibson to Norlin in 1969, production of Epiphone guitars moved from Gibson's Kalamazoo factory to Japan, and the designs and craftsmanship took a downhill turn along with it. These early solidbody, bolt-neck Epiphones aped many other

cheap Japanese imports of the early 1970s, and the brand seemed very much adrift in the sea of mediocrity until the late 1980s, when the name was once again used for more affordable 'in-house copies' of expensive Gibson instruments. Although the production of these has largely moved to Korea, with a few special-issue and historical models being made by Gibson in Nashville, the quality and appeal of the contemporary Epiphone line has given the brand far more staying power than it had upon first moving to the Far East.

Later Epiphone reissues of the Sheraton often used full-size humbuckers – the Noel Gallagher Supernova being one such model – although an accurate John Lee Hooker 1964 Sheraton with mini-humbuckers and Frequensator is also available. Along with these two players, the model has appealed to a number of guitarists seeking just a minor twist on the classic ES-335 semi-acoustic template. In 1962 Epiphone introduced the simpler Riviera model, which was similar to the Sheraton in design, electronics, and hardware, but had chrome-plated parts, single-ply binding, and simpler inlays.

Over on the other side of the pond, semi-acoustic construction was being employed by many formative guitar makers. One of the most prominent among these was Hofner, a brand taken up early in the careers of many great British guitarists when American-made instruments were

still extremely expensive and difficult to come by. The German company had been manufacturing orchestral stringed instruments since the 1880s, and introduced guitars to its roster in 1925. Despite this legacy in instrument-making, the company might have languished as an also-ran in the eyes of U.S. guitarists if not for that Hofner 'Beatle Bass' (violin bass) seen in the hands of Paul McCartney throughout the 1960s. In fact, John Lennon had also played a semi-hollow Hofner Club 40 in the early years, as Beatle fanatics will already know, although he had abandoned it for his Rickenbacker by the time the group started to gain any real fame. In the U.K. Hofner guitars were played by such a wide range of artists in the 1950s and early '60s – including Bill Shearer, Bert Weedon, Tommy

> **Early-1960s Epiphone Sheraton**

> **Body:** semi-acoustic construction with back, sides, and top of laminated maple, with a pressed arch on the top and solid maple center block; seven-ply top binding and back binding; double-cutaway with 20th-fret neck-body joint; blond (natural) finish in nitrocellulose lacquer
> **Neck:** glued-in, one-piece mahogany neck with multibound ebony fingerboard with 12" fingerboard radius, 22 medium nickel-silver frets, and 1¹¹⁄₁₆" nut width; 24⅝" scale length
> **Headstock:** symmetrical back-angled headstock, with three-a-side tuners, multiple binding, and vine inlay; bone nut
> **Bridge:** adjustable Tune-o-matic bridge and Frequensator trapeze tailpiece
> **Electronics:** dual mini-humbucking pickups constructed of single alnico bar magnet beneath, six fixed steel-slug polepieces in one coil and six threaded adjustable polepieces in the other; DC resistance of approximately 6.5k to 7.5k; nickel-plated steel cover; three-way toggle switch to select either pickup alone or both together; four 500k potentiometers for individual volume and tone for each pickup
> **Sound:** a good blend of bright, incisive, and warm; not overly aggressive, with a slight woody resonance at its core; good hum rejection

Steele, and many others – that the brand's spot near the top of the guitar-making heap was never in question, even if many young players still wanted to get their hands on the American-made instruments that all the big stars from the U.S.A. were playing.

The Club series guitars, introduced in 1954, were real crossroads designs, representing a halfway house between the hollowbody archtop guitars they followed and the solidbody electrics with which they intended to compete. Like the smaller-bodied, solid-topped Gretsch models, the Club 50 was actually a semi-solid design with plenty of air inside the wood, but its solid spruce top lacked the f-holes that would normally give such away. The Clubs were among the first Hofners with built-in pickups, but these single-coils were still raised pretty high from the body due to the more traditional set-up of the pitched neck and rather high-floating two-piece bridge.

Hofner built its guitars well, although the company had some characteristic design quirks that the Club 50 didn't escape. Earlier examples such as the one in our main photo lacked a truss-rod, although five-piece laminated construction made the necks quite solid. The tapered mortise joint with which the neck was attached to the body isn't quite as stable as a dovetailed joint, and many of these guitars need a neck re-set over time, but, fortunately, the mortise joint also makes this easy to accomplish. The Club 50 also uses the classic if slightly odd Hofner bridge design that is much like the traditional two-piece floating bridge used on many archtops, but has small snippets of fretwire set in the upper piece of rosewood to act as saddles. Interestingly, this arrangement gives the strings the same anchor point – nickel-silver fret wire set into rosewood – at both the neck and the body end, something not seen on many electric guitars.

⊗ 1958 Hofner Club 50

> **Body:** single-cutaway semi-solid construction with back and sides of maple, and carved top of solid spruce; three-ply top binding and back binding; 14th-fret neck join

> **Neck:** glued-in five-ply maple and rosewood neck with no truss-rod, with unbound rosewood fingerboard with approximately a 10" fingerboard radius, 22 narrow nickel-silver frets; 24⅝" scale length

> **Headstock:** symmetrical back-angled headstock, with three-a-side tuners; zero fret

> **Bridge:** two-piece rosewood floating bridge adjustable for height, inset with fret wire for string saddles

> **Electronics:** two low-gain single-coil Fuma pickups; individual toggle switches for pickup on/off; individual volume and tone controls for each pickup

> **Sound:** resonant, round, and woody, with a bright, crisp edge

Given the carved, solid-spruce top, which is fairly thick towards the center arch, coupled with chambered maple back and sides, the Club 50 is quite a resonant guitar, and fairly bright, too. Its single-coil Fuma pickups are pretty limited units, although not bad sounding in themselves, so some players of vintage examples have changed these out over the years for P-90s, DeArmonds, or Fender-style single-coils.

When John Lennon swapped his Club 50 for a Rickenbacker 325, the California maker not surprisingly gained a major boost in status. But, despite embodying the archetypal Beatles rhythm sound for the earlier years of the Fab Four's recording and touring career, the short-scale 325 isn't really a great example of Ricky designs for the big boys. Such honors go to the full-scale 360 or less decorative 330, both of which are archetypal Rickenbacker semi-hollow models.

Rickenbacker had been a major player at the dawn of the electric guitar way back in the 1930s, and one of the first makers of solidbody electrics – if in smaller numbers than its rival Fender would put out with its first production model in 1950 – but until The Beatles came along the company

was struggling to compete with Gibson and Fender in the rock'n'roll age. The 360 and 330 models had been around since 1958, but following the publicity boost Lennon and co gave its littler sibling, the model became a major player in the pop, British invasion, and West Coast scenes, establishing a bright, rhythmic jangle sound that has remained a classic to this day.

As part of the Capri series, the 360 sprung from the design bench of German luthier Roger Rossmeisl, who had been hired by Rickenbacker in 1954. To construct the new semi-hollow guitar, Rossmeisl joined two slabs of solid maple to a maple and rosewood through-neck, and routed out the body sides from the rear, closing up the work with a wooden back. As such, these guitars exhibit a little less acoustic energy than semi-acoustics made more in the tradition of a thin hollowbody, but the airspace definitely affects their tone. Given all that solid – if routed-out – maple and the single-coil Rickenbacker toaster-top pickups, they are brighter guitars than those of the ES-335 format, too, and that has been a big part of the brew that has given the 360 its own very individual tonal reputation.

Whether thranging out dirty, punkish rhythm work in a power-trio setting, in the hands of Pete Townshend or Paul Weller, or the sparkling jangled arpeggios of Roger McGuinn of The Byrds or Peter Buck of REM, the 360 could cut through a mix to become the defining sound of a broad range of styles. (Note that Roger McGuinn used a healthy dose of compression to get that blooming, slightly squashy sound for which he was famous.) While no doubt some very capable players have laid down some thoroughly capable leads on 360s and other Rickenbacker models, these just haven't become known as rock solo guitars. For one thing, Rickenbacker pickups don't tend naturally toward singing, vocal lead tones; for another, perhaps, the characteristically narrow, rounded Rickenbacker neck – with slightly odd varnished rosewood fingerboard – doesn't inspire wide bends and fleet-fingered riffing.

Overall, however, it's possibly just that these guitars have been thoroughly pigeonholed for the very notable rhythm styles detailed above. Run through an overdrive pedal and a cranked tube amp a Rickenbacker can wail just about as much as any of the single-coil Fenders, which have far more

1964 Rickenbacker 325S

> **Body:** double-cutaway semi-solid maple body
> **Neck:** set neck with 1⅝" nut width, 10" fingerboard radius; 20¾" scale length
> **Bridge:** same as 360, with added Accent Vibrato
> **Electronics:** three single-coil toaster-top pickups; DC resistance of approximately 5k to 7k; three-way toggle switch to select either the bridge pickup alone, all three pickups together, or neck and middle pickup together (no neck-pickup-only selection, although it can be tweaked with the blend control); blend control for fine-tuning balance of neck pickup's input into other selections
> **Sound:** bright, springy, sizzling, and somewhat loose

1959 Rickenbacker 360

> **Body:** routed-out double-cutaway maple body with single-ply top binding and recessed tail section; 21st-fret neck join
> **Neck:** three-ply maple-and-rosewood neck, neck-through-body construction, with bound and varnished rosewood fingerboard with a 10" radius, 21 narrow nickel-silver frets; 24¾" scale length
> **Headstock:** asymmetrical back-angled headstock, with three-a-side tuners; headstock-end truss-rod access
> **Bridge:** metal bridge adjustable for height and individual string intonation; simple trapeze tailpiece inset in recessed body routing
> **Electronics:** two single-coil Rickenbacker toaster-top pickups; DC resistance of around 5k to 7k; three-way toggle switch for selecting pickups individually or together; independent volume and tone controls for each pickup; later models carried a fifth blend control to fine-tune the neck pickup's contribution to the overall sound
> **Sound:** bright, snappy, round, with a crisp and percussive attack

of a reputation for lead playing. But that percussive, biting, ringing Ricky rhythm tone is such a sound unto itself that these guitars have far and away made their mark on the other side of the stage.

Although it often lingers in the shadow of Gibson, Gretsch, and perhaps even Epiphone on occasions – all of which produce roughly similar-formatted set-neck, hollow or semi-hollow guitars – Guild has earned a reputation for consistent quality over the decades of the company's existence, and picked up plenty of professional players along the way. Founded in New York in 1953 by Alfred Dronge, Guild gained favor early on mainly with jazz players at whom their early high-end archtop models were aimed. A greater range of players, however, picked up the company's well-built thinline hollowbodies, semi-acoustics, and solidbodies from the early 1960s onward, including the likes of Duane Eddy, Dave Davies of The Kinks, Muddy Waters, Buddy Guy, Lightnin' Hopkins, and Son Seals.

The latter three in this list were drawn specifically to the

Guild Starfire IV, a guitar with many similarities to the Gibson ES-335, but with a few subtle differences as well – OK, *very* subtle differences. In essence, the Starfire IV – or V with Bigsby; VI with gold hardware – is about as much like a Gibson ES-335 as *another* Gibson ES-335 from a different era might be, yet being a Guild guitar, it somehow escapes feeling like a copy.

Guild's standard humbucking pickups are not greatly unlike the Gibson standard, yet they often sound just a little brighter, edgier, and perhaps rawer than the 'buckers found on the bigger rival. Compared with a standard ES-335, a Starfire can often sound a little chimier and woodier at the same time. Of course, despite the outward similarities of style and features, the minor differences of design and construction still have a say on the overall tones of the two instruments. Note, too, that the Starfire's glued-in neck joins the semi-acoustic body about a fret and a half earlier than the ES-335, setting the neck joint a little deeper into the body, and the bridge and tailpiece along with it.

For many players the difference between a Guild Starfire IV and a Gibson ES-335 has probably come down to price: on the used market, a good U.S.-made Starfire from the 1960s will be as little as anywhere from a half to a quarter the price of an ES-335 from the same period. Guild's production quality remained pretty consistent over the years, and although the earlier guitars are often favored, examples from the 1970s were still made to high standards, and the current models have retained a good reputation, too. Specs altered slightly over the years, with earlier models often having a Tune-o-matic-style Guild bridge set into a floating rosewood base, coupled with lyre trapeze tailpieces rather than the stop-bar and stud-mounted Tune-o-matic seen currently. The latter offers a more Gibson-like performance, while the older style is tonally a little lighter and woodier.

We have already seen some guitars that are more in the semi-solid camp than the semi-acoustic, and the Fender Telecaster Thinline is a classic of the type. The Thinline's approximate constructional similarity to an earlier semi-solid design, namely the Rickenbacker 360, is not a coincidence. Toward the late 1960s Fender had started experimenting with removing some wood from a Telecaster's body to lighten the load, the weight of which was becoming unacceptable to some players, thanks to inconsistent wood stocks. A few years earlier, former Rickenbacker designer Roger Rossmeisl had been lured to Fender to help with the

company's move into acoustic guitars, and the former Ricky man – one of the main designers of the 360 – was one of the chief contributors to the grand 'let's lighten up the Tele' project that culminated in the Thinline of 1968.

The Fender Telecaster Thinline was constructed much like the Rickenbacker semi-solids: a solid slab of ash or mahogany was routed out on the bass and treble sides from the back, with an f-hole cut in the bass-side top to reveal the air space, while the treble-side chambers were covered with an enlarged pickguard. The entire operation was covered from the back with a separate slice of solid wood. The adventure lightened the instruments considerably, and the Thinline range proved a popular new addition to the Fender line.

The original model was identical to the standard Tele in electronics and hardware, but in 1971 the Thinline evolved

2000 Guild Starfire IV

> **Body:** semi-acoustic construction with back, sides, and top of laminated maple, with a pressed arch on the top and solid maple center block; top and back binding; double-cutaway with 19th-fret neck-body joint; sunburst finish in nitrocellulose lacquer

> **Neck:** glued-in mahogany neck with bound rosewood fingerboard with 12" fingerboard radius, 22 medium nickel-silver frets, and 1¹¹/₁₆" nut width; 24¾" scale length (many earlier models had three-piece maple-rosewood-maple neck with rosewood fingerboard)

> **Headstock:** symmetrical back-angled headstock, with three-a-side Grover tuners; bone nut

> **Bridge:** adjustable Tune-o-matic-style bridge and stop-bar tailpiece

> **Electronics:** dual Guild humbucking pickups constructed of single alnico bar magnet beneath, six fixed steel-slug polepieces in one coil and six threaded adjustable polepieces in the other; DC resistance of approximately 6k to 7k; chromed steel cover; three-way toggle switch to select either pickup alone or both together; four 500k potentiometers for individual volume and tone for each pickup; master volume control on some models

> **Sound:** fat, woody, resonant, with decent cutting brightness (for humbuckers) and a slightly raw edge

further to take on a pair of humbucking pickups. These new units were another element of the ever-changing Fender brew contributed by yet one more émigré from a major guitar-making rival, this time Gibson's Seth Lover, who was, as we've seen, also the designer of the legendary PAF humbucking pickup. As detailed in the first section of the book, these pickups are quite different from the Gibson PAF-style humbuckers; Lover wasn't a designer happy to rest on his laurels, and he redesigned the Fender humbucker from the ground up, to give it a response that was both hot and sharply defined, and which, naturally, had good hum rejection.

This later Telecaster Thinline also used a different bridge from the standard Tele, one which was borrowed from the hardtail Stratocaster. It still employed through-body stringing, but the bridge pickup was now mounted in the

pickguard, not a semi-floating bridge plate. Also, tuning efforts now benefited from six individual string saddles that were adjustable both for height and intonation. Non-standard Telecasters such as the Thinline also now carried the Tilt Neck design most prominently seen on 1970s Strats, along with the 'bullet' truss-rod adjustment located at the headstock end. In addition, it's worth noting that Telecasters from this era had a slightly 'wrong' body shape when compared with 1950s and '60s models, because the numerically controlled (NC) routers that CBS-owned Fender was using couldn't cut the upper bass-bout curve to the same shape as the older pin routers, and, of course, guitars of this era carry heavy polyester finishes.

In construction, these Thinlines are still very much Telecasters, although with the humbucking pickups, different bridge, and added air in the body pockets, they

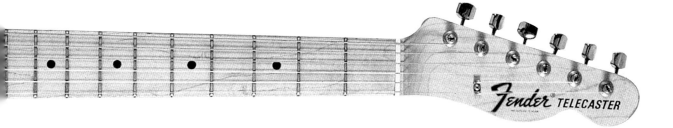

have a fuller, fatter, hotter sound, albeit one that still carries plenty of snap and bite. They almost approach some midpoint between a Fender Telecaster and a Gibson SG or Les Paul Special, although all that ash and maple still gives the Thinline more 'cluck' and sparkle.

Tom Anderson Guitarworks, founded in California in 1984 by the eponymous former Schecter employee, has grown to be one of the most respected independent guitar makers in the U.S.A. Anderson guitars are unashamedly high-end instruments, aimed at professional players and deep-pocketed enthusiasts, hand-built to specifications befitting exclusive custom shops. Fancy tone woods, elaborate chambered body construction on some models, versatile switching, and pickups wound in Anderson's own pickup shop all contribute to the ultra-refined Anderson stew. The result is a guitar with a playing feel that achieves a standard about as high as any available, and a broad tonal palette to go with it.

The approximate styles of Anderson models mainly fall in the range of Tele (T), Strat (Drop Top Classic, ProAm), and superstrat (Drop Top) body shapes, and the more Gibson-esque single-cutaway Atom has recently joined the ranks. All are available in totally solid or partially chambered body styles, the latter of which lands us here in the semi-

1969 Fender Telecaster Thinline

> **Body:** semi-solid single-cutaway ash body with single f-hole
> **Neck:** bolt-on maple neck with maple fingerboard with 7¼" fingerboard radius, 21 nickel-silver frets, and 1⅝" nut width; 25½" scale length
> **Headstock:** asymmetrical headstock with six-in-line sealed Fender tuners; bone nut; single pressed-steel butterfly string tree
> **Bridge:** through-body stringing; fixed steel bridge plate with three threaded steel saddles, strings adjustable in pairs for height and intonation
> **Electronics:** single-coil bridge pickup with six individual alnico pole magnets, DC resistance of 6k to 6.5k, with a steel base plate to aid shielding and raise inductance; single-coil neck pickup with six individual alnico pole magnets, DC resistance of approximately 6.5k; three-way switch to select either pickup or both together, two 250k potentiometers for volume and tone
> **Sound:** bright, snappy, cutting, harmonically saturated, but with a little extra openness in the mids compared with fully solidbody models

⌃ 1999 Anderson Hollow Drop Top

> **Body:** semi-solid basswood body with quilted maple top with natural maple binding; offset double-cutaway body styling

> **Neck:** bolt-on maple neck with rosewood fingerboard with conical 12" to 14" fingerboard radius (from nut to upper frets), 22 medium jumbo nickel-silver frets, and 1¹¹⁄₁₆" nut width; 25½" scale length

> **Headstock:** asymmetrical headstock with six-in-line sealed locking Grover tuners; Buzz Feiten Tempered Tuning system, involving a compensated synthetic nut for improved intonation

> **Bridge:** dual-pole fulcrum vibrato bridge with six individually adjustable, piezo-pickup-equipped saddles

> **Electronics:** single Anderson H humbucker in bridge and two single-coil sized hum-canceling pickups (a wide range of pickup options is available); piezo pickups in bridge saddles (a less often seen Anderson option); individual miniature toggle switch for each pickup to select series, off, or split-parallel (on early models the latter two options were preset at factory to suit individual clients' requirements, while more recent models have internal dip switches); blow switch to select bridge humbucker in series mode from any switching positions, master volume, master tone; piezo-saddle bridge system with independent on/off switch, volume, and independent output

> **Sound:** from hot and singing to hollow and funky, according to switching; also electro-acoustic-like sounds from the piezo bridge

solid chapter. Of course, the elimination of some wood from an otherwise solid body helps to reduce weight, something most guitarists desire, but the practice also helps to open up the sound a little, adding a certain roundness to the tone. Anderson Guitarworks builds its guitars with bolt-on necks exclusively, which might seem unusual for such a high-end luthier, but Anderson claims that such neck joints, when done right, offer just as much sustain and resonance as a glued-in neck, and most players of the company's guitars would agree. In fact, the Anderson bolt-on neck joint is an extremely tight fit, and upon examination offers more wood-to-wood contact than many glued-in neck joints used by other makers.

Anderson offers a wider range of tone-wood options than most makers, which includes a dazzling number of multiwood body choices. Calculate the variables offered by

1989 Aria TA-60

> **Body:** laminated maple top, back, and sides, with partial center block of solid maple; double-cutaway design with 17th-fret neck joint
> **Neck:** bolt-on maple neck with rosewood fingerboard, 22 medium jumbo nickel-silver frets
> **Headstock:** back-angled headstock with three-a-side sealed Aria tuners; plastic nut
> **Bridge:** Tune-o-matic-style bridge with stop-bar tailpiece
> **Electronics:** two Aria AL-7 humbucking pickups; three-way toggle switch to select either pickup alone or both together; independent volume and tone controls for each pickup
> **Sound:** thick, round, ever so slightly muddy when pushed

a top of maple, koa, spruce, walnut, mahogany, rosewood, alder, or swamp ash, on a body of any of the same, topped off with a number of neck and fingerboard options, and you really have to suck it and see as far as putting the resultant sound into words. As would be expected, the company has plenty of experience in guiding prospective clients through the wood-options jungle.

Dwight Yoakam producer and guitarist Pete Anderson – no relation – is one of Anderson's more famous players, but the roster also includes Steve Kimock, Vernon Reid, Dan Huff, and the marque is popular particularly among session players. Some players who are fond of the more traditional guitar styles find the more elaborate Anderson models a little over-refined, but few can argue with their craftsmanship or playability.

While Yamaha established its electric guitar making credentials most firmly in the late 1970s with the SG-2000, as we examined in the previous chapter, its semi-acoustic SA range has provided an equally accomplished alternative to the Gibson ES-335 for players seeking more affordable instruments of that style. However, while the SG-2000 was a very different guitar from a Les Paul, despite certain outward similarities, the SA-2000 and related models were to a greater extent copies of the ES-335. There are a few uniquely Yamaha touches, of course, mainly by way of elements of styling and some subtle construction points, but their main appeal was the out-and-out impression of quality that the models radiated, especially in the late 1970s and early '80s when the Gibson 'originals' were often deemed inferior products by some musicians.

The standard Yamaha pickups used on these guitars were one of their weak points – not that they were poor by any means, just fair and occasionally lackluster – and serious players often changed these out for retrofit DiMarzio, Seymour Duncan, or even actual Gibson humbuckers. The SA-2000, simpler dot-neck SA-1100, and fancier SA-2200 became favorites among LA session players, and helped to further bring Japanese guitar making neck and neck with American makers in terms of credibility.

Plenty of intermediate gigging guitarists also turned to the Aria Pro II range for their semi-acoustic needs. These ranked perhaps a rung or two down the ladder from Yamaha's ES-335 beater, and were less direct copies as well, but oozed quality in their price bracket. Earlier models in the semi-acoustic Titan Artist series were closer to the ES-335 template, albeit with subtle differences in body horn, f-hole, and headstock shape. Later models, such as the 1989 TA-60 shown on the previous page, strayed even further from the archetype. Toward the late 1980s production was shifted from Japan to Korea, and body horns are now a little more rounded, although still narrower than the Gibson's – or, indeed, the Yamaha's – but the neck has now been set further into the body, with a 17th-fret neck joint that, perhaps most significantly of all, is now a bolt-on joint rather than the former glued-in joint. The change also moves the bridge deeper into the body, and, of course, all of these changes alter the guitar's sound some.

Aria still produces the TA series, and these guitars continue to be manufactured in Korea, but the company has returned to set-neck construction for the semi-acoustics, and the quality of the Korean efforts has improved a lot in recent years. Aria currently offers TA models with both humbucking and P-90-style pickups, with both genuine and painted-on f-holes.

The Charvel and Jackson brands are best known for the pointy headstocked superstrats they have manufactured in both the U.S.A. and Japan for the heavier reaches of the rock market, but one of these sibling companies' sidesteps into the semi-solid world also gained some followers. The Charvel Surfcaster was issued in 1991, patterned after a Jackson guitar made for a custom-order client, and was a design very much at the forefront of the retro-original design movement that swept through the latter part of the 1990s and early 2000s.

Blending elements from offset-waist-era Fender, Rickenbacker, Gretsch, and Danelectro, the Surfcaster had a deceptive bolt-on maple neck with a bound rosewood fingerboard, and spliced-on back-angled headstock, with roller nut on the vibrato-equipped models to help keep wobbles in tune. Rather unusually – unusual being a term that applies to much of the Surfcaster's design – the guitar's fingerboard ended in an angle that ran parallel to that of its pickups and carried 22 full frets plus two partial frets in the 23rd- and 24th-fret positions on the treble side.

The body was made from a partially routed blank of solid wood, and covered with a maple veneer top with single 'slash' sound hole. Two Danelectro-style lipstick tube pickups offered a bright if low-output performance that

◀ 1990 Yamaha SA-1100

> **Body:** semi-acoustic construction with back, sides, and top of laminated maple, with a pressed arch on the top and solid maple center block; top and back binding; double-cutaway with 20th-fret neck-body joint

> **Neck:** glued-in, one-piece mahogany neck with bound rosewood fingerboard, with 12" fingerboard radius, 22 medium nickel-silver frets, and 1¹¹⁄₁₆" nut width; 24¾" scale length

> **Headstock:** symmetrical back-angled headstock, with three-a-side sealed Yamaha tuners

> **Bridge:** adjustable Tune-o-matic-style bridge and stop-bar tailpiece

> **Electronics:** dual Yamaha humbucking pickups constructed of single alnico bar magnet beneath, six fixed steel-slug polepieces in one coil and six threaded adjustable polepieces in the other; DC resistance of approximately 7.5k; chromed steel cover; three-way toggle switch to select either pickup alone or both together; four 500k potentiometers for individual volume and tone for each pickup

> **Sound:** thick, rich, and vocal from the neck pickup, punchy and cutting from the bridge, with a slightly airy, woody resonance in all positions; good sustain; good hum rejection

◢ 1991 Charvel Surfcaster

> **Body:** semi-solid body of routed ash with a laminated maple top; three-ply top binding; double-cutaway with offset neck-body joint

> **Neck:** bolt-on, two-piece maple neck with bound rosewood fingerboard with 12" fingerboard radius, 23½ jumbo nickel-silver frets, and 1¹¹⁄₁₆" nut width; 25½" scale length

> **Headstock:** spliced-on, asymmetrical back-angled headstock, with three-a-side sealed Gotoh tuners

> **Bridge:** two-post Gotoh fulcrum vibrato bridge

> **Electronics:** dual low-output single-coil lipstick-tube pickups with alnico magnets; three-way toggle switch to select either pickup alone or both together; master volume and tone switches; push-push tone pot for out-of-phase pickup wiring

> **Sound:** snappy, bright, and funky, with good bite and a slight edge of snarl

accentuated the intended twang factor of this funky design. When Japanese electronics giant Akai acquired Charvel-Jackson in 1997 it closed down the Charvel brand, but the popular Surfcaster model was initially retained under the Jackson name. Many Jackson examples carry humbucking pickups in the bridge position, and non-vibrato models later employed through-body stringing across a Tune-o-matic-style bridge. The Jackson Surfcaster has recently been discontinued.

Although fully hollowbody electric archtops will be considered in the next chapter, let's take a look right now at one guitar that has a body that is *almost* completely hollow. The Paul Reed Smith McCarty Hollowbody model evolved out of the company's attempts to build its full-bodied (fully hollow) Archtop model, and, in terms of construction, is the same guitar except for an inch less body depth. That said,

both models have a narrow but solid block of wood between the back and top in the position of the bridge, which is what enables PRS to use a stud-mounted wrapover bridge on these guitars in the first place, something that would be impossible on a traditionally crafted full-bodied or thinline acoustic archtop guitar.

PRS's approach to the Hollowbody is an extension of the practice of routing-out solid wood that some manufacturers employ in making a semi-solid guitar, such as the Rickenbacker 360 or the Fender Telecaster Thinline. PRS just takes the technique a step – or several – further, and uses CAD/CNC (computer-assisted design/computer numerically controlled) routers to hollow out all of the body space between the top and back except for the narrow block beneath the bridge, and to carve the outer top and back arches as well.

The result is a hollowbody that has much greater

1999 PRS McCarty Hollow Body II

> **Body:** 1¾"-deep PRS-shaped offset double-cutaway body made from hollowed-out mahogany back with carved, arched solid two-piece figured maple top, with natural maple binding top and back

> **Neck:** glued-in one-piece mahogany neck with paua-edged rosewood fingerboard with Artist Package paua bird inlays with 10" radius, wide-fat profile, 22 medium-jumbo nickel-silver frets, 1¹¹⁄₁₆" nut width; 25" scale length

> **Headstock:** back-angled PRS-shaped headstock with three-a-side ebony tuner buttons, with Artist Package rosewood facing and inlaid signature; headstock-end truss-rod access

> **Bridge:** two-post, stud mounted PRS compensated wrapover tailpiece

> **Electronics:** two McCarty archtop humbucking pickups (slightly lower output than standard McCarty humbuckers) constructed with a single alnico bar magnet each in the traditional PAF fashion, gold-plated metal covers

> **Sound:** thick, full, round, and sweet, with an airy and slightly acoustic resonance and good sustain

strength than pressed, laminated archtop designs thanks to its use of solid woods only, but which also offers a great deal of acoustic resonance. Mounting a wrapover bridge on these guitars also gives a rare solidity to the body-end string anchoring of these archtops, and allows an easy-bending playing feel that is rare for the construction style.

The PRS McCarty Hollowbody models have been better received than the archtops, perhaps because they aren't quite as big a step away from that to which players of solidbody McCarty models are used, and from the front appear to be much the same guitar with a couple of f-holes added. The semi-acoustic body changes the guitar's tonality considerably, smoothing out the attack, rounding off the characteristic solidbody sharpness, and adding an extra degree of wood and warmth to the tone, too. Thanks to the fact that the body is precisely carved from solid woods and to the solidity of the bridge block, this model is also far more resistant to feedback than many other fully hollow thinline archtops, such as the Gibson ES-330 or Epiphone Casino.

5

Acoustic-Electric Archtops

Fender might have bagged the honors as the formative maker in the solidbody electric department, but Gibson has always been the name to beat for hollowbody archtop electrics, whether they be semi-acoustic models like those covered in the previous chapter or the fully acoustic designs we will examine here. Orville Gibson invented the archtop guitar way back in the 1890s, for heavens' sake, so it seems only right and fitting that the first widely available electric Spanish guitar be a Gibson – the ES-150, to be precise, first offered with built-in pickup in 1936, and taken up most famously by jazz great Charlie Christian.

While the electric guitar in the broad sense evolved away from the fully acoustic template for the very reasons covered in the chapters on solidbody and semi-acoustic guitars, the properly hollow full-depth and thinline archtop electric guitar still has its own vibe and its own tone, and possesses a great appeal for a great many players to this day. Howling feedback and a propensity toward boominess be damned: nothing else sounds quite like a big jazz box with a magnetic pickup or two bolted into it – or, indeed, floating above it. In many cases, to be sure, 'vibe' is the operative word here: there's an acoustic life and motion in the vibration of a hollow guitar against the player's torso that can create an intimacy and interaction to the musician-instrument relationship that just isn't replicated satisfactorily in a solid slab of wood. And, of course, they just sound different.

Gibson's electrified debutante is something of an oddball today, mainly because the company evolved away from the cumbersome 'Charlie Christian' blade pickup that appeared on the first ES-150 and a few other models, although the pickup itself was available by special-order as late as the 1970s. Nevertheless, the ES-150 embodies the spirit and sound of the pre-war jazz box, and certainly helped to spark the amplification revolution that brought guitarists out of the rhythm section and into the spotlight. The specs of the guitar itself read like those of so many entirely acoustic models before it: carved, arched top made from solid spruce, maple back and sides with mahogany neck and maple fingerboard, floating two-piece rosewood bridge with

trapeze tailpiece. But, of course, it was that big blade-pole pickup that all the fuss was about.

Viewed from the top of the guitar when installed, the Charlie Christian pickup looks like a pretty standard P-90-sized unit with a single blade instead of individual polepieces. Its three oddly distant mounting screws hide this design's real surprise, however: the design employs a large carbon steel magnet suspended under the top of the guitar, which contacts the blade polepiece, and hence the coil, side on. The large magnet was required because carbon-steel magnets are weaker than the alnico or ceramic units made today. Despite the size of the magnet and the wide coil, most Charlie Christian pickups measured today show a DC

1937 Gibson ES-150

> **Body:** 16¼"-wide non-cutaway fully hollow body with flat maple back, maple sides, and X-braced arched solid spruce top, bound top and back
> **Neck:** glued-in one-piece mahogany neck with bound rosewood fingerboard with 12" radius and pronounced V profile, 14th-fret neck-body joint, 19 narrow-gauge nickel-silver frets, and 1¹¹⁄₁₆" nut width; 24⅝" scale length
> **Headstock:** symmetrical 17-degree back-angled headstock with three-a-side Grover tuners; bone nut
> **Bridge:** floating two-piece rosewood bridge with thumb wheels for height adjustment; trapeze tailpiece
> **Electronics:** single Charlie Christian pickup made with large carbon-steel magnet and single blade polepiece; DC resistance approximately 2.5k to 3.5k (perhaps roughly 6k when new); controls for volume and tone
> **Sound:** warm, deep, and full-throated, but with decent brightness and definition; plenty of woody resonance

resistance reading of only around 2.5k to 3.5k, although it has been suggested that the aging of the magnet contributes to this low spec, and that many started life in the late 1930s in the 6k range. Their sound is fairly warm and full, yet with a reticent brightness that gives pretty good note definition to the ES-150.

When designing the ES-150, Gibson had already begun to recognize that making a guitar primarily to be heard amplified was different from making one to be heard acoustically, an understanding that would bloom a decade later in the form of the ES-175. At the same time, however, this was a pretty conservative company dipping a toe in the radical new waters. The ES-150 was, therefore, made as a much more basic guitar than the top-of-the-line L-5 or L-7, for example, with unfigured woods, a flat back, and minimal adornments. It still carried the laboriously hand-carved, X-braced, solid spruce top, which, without that heavy pickup hanging from it, would have helped to make for a tuneful acoustic performance in itself.

By 1946 Gibson's standard pickup eventually evolved into the P-90, via a version with non-adjustable polepieces used in the early 1940s, and this is far more common on early, pre-humbucker Gibson archtop electrics. But the Charlie Christian pickup set a tonal standard from the

start, and still holds a place in the hearts of many jazz aficionados.

As it gradually became clear that the pitbull of electrification wasn't about to unclamp its jaws in a hurry, Gibson moved its Electric Spanish line upscale, eventually offering pickups on more elaborate and more elegantly adorned instruments. Meanwhile, plenty of players did the job for themselves, retrofitting floating pickups – often still called 'guitar microphones' in the day – to guitars that were built as acoustic instruments. The floating pickup is held in place by a bar or bracket that is attached to the end of the neck, or occasionally to the pickguard or finger-rest, and therefore doesn't touch the top of the guitar at all.

The result of this is a little different from mounting a pickup in a cut-out right inside the top of the guitar, and is still preferred by many jazz purists. A floating pickup maximizes the resonance of the guitar, which is to say it doesn't impede its acoustic performance, and runs more toward amplifying an acoustic guitar than electrifying one. Of course, any such pickup is still using the magnetics of string vibration to create the low-voltage signal that will be amplified, but with a fully hollow body and unimpeded top, that string vibration rings with a much woodier and more acoustic tone.

Gibson introduced the top-of-the-range, 18″-wide Super 400 in 1934, but the electric Super 400CES didn't

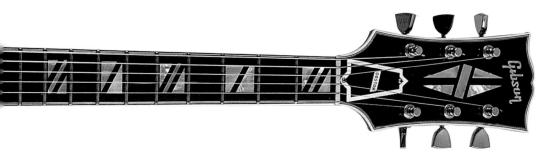

arrive until 1951. So what did the hardworking professional in the orchestra do, who needed a big, high-end archtop to play through an amp? He mounted a floating pickup, naturally, and in most cases a DeArmond Model 1000 Rhythm Chief or adjustable 1100 Super Chief made by Rowe Industries of Toledo, Ohio. These pickups are famed in jazz circles, and, having been out of production for the best part of three decades, are getting costly on the used market. They have a clean, full, punchy sound that helps to counter the potential boominess of some of these big-bodied jazz boxes, and gives them a little cut and bite, even in the neck position where such pickups are usually used.

The Super 400 itself had all the refinements Gibson could muster in a big-bodied archtop, what the company called 'advanced' at the time of the model's release, since the dimension had been increased from the previous standard maximum sizes. Naturally, the Super 400 had a carved, arched spruce top – originally with cremona brown sunburst finish or, later, a natural blond – and maple sides and back. The top was originally X-braced, but Gibson moved to parallel bracing during 1939, around the same time that a

---

⌃ 1969 Gibson Super 400CN

> **Body:** 18"-wide single-cutaway fully hollow body with arched maple back, maple sides, and parallel-braced arched solid spruce top, with seven-ply top binding, three-ply back binding
> **Neck:** glued-in five-piece mahogany neck with triple-bound ebony fingerboard with 12" radius, 14th-fret neck-body joint, 20 medium nickel-silver frets, and 1¹¹⁄₁₆" nut width; 25½" scale length
> **Headstock:** symmetrical 17-degree back-angled headstock with three-a-side Grover tuners; bone nut
> **Bridge:** floating two-piece ebony bridge with thumb wheels for height adjustment; trapeze tailpiece
> **Electronics:** single DeArmond Model 1000 Rhythm Chief pickup with alnico bar magnet; controls for volume and tone
> **Sound:** full, rich, and resonant, but with good clarity and note definition

cutaway version of the Super 400 was made available. These are big, deep, rich-sounding archtops – both acoustically or amplified – and the early X-braced versions have a little more resonance when compared with the parallel-braced examples' more percussive attack. With a well-installed DeArmond Rhythm Chief, this is the crème de la crème of refined jazz tone.

Throughout much of the 1930s and '40s, Epiphone proved to be an arch rival to Gibson, and, along with a handful of other smaller makers, helped to keep the boys from Kalamazoo from total domination of the archtop market. Until it was bought out by Gibson in 1957, Epiphone maintained very much its own identity, and while some models were similar in size and form to popular Gibson archtops, the exact body lines and many subtle details helped to set them apart. Plenty of name artists chose Epiphones over Gibsons back in the jazz age, and the New York company was almost as quick to enter the

amplification race. Epiphone's first electric archtop, the short-lived Electar Spanish, was introduced in 1937 with a big horseshoe pickup, but it was discontinued in 1939. The Coronet, Century, and Zephyr that were brought out in that same year to replace it, however, all carried pickups that look a little less antique today, and the latter two models survived into the Gibson era.

Epiphone often used solid maple tops on its guitars rather than the spruce that was standard on the majority of archtops; there was also a tendency to position the pickups on many of these early models in the bridge position rather than at the end of the fingerboard. Together, these design features helped to make them bright and cutting compared with other big-bodied archtops. The pickup positioning in particular makes some sense when considered in the context of the time, when manufacturers were scrabbling to come up with designs that would help players cut through the dense mix of a big swing band. But the neck-position

1954 Epiphone Zephyr Emperor Regent

> **Body:** 18½"-wide, deep single-cutaway, fully hollow body with arched laminated maple top, back, and sides, with five-ply top binding, back binding

> **Neck:** glued-in five-piece maple neck with multibound rosewood fingerboard with 12" radius, 14th-fret neck-body joint, 20 narrow nickel-silver frets, and 1⅜" nut width; 25½" scale length

> **Headstock:** symmetrical back-angled headstock with three-a-side closed-back Epiphone tuners; bone nut; 'tree of life' inlay

> **Bridge:** floating two-piece rosewood bridge with thumb wheels for height adjustment; two-tiered Frequensator trapeze tailpiece.

> **Electronics:** three Epiphone New York single-coil pickups with side-on alnico bar magnets and adjustable threaded polepieces; six-pushbutton Vari Tone pickup selector switching, with a different pickup or combination achieved by each button: 1) bridge, 2) neck and bridge, 3) neck, 4) all three, 5) neck and middle, 6) middle; single master controls for volume and tone

> **Sound:** generally deep and airy with blooming sustain, and punchy in the classic big-bodied jazzer vein, with degrees of brightness or warmth determined by pickup selection

pickup has become the standard of jazz tone, and Epiphone pickups moved toward the middle and neck positions by the mid 1940s.

High-end Epiphones of the late 1940s and early '50s were becoming adventurous guitars, often with three pickups and an array of unusual switches for numerous tonal options. By this time Epiphone had followed Gibson's example in making many of its electric archtop guitars out of laminated woods. Labor troubles at the New York factory put a serious dent in production at a crucial point in the company's struggle to keep up with Gibson, and Epiphone eventually received an offer it couldn't refuse. Most of the high-end, big-bodied Epiphone electrics from the pre-Gibson and early Gibson eras are great instruments that are highly desired by jazz players, while many low-end Epiphone archtops are good-value vintage American guitars for players on tighter budgets.

Just as a disproportionate amount of the bolt-neck chapter belonged to Fender, Gibson rules the roost here in archtop land. As has already been mentioned, the company's founder invented the form, and Gibson also did more than any other maker to further advance the design of the archtop through the first half of the 20th century. This is an examination of tone, not a book on guitar history, so entries here aren't always taken chronologically. The Gibson ES-175 is just such case, and in the evolutionary sense it comes before the laminated-woods Epiphone Zephyr Emperor Regent just featured – although that example was used as the culmination of changes made to an earlier and somewhat different single-bridge-pickup Zephyr model.

The ES-175 of 1949 was a considerable step forward, and epitomized Gibson's acceptance of the requirements of amplifying a guitar that was still, at heart, a big-bodied archtop acoustic.

If pickups and controls were going to be mounted in holes cut in the guitar's arched top, and if the player was going to use the instrument through an amplifier 95 per cent of the time, why go to the trouble and expense of laboriously hand-carving an arched top out of solid spruce or maple? Apparently there was no reason to do so. The use of laminated maple top, back, and sides on the ES-175 helped bring in a professional electric archtop at a much more affordable price than, for example, a carved-top

acoustic such as a Super 400 or an L-5. At the same time, such construction provided a slightly brighter tone and was a little – although not a whole lot – more resistant to feedback. Functional, affordable: they couldn't lose.

The ES-175 was an instant hit, and has remained the standard for the hardworking electric-jazz man. If you've heard more than a handful of classic jazz guitar recordings, it's a pretty sure bet you've heard an ES-175 or two in there among them. Kenny Burrell, Joe Pass, Jim Hall, and a multitude of others coined classic electric jazz tones on an ES-175, while Pat Metheny has used the model throughout his career for modern jazz and fusion, and Steve Howe of Yes has proved it a versatile prog-rock-fusion instrument as well.

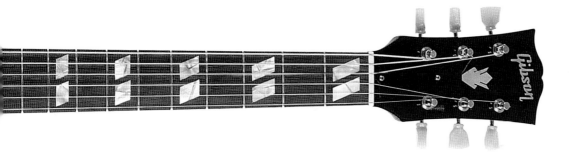

1953 Gibson ES-175D

> **Body:** 16¼"-wide, 3½"-deep fully hollow single-cutaway body with laminated maple top, back, and sides; pressed-arch top with parallel bracing, bound top and back

> **Neck:** glued-in three-piece maple neck with bound rosewood fingerboard with 12" radius, 14th-fret neck-body joint, 19 narrow nickel-silver frets, and 1¹¹⁄₁₆" nut width; 24⅝" scale length

> **Headstock:** symmetrical back-angled headstock with three-a-side tulip button Kluson tuners; bone nut

> **Bridge:** floating two-piece rosewood bridge with thumb wheels for height adjustment; trapeze tailpiece

> **Electronics:** two P-90 pickups; three-way toggle switch for either pickup or both together; four 500k potentiometers for independent volume and tone controls for each pickup

> **Sound:** warm and full, yet punchy and relatively well defined, with a slight midrange hump and a sizzly edge (with humbuckers, the tone is rounder but a little less punchy)

Gibson's P-90 pickup arrived in the world just three years before the ES-175, and that guitar first carried one and later an optional two – on the ES-175D of 1953 – of those fat single-coil units, until the PAF humbucker hit the scene in 1957. Some players still prefer the punchy, tactile, well-defined, and ever so slightly gnarly sound of the P-90 on their ES-175, although the singing and smooth-as-butter PAF defines 'the jazz tone' for plenty of others, and, sure, plenty of others still will swear blind that you need a carved-top L-5 or Super 400, or for that matter D'Aquisto or Benedetto, to produce the creamiest jazz tones available. But players vote with their fingers, or a combination of fingers and wallets, and more working jazz guitarists have laid down their chops across the fingerboard of an ES-175 than probably any other single model of archtop acoustic-electric.

The Guild company, a newcomer to the scene in the early 1950s, hit the ground running and became a respected maker – of archtop jazz guitars in particular – right from the start. When troubles with labor relations in New York forced the original, independent Epiphone company to move to Philadelphia for a time, the departure left a lot of skilled guitar makers in the city with nowhere to go for work – until Guild came along soon after. Being a jazz guitarist himself, Guild founder Alfred Dronge had a lot of friends among the big players on the New York club and studio scenes, and it seems he had little trouble convincing some of them to give his guitars a try. By the late 1950s and early '60s jazz stars Johnny Smith and George Barnes were on the roster, and Guild was accepted as an alternative to any of the leaders in the archtop market.

The Stuart X-500 was introduced in 1953, with the X-550 variation following shortly after, and stayed in the Guild catalog until 1994. It has been offered again in recent years as the upgraded Benedetto Signature Guild Stuart. It was designed as a more elaborately decorated version of the two-pickup X-400, with engraved lyre tailpiece, ebony fingerboard, and large abalone block position markers with V-shaped inserts that are clearly inspired by the Epiphone Zephyr Emperor Regent. Otherwise, the guitar is made along the lines of many of the electric archtops of the day, with a laminated arched spruce top, and maple back and sides.

These were big, warm, toneful jazz boxes unplugged, and with the full yet cutting P-90-style Guild pickups they were powerful instruments in both the big-band or small-combo setting. Guild's quality has remained fairly consistent through the years, despite factory relocations

first to Hoboken, New Jersey, in 1956, then to Westerly, Rhode Island, in the late 1960s after Guild was purchased by Avnet, and finally to Corona, California, shortly into the new millennium, after the company's purchase by Fender. The two finest Guild archtop electrics of all time, the Johnny Smith Award and Stuart (now designated X-700) are currently hand-built to exacting standards alongside Fender Custom Shop production in the Corona factory, under the supervision of master luthier Robert Benedetto. The Stuart now carries a carved solid spruce top, with a commensurate price tag.

In the late 1940s and '50s, Gretsch had made some efforts to compete in the archtop electric market with its Elelctromatic and Synchromatic models, and even gained a few big-name players. But with the rock'n'roll boom came a new emphasis on electric guitars, and the New York company redirected its efforts mainly at that market as well as the electric-country scene. In itself, that's probably a good thing; despite having the audacious looks and the general vibe of many of the leading archtop models, the big-bodied Gretsches were rarely as well made as the upscale offerings from Gibson, Epiphone, Guild, or any of half a dozen other prominent smaller American makers. As the emphasis fell on amplified sounds, however, Gretsch made headway with raw, hot sounds, hotrod looks, and flashy colors.

Gretsch's most important endorser was one country-jazz star by the name of Chet Atkins, and the company's early inroads into both the country and rock'n'roll markets came via guitars with his name attached. The Chet Atkins Hollow Body of 1955 – designated with the model number 6120 – was a fully hollow archtop electric made with laminated body woods roughly along the lines of the earlier Gibson ES-175, but with a rounded Venetian cutaway, bodacious cowboy cosmetics, and a Bigsby vibrato unit as standard. Unplugged, this was even less of an acoustic performer than Gibson's laminated jazz box, but through a semi-cranked amp it provided one of the formative voices of the birth of rock'n'roll. Full and thick but surprisingly punchy and twangy along with it, the original 6120 offered a sound that satisfied smooth picker Atkins only briefly, and he soon sought more refinement in the form of the Filter'Tron humbucker and other advances to the model. In the hands of a Duane Eddy or an Eddie Cochran, however, it was the sound of a revolution.

‹ 1958 Guild Stuart X-550

> **Body:** 17"-wide fully hollow single-cutaway body with arched spruce ply top, maple back and sides; multi-ply top and back binding
> **Neck:** glued-in five-piece maple neck with bound ebony fingerboard with 12" radius; 14th-fret neck-body joint, 20 medium nickel-silver frets, and 1¹¹⁄₁₆" nut width; 25⅝" scale length
> **Headstock:** symmetrical back-angled headstock with three-a-side pearl button Grover tuners; bone nut
> **Bridge:** floating two-piece ebony bridge with thumb wheels for height adjustment; lyre-shaped trapeze tailpiece
> **Electronics:** two wide single-coil pickups, made with alnico bar magnets beneath and six adjustable threaded steel polepieces; three-way toggle switch for either pickup or both together; controls for independent volume and tone controls for each pickup
> **Sound:** full, airy, and resonant, with good balance and clarity, and just a little bite for cutting power (later Stuarts with Guild humbuckers sound a little fuller and warmer, although with a shade less snap and cut)

The DeArmond 200 single-coil pickups – also referred to as Gretsch Dynasonics – that this guitar carried for its first few years are a big part of the magic. They are both bright and fat, with good midrange oomph, and that ever so slight air of lo-fi response that often suits rock'n'roll so well. Combined with the many quirks of the Gretsch guitar – including the fairly loose anchor points and less-than-optimally resonant construction, all of which somehow adds up to a magically brash, compelling tone when amplified – they became the soundtrack of teen rebellion.

The Filter'Tron humbucking pickups added to the 6120 during 1958 are seen as an improvement by some players, and they do make these guitars a little smoother and hotter. You hear this sound in the playing of Brian Setzer in particular. At the same time, however, the construction of the 6120's body was changed slightly: the parallel top and back bracing now met at a point toward the middle of the guitar to form a narrow sound post. This was done in an effort to tighten up the front and back a little and get them vibrating in unison in order to cut down on undesirable howling feedback. The practice also improves sustain a little in post-'58 Chets, but some fans of the earlier guitars say the sound post dampens the openness and airiness of the earlier models.

In the early 1960s Guild made an effort to attack Gretsch head on in the rock'n'roll market by swiping 6120 player Duane Eddy to endorse a new model in 1962 that, frankly, was equipped very much like a pre-1957 Chet Atkins Hollow Body, complete with DeArmond single-coil pickups and Bigsby vibrato. An Everyman version of this guitar, however, was the Starfire III, a single-cutaway thinline hollowbody that came with DeArmonds – later Guild humbuckers – and often a Bigsby. We have already visited Guild's quality of

1955 Gretsch Chet Atkins Hollow Body

> **Body:** 16"-wide, 2⅞"-deep fully hollow single-cutaway body with pressed arched maple ply top and maple ply back and sides, multi-ply top and back binding; transparent nitrocellulose finish

> **Neck:** glued-in maple neck with bound rosewood fingerboard with 12" radius, 14th-fret neck-body joint, 21 narrow nickel-silver frets, and 1¹¹⁄₁₆" nut width; large mother of pearl block position markers etched with western themes; 24¾" scale length

> **Headstock:** symmetrical back-angled headstock with three-a-side tuners; aluminum nut

> **Bridge:** fixed-arm Bigsby vibrato tailpiece with cast aluminum one-piece compensated rocker bridge, mounted on floating rosewood base; adjustable for height only (or approximate intonation by moving the base)

> **Electronics:** two single-coil DeArmond 200 pickups, made with six adjustable alnico slug polepieces, DC resistance approximately 8.5k; three-way toggle switch for either pickup independently or both together; four controls for individual volume for each pickup, master tone, plus master volume (on treble bout)

> **Sound:** thick, cutting, twangy, and a little bit raunchy, with a whisper of air and openness to round out the package

1958 Gretsch Chet Atkins Hollow Body

> **Body:** same dimensions as 1955 model, but internal top and back braces now meet to form a sound post

> **Neck:** bound Neo-Classic ebony fingerboard with small thumbnail position inlays

> **Headstock:** symmetrical back-angled headstock with three-a-side tuners; aluminum nut

> **Bridge:** movable-arm Bigsby vibrato tailpiece with chromed brass bar rocker bridge, mounted on floating rosewood base

> **Electronics:** two humbucking Gretsch Filter'Tron pickups, made with alnico bar magnets and 12 adjustable threaded polepieces; DC resistance approximately 4k (note, however, that other constructional differences mean the Filter'Trons are more than 'just half as powerful' as DeArmonds); three-way toggle switch for either pickup independently or both together; three-way master tone switch; three controls for individual volume for each pickup, plus master volume (on treble bout)

> **Sound:** smoother than DeArmond-pickup model, but with a little edge and still plenty of brightness and twang; improved sustain compared with the 1955–57 models

construction, and these were well-made utilitarian guitars that, in many ways, probably surpassed the famous Gretsch rivals, although they certainly didn't have the looks.

The thinner body, mahogany ply instead of maple, and other constructional differences mean these Starfires don't sound exactly like the Gretsches they resemble, but they're in the ballpark at least, and if not for the 6120's fame and the fact that it established the sound, you'd be hard pressed to say the Starfire III with DeArmond pickups was inferior in any tangible way. DeArmond-loaded Starfires have become a little more popular recently, perhaps for this very reason, but when you can find one it's still usually just a fraction of the price of an original Gretsch 6120 with DeArmonds. The Starfire III is also a good bargain with Guild humbucking

pickups, and, if anything, it's a more versatile instrument in this attire.

Other Guilds, such as the thinline T-100D 'Slim Jim' and full-bodied CE-100, can be pretty good bargains, too, and they often make great jazz, blues, or rockabilly guitars. The single-coil pickups on earlier versions of these are sometimes inferior to the DeArmonds on the Starfire III pictured, but they can sound great even so, and the wide, P-90-like single-coil units on some earlier Guilds, like the Stuart pictured, are very good-sounding pickups by any standards.

Fender-owned Guild continues to offer a humbucker-equipped version of the Starfire III, made in the Fender factory in Corona, California. It's hard to argue with the quality of the current model, but it provides one of the rare

1961 Guild Starfire III

> **Body:** fully hollow, single-cutaway thinline body made with pressed arched top of laminated mahogany, back and sides of laminated mahogany, bound top and back

> **Neck:** glued-in mahogany neck with bound rosewood fingerboard with 12" radius, 14th-fret neck-body joint, 20 narrow nickel-silver frets, and 1¹¹⁄₁₆" nut width; 24¾" scale length

> **Headstock:** symmetrical back-angled headstock with three-a-side Grover tuners

> **Bridge:** Bigsby vibrato tailpiece with cast aluminum one-piece compensated rocker bridge, mounted on floating aluminum base, adjustable for height only (or approximate intonation by moving the base)

> **Electronics:** two single-coil DeArmond 200 pickups, made with six adjustable alnico slug polepieces; DC resistance approximately 8.5k; three-way toggle switch for either pickup independently or both together; four controls for individual volume and tone for each pickup

> **Sound:** bright and snappy, but with a little grit and edge; decent warmth, especially in the neck position, and a certain open hollowness overall

inverse relationships in new versus vintage American-made electric guitars, in that an original from the early 1960s can often be had at about half the list price of a new model.

Often mistakenly considered a poor-man's ES-335 with P-90 pickups and slightly simpler ornamentation, the Gibson ES-330, which arrived in 1959, just one year after the ES-335, is actually a very different guitar. Swapping humbuckers for P-90s would in itself make for different voices, but the ES-330 is an entirely hollow thinline archtop, lacking the ES-335's center block of solid maple, and it also has a neck-body joint around the 16th to 17th frets, rather than the 20th as on the ES-335. This in itself – regardless of the lack of a center block – would change the guitar's acoustic voice some. It puts the guitar's bridge nearer to the center of the large, lower bout – in the position of the traditional big-bodied archtop, in fact, aligned with the center points of the two f-holes – and gives the guitar a deeper response as a result. Compared with most hollowbody archtops, thinline or otherwise, the ES-330 is unusual in having its Tune-o-matic bridge mounting set

right into the wood of the top, and, in fact, into the parallel top braces beneath it, rather than in a floating bridge base.

Being a truly hollowbodied guitar, albeit a thin one, the ES-330 is more prone to feedback than its sibling, but less so than a full-depth archtop electric, and it also cops a little more of the jazz box's woody warmth. Of course, the ES-330 lacks the sustain of the maple-stuffed ES-335, so it's less of a rock-fusion wailer, but it has spanned the genres from cool jazz to alt-country grind and twang, and has been preferred by many players who want a little more wood, air, and grit with their thinline thrills.

Even so, the ES-330 hasn't had nearly the number of famous users as the ES-335. Grant Green played much of his sparsely swinging jazz on one, and they have been chosen by a few worthy indie and alternative guitarists, but major rock and blues names don't spring readily to mind. Ironically, considering Epiphone was Gibson's more budget sister brand, the ES-330 package became much more desirable and famous in the guise of the Epiphone Casino, launched in 1961, thanks entirely to its use by The Beatles. All three string-strumming members of the Fab Four used a Casino for a time in the mid 1960s, particularly on the *Revolver* album and during the band's final live performances in 1966, and Paul McCartney's own Bigsby-equipped

Casino has remained one of his favorite guitars to this day. The Beatles' use of the model has put it in more notable hands than the ES-330 over the years, and artists as diverse as Matthew Sweet and Steve Earle have favored it.

Both the Casino and the ES-330 yield a thick, rich yet cutting tone through a semi-cranked tube amp for rock'n'roll or raw-roots playing. Those hot P-90s can really drive an amp to break up, and the added acoustic energy gives the ES-330 or Casino tone extra body and power. These guitars can howl with feedback, too, if not hand-muted during loud passages – or not kept a distance from the amp at almost any time – but on certain magical examples this feedback can be, surprisingly, quite harmonic and useful, if that's your bag. Gibson discontinued the ES-330 in 1970, but thanks to the higher-end demand generated association with The Beatles, the company currently manufactures its special-issue John Lennon 1965 Casino and John Lennon Revolution Casino in the U.S. factory, whereas the majority of Epiphone electrics come from Korea.

A lot of B-list (or C-list, or D-list...) archtops have proven to be great funky fun over the years, generating no shortage of compelling garage-band excitement, and some genuinely sterling tracks as well on occasion. Given the limited sustain and often rather choked resonance displayed

1961 Gibson ES-330

> **Body:** fully hollow, double-cutaway thinline body made with pressed arched top of laminated maple, laminated maple back and sides; single-bound top and back
> **Neck:** glued-in mahogany neck with bound rosewood fingerboard with 12" radius, 16th-fret neck-body joint (approximately), 22 jumbo nickel-silver frets, and 1¹¹⁄₁₆" nut width; 24⅝" scale length
> **Headstock:** symmetrical 17-degree back-angled headstock with three-a-side Kluson tuners
> **Bridge:** fixed Tune-o-matic bridge and trapeze tailpiece
> **Electronics:** two single-coil P-90 pickups, made with two alnico bar magnets each and six adjustable threaded polepieces; DC resistance in the range of 7.5k to 8k; three-way toggle switch for either pickup independently or both together; four controls for individual volume and tone for each pickup
> **Sound:** deep, rich, a little gritty, and hot; some pronounced midrange emphasis but pretty good balance overall, and an air of openness from the fully hollow body

Paul McCartney's 1961 Epiphone Casino

Paul McCartney's own Epiphone Casino displays the similarity between this model and the Gibson ES-330. In fact, the only differences are cosmetic, such as the dot fingerboard inlays on the Gibson – these were small blocks on the ES-330, too, after 1961 – and the Bigsby vibrato and vinyl saddles on the Casino's Tune-o-matic bridge, both of which were also options on the ES-330.

even by many quality brand thinline archtop electrics, older budget examples of the breed often come closer to aping lauded vintage tones in this category than do cheapo solidbodies and semis.

Harmony introduced its thinline hollowbody Rocket the same year that Gibson's ES-330 came out, although the budget brand's instrument was a single-cutaway model until 1967. The more elaborate double-cutaway, three-pickup H75 and H77 arrived in 1960, and fast became the ES-335

copy of choice for many a thin-walleted string slinger. These Harmony models had the full end-of-fretboard neck-body joint that the ES-330 lacked, but carried single-coil pickups, and rather clunky sounding ones at that – although when played in anger they could still make a righteous noise.

Such guitars undoubtedly accounted for no end of grizzly blues, proto-grunge, and rock'n'roll, although the proof of this is largely unrecorded. Particularly with a Bigsby attached, an H75 or H77 makes an evil rockabilly or

psychobilly weapon, and that slim but hollow body and the three rather primitive, microphonic pickups can howl and squeal when desired – and when not.

Of course, these Harmony models, such as the H77 in our photo, were far inferior in construction to the Gibsons they aped. They used cheaper grades of maple ply for the body, somewhat more crudely shaped necks, and inferior DeArmond pickups. (DeArmond made many pickups at many grades, and these weren't top of the tree, but can sound very cool at times nonetheless.) Which is not to say it wasn't a major effort on Harmony's part to offer a top-shelf guitar. The H77 had five-ply binding around its top, three-ply binding around the fingerboard and headstock, large mother-of-pearl-block neck inlays, and mock-tortoiseshell pickguard and headstock facing. Although the latter often began to peel away some years down the road, you have to give them an A for effort.

Also, these were bolt-neck guitars; the format is less often seen in the genre, although there's no real reason a quality semi or thinline hollowbody can't be made with a screwed-on neck. It's certainly true that plenty with glued-in necks, even from makers such as Gibson, Guild, and Gretsch, have required neck re-sets over the years. Still, in Harmony's case the detachable neck was used for ease of manufacture and cost savings. Ironically, while the style puts off some players in search of an affordable but 'properly made' semi, a bolt-on neck can make a 40-year-old guitar easier to service and repair, if such is required – and it often is.

We visited Hofner guitars in the previous chapter, and the German company deserves another entry here on behalf of its many truly fine hollowbody archtop electrics. Hofner electrics made their greatest inroads into early pop and rock culture in Great Britain in the 1950s, thanks to a ban on U.S. imports that lasted from 1951 until 1959. You can bet

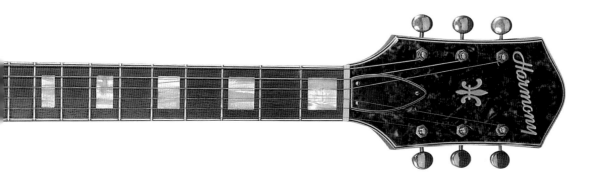

the kids flipped for Fender when they finally hit those shores – notably in the form of Hank Marvin's Fiesta Red Stratocaster – but in the meantime Hofner had become one of the quality electric brands to which to aspire, and was played by many major British names right into the early 1960s and beyond.

The London-based Selmer company, which imported Hofner guitars, distributed many U.K.-only models, and perhaps most prominent among them was the full-bodied President archtop. The President carried the same single-coil pickups as the Club 50 that we have already examined, and was made as an upscale electric jazz guitar, with laminated spruce top – earlier acoustic Presidents were solid spruce – laminated maple back and sides, and elegantly understated binding and inlay work. The ingredients and workmanship are primed to make the President a fine jazz guitar by any standards, although the thin, slim neck and zero fret set-up make it a little odd feeling to many players today. Nevertheless, these were very good guitars indeed, and became the choice of a near countless list of professionals in Britain before the big U.S. brands arrived. If names such as Roy Plummer, Frank Deniz, Tommy Steele, Dickie Bishop, and Bill Shearer mean little to American guitarists today, they meant a lot to guitar-playing British teenagers in the late 1950s, and helped to sell a lot of Hofners.

⌃ 1964 Harmony H77

> **Body:** fully hollow, double-cutaway thinline body made with pressed arched top of laminated maple, laminated maple back and sides; five-ply top binding
> **Neck:** bolt-on maple neck with bound rosewood fingerboard with 12" radius, 19th-fret neck-body joint (approximately), 20 narrow nickel-silver frets, and 1 11/16" nut width; 24 3/4" scale length
> **Headstock:** back-angled symmetrical headstock with three-a-side open-back tuners
> **Bridge:** floating two-piece rosewood bridge with notched plastic saddle insert, thumbscrew adjustment for height only; trapeze tailpiece
> **Electronics:** two single-coil DeArmond pickups, made with alnico bar magnets and six adjustable threaded polepieces; relatively low output; three toggle switches for on/off for each pickup; six controls for individual volume and tone for each pickup
> **Sound:** open, round, and spanky, with a slight graininess and edge and good dynamics; fairly bright in the bridge-pickup setting, fat, throaty, and creamy in the neck; mediocre sustain, and prone to feedback

The better Hofner archtop models have retained something of a following, in Europe in particular, and enjoy a moderate status as collectable guitars, although they are mostly still a lot more affordable than quality vintage American makes. The Hofner company has revived the President in a somewhat different format, with a more contemporary neck feel and a single humbucking pickup.

Gretsch originally developed its most ostentatious model, the White Falcon, as a 'Guitar of the Future' for display at the 1955 NAMM (National Association of Music Merchants) convention, where they propped it up on a rotating platform under spotlights. The company hadn't expected to go into major production of the elaborate white-and-gold-sparkle creation, but rather considered it a teaser to lure dealers and players to more standard Gretsch

guitars. The model caught a little more attention than anticipated, however, and the White Falcon went into full production, and, given the mid-1950s sticker price of $600 for a White Falcon as against $385 for a Chet Atkins Hollow Body, this was a major investment for any player of the day.

The first White Falcons had the body lines of the Chet Atkins Hollow Body – although it was an inch wider and had a 25½" scale – but looked like they had been dressed by Liberace after one too many sloe-gin fizzes. An arctic-white paint job was accompanied by gold sparkle body and neck binding and headstock decoration, jewel-inlaid control knobs, and 'hump-back' abalone position markers engraved with rather basic winged designs. By the end of the 1950s these guitars were a hair more sedate, but only just. Gretsch was still aiming its

1959 Hofner President

> **Body:** full depth single-cutaway hollowbody made with pressed arched top of laminated spruce, laminated maple back and sides, five-ply top binding

> **Neck:** glued-in five-piece maple-mahogany-beech neck with bound rosewood fingerboard, 14th-fret neck-body joint, 22 narrow nickel-silver frets; no truss-rod (although later models had them)

> **Headstock:** back-angled symmetrical headstock with three-a-side tuners and floral abalone inlay; zero fret

> **Bridge:** floating two-piece rosewood bridge with plastic saddle insert, thumbscrew adjustment for height only; trapeze tailpiece with individual anchor arms for each string

> **Electronics:** two single-coil Fuma pickups, three slide switches for individual pickup on/off and preset rhythm/lead tone selection; individual volume controls

> **Sound:** rich, smooth, and warm, with plenty of wood and body, but good definition, too; plenty of brightness from bridge position

sights at the jazz market, with considerable help from star player Jimmie Webster, but was hitting the mark far more in the country and rock'n'roll markets. It's easy to see how, esthetically, the White Falcon falls more easily into the latter camps, and it was never really accepted by the jazz community for its tonal capabilities either. This high-end model has become extremely collectable in all vintage circles, but has been played by many more notable rockers than jazzers: Crosby, Stills, Nash, and Young between them donned three White Falcons simultaneously at times in the early 1970s; Gretsch mainstay Brian Setzer has played one on occasion; and Billy Duffy made a major noise with British goth-rock band The Cult wielding a White Falcon.

All of these, it so happens, were Filter'Tron equipped examples like that in our main photo. The Gretsch humbuckers have generally been preferred by players seeking to accomplish major rock sonics with this guitar – or any Gretsch, for that matter – while rockabilly players swear by the earlier DeArmonds. Ultimately, the construction and design of a White Falcon don't distinguish it much from a Chet Atkins model 6120 once you get the two of them into an amplifier, but you've got to figure all that bright white and gold sparkle is going to channel a little something different through your fingertips most days.

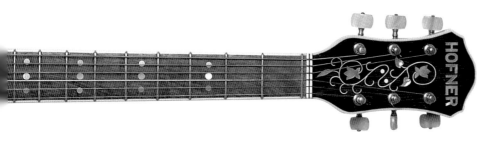

As the Japanese makers began proving their way with quality electrics in the late 1970s and early '80s, they sought a diverse list of players to endorse their products that spread beyond the rock and pop fields. Ibanez achieved this pretty convincingly by signing up George Benson. Benson had come up through the bebop tradition, and had been one of the most talented young jazz guitarists of the 1960s. Then he started to open his mouth to sing a little more often in the 1970s, and became a major crossover artist in the pop and R&B markets as well.

Benson endorsed the small-bodied GB10 and large-bodied GB20, both introduced in 1977. The former remains in the catalog today, while the GB20 went out of production after 1983. A range of others have taken its place

over the years – the GB5, for example – while the most recent is the large-bodied GB200.

The GB10 has two floating mini humbuckers, one attached to the end of the neck, the other to the pickguard in front of the bridge, while the GB20 had just the floating neck humbucker. The current GB200 has two full-size humbuckers mounted in holes cut in the top of the guitar. All three have arched spruce ply tops, and maple ply back and sides, and are fully hollow instruments.

Given these constructional details, the GB10 is a slightly unusual combination of acoustic and electric archtop formats: it uses the floating pickups more commonly seen on big-bodied jazz archtops with carved solid spruce tops in order to avoid impeding their acoustic vibration. However,

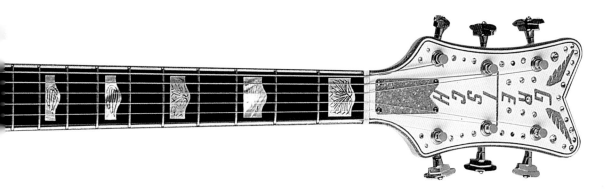

⌃ 1958 Gretsch White Falcon

> **Body:** 17"-wide, 2¾"-deep fully hollow single-cutaway body with pressed arched maple ply top, and maple ply back and sides, multi-ply top and back binding with outer layer of gold sparkle

> **Neck:** glued-in maple neck with bound ebony fingerboard with Neo-Classical thumbnail position inlays, 12" radius, 14th-fret neck-body joint, 21 narrow nickel-silver frets, 1¹¹⁄₁₆" nut width; 25½" scale length

> **Headstock:** symmetrical back-angled headstock with three-a-side Grover Imperial tuners

> **Bridge:** Space Control roller bridge on floating ebony base, with G-brand Gretsch trapeze tailpiece

> **Electronics:** two humbucking Gretsch Filter'Tron pickups, with alnico bar magnets and 12 adjustable threaded polepieces; DC resistance approximately 4k; three-way toggle switch for either pickup independently or both together; three-way master tone switch; three controls for individual volume for each pickup, plus master volume

> **Sound:** big, bold, and smooth, but with good bite and definition; plenty of cutting power in the bridge position, but full and round in the neck position; only mediocre sustain – until feedback kicks in

this smaller-bodied guitar has a laminated top, and one which has four control knobs and a toggle switch mounted in it. Even so, this is a clever piece of design from Ibanez, and the GB10 goes a long way toward capturing a full, rich, classic big-box sound in a more compact instrument designed for a broader range of live and studio applications. The bigger GB200 and the GB5 that preceded it strike a little closer to the classic electric archtop format established by the Gibson ES-175D, given the combination of a

laminated top and humbuckers set right into the body, although in dress at least it seeks to make association with fancier Gibsons, such as the L-5CES.

Our only real foray into the world of the flat-top acoustic electric guitar comes via an entry from a genre that is often called a hybrid because it blends elements of pure amplified acoustic and electric tones. Yamaha's full-bodied archtop model, the AEX-1500, with a mini humbucker at the neck and a piezo-equipped bridge with on-board

⌃ 1978 Ibanez GB10

> **Body:** 14"-wide, 3⅛"-deep, fully hollow single-cutaway body with pressed arched spruce ply top, and maple ply back and sides, multi-ply top and back binding

> **Neck:** glued-in maple neck with bound ebony fingerboard with 12" radius, 15th-fret neck-body joint, 21 medium nickel-silver frets, and 1¹¹⁄₁₆" nut width; 24¾" scale length

> **Headstock:** symmetrical back-angled headstock with three-a-side tuners; bone-and-brass nut

> **Bridge:** two-piece floating ebony bridge

> **Electronics:** two Ibanez GB Special mini humbucking pickups, made with alnico bar magnets, six fixed steel-slug polepieces and six adjustable threaded polepieces, gold-plated steel covers; DC resistance approximately 6.5k; three-way toggle switch for either pickup independently or both together; controls for individual volume and tone for each pickup

> **Sound:** full, rich, and warm, with good definition and plummy attack; acoustic sustain is rather limited

preamp, has been taken up by some artists seeking to blend traditional jazz-box sounds with more traditional acoustic tones, most notably Martin Taylor. But the flat-topped, thin-bodied AEX-500 is a far more affordable model that brings similar versatility to the masses.

Yamaha was at the forefront of the electro-acoustic genre, and its piezo pickup and preamp systems have long been recognized as good performers. The AEX-500 carries the same preamp used on Yamaha's popular APX electro-acoustics, with its own volume control and three-band EQ,

plus volume and tone controls for the neck-mounted mini humbucker, a three-way switch to select between either or both pickup systems, and a mix control to determine the balance between the two when both are selected.

Such guitars initially became popular with players who needed swift transitions between electric and acoustic sounds in the live situation, but the ability to blend the two – and hence to run new tonal combinations through unusual effects chains – has made them a creative tool for adventurous players. More affordable versions of hybrid

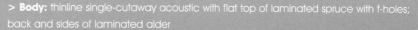

> ⌄ 1999 Yamaha AEX500

> **Body:** thinline single-cutaway acoustic with flat top of laminated spruce with f-holes; back and sides of laminated alder
> **Neck:** bolt-on maple neck with unbound rosewood fingerboard with 13¾" radius, 14th-fret neck-body joint, 20 medium nickel-silver frets, and 1¹¹⁄₁₆" nut width; 24¾" scale length
> **Headstock:** symmetrical, back-angled headstock with three-a-side enclosed Yamaha tuners; synthetic nut
> **Bridge:** glued-on flat-top-style rosewood bridge with piezoelectric saddle pickup; trapeze tailpiece
> **Electronics:** single floating mini-humbucking pickup mounted at the end of the neck, plus piezo bridge pickup; active volume and three-band EQ for piezo system; passive volume and tone controls for magnetic pickup; three-way toggle switch to select either or both, plus blend control to determine mix
> **Sound:** from bright, snappy electro-acoustic sounds to fatter jazz-style tones, and a broad blend of the two

designs usually offer some sonic compromises when compared with quality guitars that are purely electro-acoustic or magnetic-pickup-based electrics, but it's hard to argue with their versatility or the possibilities opened up merely by having the ability to blend these sounds.

Although Gibson invented the archtop, New York luthier John D'Angelico is credited with having raised the art to a state of elegance and achievement that is often only attainable by the individual craftsman working in a small shop. D'Angelico was raised in the violin-making tradition, but began making guitars for himself in the early 1930s, completing only 1,164 instruments up until the time of his death in 1964.

The finest D'Angelicos were made as hand-carved acoustic archtops, although, of course, many have had floating pickups added to them. D'Angelico also offered electric models as the demand for these increased, but he viewed the genre as a step down from acoustic building, and often used lesser plywood bodies bought in from the nearby Codé or United Guitars companies, while still making the

necks himself. This practice follows the same thinking used by many companies in manufacturing electric models, and recognizes that the mere act of mounting pickups in the top of an archtop hollowbody is going to compromise it as an acoustic instrument, and render it mainly fit for amplification.

A large proportion of D'Angelico's guitars were made to order, however, and no doubt some electrics were requested with hand-made D'Angelico bodies. The electric in our photo appears to have been one such guitar, and it has a well-made body with carved solid maple top, and maple back and sides. There are also some other notable

D'Angelico touches, although it lacks the full elaboration of an acoustic archtop such as a New Yorker or an Excel, guitars that were played by the likes of Chet Atkins, Oscar Moore, and Johnny Smith.

In recent years the D'Angelico name has been used by the company D'Angelico Guitars Of America to market instruments made in Japan under the supervision of master luthier Hidesato Shino. The newer D'Angelico Excel series has also been sourced from a factory in Incheon, Korea. All of these are considered to be well-made guitars by mass-manufacture standards, but, of course, are very different from the originals. D'Angelicos made from 1932 to 1964

⌃ 1960 D'Angelico Electric

> **Body:** 16¾"-wide, 3½"-deep, fully hollow, single-cutaway body with carved solid maple top, maple back and sides, multi-ply top binding
> **Neck:** glued-in maple neck with bound rosewood fingerboard with 12" radius, 14th-fret neck-body joint, 20 narrow nickel-silver frets, and 1¹¹⁄₁₆" nut width; 24¾" scale length
> **Headstock:** symmetrical back-angled headstock with three-a-side Grover Imperial tuners; bone nut
> **Bridge:** floating two-piece rosewood bridge, adjustable via thumb screws for overall height;

D'Angelico trapeze tailpiece
> **Electronics:** two full-size humbucking pickups, made with alnico bar magnets, six fixed steel-slug polepieces and six adjustable threaded polepieces; three-way toggle switch to select each pickup individually or both together; individual volume and tone controls for each pickup
> **Sound:** bright and well-defined overall, but with good air and balance; lots of warmth and richness from the neck pickup with a sharper performance from the bridge unit

are among the most valuable instruments on the vintage guitar market today, although it's interesting to note that D'Angelico originally sold these instruments for only around the same prices as the higher-end Gibson archtop models, despite their very limited and often custom-order production.

James D'Aquisto became an apprentice to John D'Angelico while still in his teens, and helped to make guitars in the New York workshop for a little over ten years before his mentor's death in 1964. D'Aquisto bought the D'Angelico business, and set out under his own name with the appropriately transitional task of completing ten guitars that D'Angelico himself had started. Unsurprisingly, guitars from D'Aquisto's early years are very much in the D'Angelico style, but the younger luthier evolved into an adventurous and forward-looking guitar maker in his own right, and helped to usher in the modern era of archtop construction. D'Aquisto died in 1995 at the age of 59 – the same age at which his former mentor had passed away – with a decade-long list of would-be customers still waiting to be supplied.

Toward the end of his career, D'Aquisto was making guitars with modernistic open headstocks, oblong segmented soundholes, and a minimum of non-wood adornment, all with the aim of enhancing the resonance and acoustic tone of the instrument. Mid-period D'Aquistos show a clearer lineage to the D'Angelico template but also begin to display a number of individual touches that became characteristic of the apprentice-turned-master. For example, the D'Aquisto New Yorker pictured still has a body shape very close to

that of the D'Angelico original of that model, and the headstock shape and neck adornment are still similar as well, but the f-holes are now fatter and actually more S-shaped, the base of the floating ebony bridge is wider, and the metal trapeze tailpiece has been replaced with one of ebony.

As also propounded by Robert Benedetto, D'Aquisto was by this time already concluding that the more non-wood ingredients with which you load down your guitar, the more you impede its acoustic vibration. On later D'Aquistos, virtually the only metal on the whole guitar would be found in the tuners – and these with ebony buttons – frets, and the very small screws used to hold the

truss-rod cover in place. No abalone, plastic, or other material was used at all for binding or neck adornment in many cases. Although he made some chambered and solidbody electrics, the classic D'Aquisto electric remains the guitar made as a carved-top acoustic archtop with floating magnetic pickup added, and his versions of such are among the epitome of the form for the jazz player seeking exceptional tone and playability.

Robert Benedetto is a high-end archtop maker in the tradition of D'Angelico and D'Aquisto, and is undoubtedly one of the most respected makers working today; he has gone on to attain even wider recognition in recent years through his work with Fender Musical Instruments. Benedetto came on board to oversee Fender's relaunch of a limited range of Guild archtops as high-end, hand-carved models – as mentioned earlier in this chapter – and now also heads a line of Fender-licensed Benedetto acoustic and electric archtop models made by a select team of luthiers in the Fender Custom Shop in Corona, California.

New carved-top Benedetto archtop-electrics such as the Fratello and the Manhattan sell in the $20k-plus range – and if that sounds like a lot of cash, be glad you're not a concert cellist or violinist. The more recently introduced Bravo model brings Benedetto quality more within reach in the form of a hand-made, medium-depth archtop with

> ⊙ **1978 D'Aquisto New Yorker Special**

> **Body:** 17"-wide, 3⅛"-deep, fully hollow, single-cutaway body with carved solid spruce top, solid maple back and sides, multi-ply top binding
> **Neck:** glued-in maple neck with bound ebony fingerboard with 12" radius, 14th-fret neck-body joint, 22 medium nickel-silver frets, and 1¹¹⁄₁₆" nut width; 25½" scale length
> **Headstock:** symmetrical back-angled headstock with three-a-side Grover tuners; bone nut
> **Bridge:** floating two-piece ebony bridge, adjustable via thumb screws for overall height; D'Aquisto-made ebony trapeze tailpiece
> **Electronics:** single mini-humbucking pickup suspended from the bound ebony finger rest (pickguard), made with alnico bar magnet, six fixed steel-slug polepieces and six adjustable threaded polepieces, with metal cover; single volume control
> **Sound:** full-throated and sweet, with considerable warmth and richness, and a good balance between bass and treble registers; excellent sustain for a hollowbody archtop

laminated spruce top and laminated maple back and sides, for a list price of $5,000 at the time of writing.

In format, the Bravo has evolved out of the same philosophy as that which created the seminal guitar of the genre, the Gibson ES-175 (which, it's worth noting, currently lists for $92 more than the Bravo): if a guitar's mission is primarily to be amplified, there's a lot of sense in using laminated woods and mounting the pickup right in the top itself. Of course, you can spend the extra $15,000 for a solid-topped Manhattan with floating neck pickup, but if – aside from some subtle shades and nuances – you often aren't going to get much benefit from the tonal differences anyway, the Bravo might do the job just as well for you. On the other hand, if you're looking for the full smorgasbord of acoustic-based tonal delights as tapped by a Benedetto La Venezia, it isn't fair to expect to find it here.

With all of this in mind, the Bravo is neither a budget version of an upmarket Benedetto nor a quality copy of an ES-175. Benedetto himself designed the model as a rethink of the format, and there are a number of fine touches that set it apart somewhat from its predecessors. The guitar's laminated top is made of three plies of spruce, rather than

the maple used in most laminated-top archtops, and it follows the Benedetto-preferred 25″ scale length rather than the traditional Gibson length of 24⅝″. The Bravo borrows elegant trademark touches from more expensive Benedettos in the form of its virtually unadorned ebony fingerboard, two-piece floating ebony bridge, ebony button Schaller tuners, and ebony control knobs, but achieves savings elsewhere by using a plastic finger rest (pickguard), a metal rather than ebony trapeze tailpiece, and a black plastic headstock facing. The result is a subtle marriage of class and functionality for the working musician.

⬇ 2005 Benedetto Bravo

> **Body:** 16″-wide, 2½″-deep, fully hollow, single-cutaway body, archtop made with formed top of laminated spruce with parallel spruce bracing, and back and sides of laminated flame maple

> **Neck:** glued-in three-piece maple neck with bound ebony fingerboard with 12″ radius, 14th-fret neck-body joint, 22 medium nickel-silver frets, and 1¾″ nut width; 25″ scale length

> **Headstock:** symmetrical back-angled headstock with three-a-side Schaller tuners

> **Bridge:** two-piece floating ebony bridge; gold-plated metal trapeze tailpiece

> **Electronics:** single Benedetto A-6 humbucking pickup made by Seymour Duncan, with single alnico V bar magnet with six fixed steel-slug polepieces and six adjustable threaded polepieces; DC resistance of 5.9k per coil, 11.8k total; single volume and tone control

> **Sound:** airy, warm, and full-bodied, but with good note definition and presence

6

12-String Electrics

The considerations in making a 12-string electric guitar are much the same as for any other electric, although the extra strings will, of course, have implications for neck width, headstock size, bridge design, and the string tension that is applied to the neck. The success or failure of even the better-known models has often depended on the ways in which these issues were dealt with, and sometimes – as we will see – whether makers simply increased the required dimensions to handle the extra strings, or found new ways to construct an instrument that would ultimately end up feeling more familiar to six-string players.

For all of the company's cut-rate-catalog chic and downmarket appeal, Danelectro achieved a considerable coup in 1961 by offering the first mass-produced electric 12-string guitar, the Bellzouki, a signature model for New York session guitarist Vincent Bell. (Gibson had produced an electric 12 three years earlier, if you didn't mind hauling a six-string around with it, as we shall see later.) The top model carried two of the familiar lipstick-tube pickups and the basic steel-plate bridge with wedge-shaped rosewood saddle piece, this time cut for 12 string slots. The body, however, was shaped in a bouzouki-like teardrop, but for a crude waist formed by curves at the bass and treble sides that allowed the musician to play the guitar seated without it constantly sliding to the floor. The single-pickup model had a pure teardrop shape –

perhaps you were allowed to just let the cheaper one slide off you – and, of course, fewer controls.

The Bellzouki was adopted by a number of other session players – eagerly accepted by a breed of musicians that was always looking for a hot new sound in order to keep in the game – and became one of the early tools of the new space-age and psychedelic eras of pop, before the task of generating new sounds became dominated by electronic effects, such as fuzz and wah-wah. (Incidentally, Vincent Bell was also behind the development of the Coral Electric Sitar, introduced in 1967 by the spin-off brand after Danelectro was purchased by MCA.)

Danelectro lipstick-tube pickups take very well to the 12-string sound, and the Bellzouki is bright, ringing, and

1965 Danelectro Bellzouki

> **Body:** semi-solid body constructed of Masonite top and back, with pine center block, shaped as a 'four-pointed teardrop'
> **Neck:** bolt-on, one-piece poplar neck and rosewood fingerboard with approximately 9½" radius, 21 nickel-silver frets, and 1⅝" nut width; 25" scale length
> **Headstock:** large, back-angled 'duck's-foot' headstock with six-per-side 'skate-key' tuners
> **Bridge:** height-adjustable steel bridge plate with one-piece, non-adjustable rosewood saddle
> **Electronics:** two identical single-coil 'lipstick tube' pickups, each with single alnico bar magnet; DC resistance of approximately 4.25k to 4.75k; three-way toggle switch for pickup selection, controls for individual volume and tone for each pickup, plus master volume
> **Sound:** light and bright, but with a sweet blend of sparkle and depth, and a gently percussive attack; an abundance of jangle, without much harshness

cutting, but with just enough softness to keep all that treble content from getting strident. With so much string vibration going on – which is to say, so much steel vibration for the magnetic pickups to work with – an electric 12-string like the Dano model seems to come across pretty well even without the use of selected tone woods and high-end construction, especially when used primarily for jangle and effect in a heavily orchestrated pop record. The forward-looking Bellzouki helped to usher in an era, and set the standard for 12-string tuning, with the lower four 'normal' strings doubled with strings an octave higher, and the high string 360 model examined in the chapter on semi-acoustics, but has been very cleverly adapted for the extra wires. Rickie designers perhaps correctly deduced that guitarists would be more

accepting of the new model if it looked and felt much like the six-strings with which they were familiar. They designed the 360/12's headstock to be the same length as that of the standard model, and squeezed the extra six tuners in by setting them at right angles to the usual six, with their posts extending through partial slots in the headstock – in effect, a design that looked something like a steel-string headstock and classical guitar headstock combined in one.

Rickenbacker also kept to the narrow neck dimensions of its standard 360, so it was actually easier for players to get to grips with the new model than with many of the wide-necked acoustic 12-strings that existed at the time. The other side of this coin, of course, is a fingerboard crammed with strings and relatively little air

George Harrison's 1964 Rickenbacker 360/12

> **Body:** routed-out double-cutaway maple body with single-ply top binding and recessed tail section

> **Neck:** three-ply maple and rosewood neck, neck-through-body construction; bound and varnished rosewood fingerboard with a 10" radius, 21st-fret neck join, 21 narrow nickel-silver frets; 24 3/4" scale length

> **Headstock:** asymmetrical back-angled headstock with six-a-side Kluson tuners, three mounted in standard fashion, three at right angles with buttons pointing to the back of the headstock; headstock-end truss-rod access

> **Bridge:** metal bridge with six individual saddles, slotted for two strings per saddle, adjustable for height and string-pair intonation; simple trapeze tailpiece inset in recessed body carve

> **Electronics:** two single-coil Rickenbacker toaster-top pickups; DC resistance of around 5k to 7k; three-way toggle for selecting pickups individually or together; independent volume and tone controls for each pickup; later models carried a blend control to fine-tune the neck pickup's contribution to the overall sound

> **Sound:** bright, snappy, round, with a crisp attack, a slightly sizzling front end, and decent sustain

for thicker fingers to find their way between them. As easy as it is even for smaller hands to wrap around the neck of a 360/12, the result can also feel something like an unbroken sea of strings to unfamiliar fingertips. However, it doesn't take long to get used to it, and these guitars are still among the easiest-playing 12-string electrics ever made.

Tonally, for many ears, the 360/12 has more going for it than a Bellzouki or many other upmarket electric 12s: there's plenty of definition and brightness to churn out that classic 12-string jangle and chime, along with a compelling richness and just a little sizzle to give some density and character to notes. There can be a lot of power in this guitar, too, especially through a semi-cranked tube amp, as a listen through so many of the tracks on The Beatles' *A Hard Day's Night* will remind you. From Harrison, to Roger McGuinn, to Tom Petty and his lead guitarist Mike Campbell, to Peter Buck, a Rickenbacker has been responsible for more archetypal chime and shimmer in great pop and rock music than any other electric 12-string.

Both Gibson and Fender introduced electric 12-strings in 1965, in the form of the ES-335-12 and Electric XII

respectively. (Do you think they noticed Rickenbacker's 360/12 or something?)

The ES-335-12 was virtually the same as the six-string model of the era, aside from the elongated headstock and other minor changes required to accommodate the extra strings. Gibson used double-notched nylon saddles on a standard Tune-o-matic bridge for the string pairs, and used a modified trapeze tailpiece that was otherwise not unlike that recently fitted to the standard ES-335 model. Of course, the ES-335 of the mid 1960s had block inlays instead of dots, and the slightly different Patent Number humbucking pickup instead of the hallowed PAF.

The ES-335-12 had a reasonable reception from the playing public, but it failed to steal much of Rickenbacker's thunder, maybe in part because it was too thunderous: that Gibson semi-acoustic body style combined with fat-sounding pickups make for a thick, ballsy 12-string electric. The tone suited some players looking to make a big noise with a guitar of this format, but the Rickenbacker had already established a ringing, crystalline tone – as did the Danelectro before it – that was quickly recognized as the standard of its type. The

1969 Gibson ES-335-12

> **Body:** double-cutaway, semi-acoustic construction with back, sides, and top of laminated maple, with a pressed arch on the top and solid maple center block, top and back binding, finished in nitrocellulose lacquer
> **Neck:** glued-in, one-piece mahogany neck with bound rosewood fingerboard with 12" fingerboard radius, 20th-fret neck-body joint, 22 medium nickel-silver frets, and 1¹¹⁄₁₆" nut width; 24¾" scale length
> **Headstock:** symmetrical 17-degree back-angled headstock (14 degrees from 1966) with six-a-side Kluson tuners; bone nut
> **Bridge:** adjustable Tune-o-matic bridge with six

double-notched vinyl saddles and adapted trapeze tailpiece
> **Electronics:** dual humbucking pickups constructed of single alnico bar magnet beneath, six fixed steel-slug polepieces in one coil and six threaded adjustable polepieces in the other, nickel-plated steel covers; DC resistance of 7.5k; three-way toggle switch to select either pickup alone or both together; four 500k potentiometers for individual volume and tone for each pickup
> **Sound:** thick, rich, and vocal from the neck pickup, punchy and cutting from the bridge, with a slightly airy, woody resonance in all positions, perhaps a little thick for some full chords; good sustain; good hum rejection

ES-335-12 was discontinued in 1971. Examples made during its original six-year run often sell for a little less than six-string ES-335s of that era, which are highly prized, so players willing to pay for a nut change and to put up with the elongated headstock can sometimes acquire a bargain in this fashion.

Fender's Electric XII was designed a little more for the jangle, and was also a ground-up redraw of the electric 12-string format rather than just a modified six-string, as were many other makers' 12-strings. Even so, it only

lasted until around 1969. The guitar had a solid body taken from the Jazzmaster/Jaguar template, and the full 25½" scale length. The 'hockey-stick' neck, however, had a headstock that was even more ungainly than those of most 12-strings, with a kind of melted, Gumby-like twist at the end to accommodate the Fender logo. It was compact and comfortable for a 12, however, much like the Rickenbacker's, and ran from a relatively narrow nut width to a wider section at its upper reaches.

The split single-coil pickups used by Fender on this

> ◔ **1965 Fender Electric XII**

> > **Body:** offset waist, double-cutaway solid alder body with rib and forearm contours
> > **Neck:** bolt-on maple neck with unbound rosewood fingerboard, 21 narrow nickel-silver frets, 7¼" radius, 1⅝" nut width; 25½" scale length
> > **Headstock:** 'hockey stick' headstock, with six-a-side enclosed Fender tuners; elongated string retainer for middle six strings
> > **Bridge:** through-body stringing, fixed bridge with 12 individual saddles adjustable for intonation and overall height
> > **Electronics:** two split single-coil pickups with fixed alnico magnet polepieces; DC resistance approximately 9k; four-way rotary switch to select either pickup individually or both together in series
> > **Sound:** bright and cutting, but also very thick and edgy, with reasonable note definition; a good blend of jangle and grunt for an electric 12-string

guitar are powerful units, but still have a lot of the brightness and twang factor that the narrow magnetic window tends to capture. Through-body stringing helps to give this instrument excellent sustain, and the clever bridge design allows for individual saddle adjustment, a rarity on 12-strings. By any standards, it's an excellent electric 12-string guitar, but – as is so often the case when a manufacturer follows a craze rather than initiating it – the model came along when the brief 12-string-electric wave was already receding, and as with the perfectly good Gibson ES-335-12, there just wasn't enough interest to keep the model afloat for long. Simply being the 12-string of The Beatles and The Byrds was enough to keep the Rickenbacker selling, but the Fender and Gibson models missed their chance to attain true classic status.

Clearly Fender didn't notice very quickly that the 12-string craze was already on the wane, because it followed the Electric XII with a 12-string version of the new thinline hollowbody Coronado in 1966. The Coronado line was Fender's first clear venture into Gibson-dominated territory, and was obviously a direct attack on the popular 300 series, but the guitars were fully hollow like the ES-330, lacking the solid center block of the ES-335, ES-345, and ES-355. Most players would also agree that the Fender hollowbody thinlines lacked the grace and style of the Gibsons, and as such they constitute the exception that proves the rule: Fender was very good at bolt-neck solidbodies; as for bolt-neck thinlines, well…

To my eyes they look like a step backward in guitar design, like some of the slightly ungainly – if reasonably

playable – semi-copy designs that came from lesser American or European makers in the late 1950s and 1960s, although readers might disagree. However, even more people would probably concur that the Coronados only got uglier with the introduction of the Wildwood range in 1967. The Wildwoods were made with colored laminates from beech trees that had been injected with dyes during growth in order to produce dramatic and often unpredictable shadings and grain patterns in the harvested wood. The results yielded some of the most dated-looking Fender electrics ever created.

The Coronado was designed by Roger Rossmeisl, the former Rickenbacker designer who would later participate in the design of the Telecaster Thinline. Fender had originally hired Rossmeisl to establish the manufacturing of acoustics, and put him on to the task of going head to head with Gibson after the acquisition of Fender by CBS.

With its 17th-fret neck-body joint and dual single-coil pickups, the Coronado was similar to the Gibson ES-330 in more ways than one. However, it was dissimilar in one very important way, too: it had a bolt-

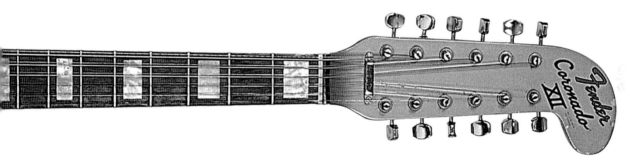

⌃ 1968 Fender Coronado XII

> **Body:** 16"-wide, fully hollow double-cutaway body with laminated maple body with pressed-arch top, three-ply top and back binding
> **Neck:** bolt-on maple neck with bound rosewood fingerboard, 21 narrow nickel-silver frets, 7¼" radius, 1⅝" nut width; 25½" scale length
> **Headstock:** 'hockey stick' headstock, with six-a-side enclosed Fender tuners; elongated string retainer for middle six strings
> **Bridge:** six adjustable individual double-notched steel

saddles, mounted in height-adjustable steel bridge section on floating rosewood base; trapeze tailpiece
> **Electronics:** two DeArmond low-output single-coil pickups; three-way toggle switch to select either pickup alone or both together; independent volume and tone controls for each pickup
> **Sound:** edgy and cutting but somewhat thin, with some good grit for rock'n'roll and a hair of openness and woody resonance; prone to feedback at any elevated volumes

on neck, as had been used in Rossmeisl's flat-top Fender acoustics. For all it's gawkiness the Coronado is an easy playing and pretty decent sounding thin-bodied hollowbody archtop, and a few did land in the hands of players seeking some Fender characteristics in a classically Gibsonesque format, but it never really made a dent in the Big G's market share in that domain. The pickups on these guitars don't do them any favors, either. For the first time in the company's history to date, Fender bought in pickups from an outside supplier, DeArmond, and as used on the Coronado they proved to

be weak and frequently microphonic, contributing to the hollow guitar's innate tendency to howl and feed back. The Coronado line, including the XII, was discontinued in 1971 or '72.

The Baldwin Double Six, a 12-string adaptation of the Marvin model of the mid 1960s, arrived right on top of the major brands' electric 12s in 1965. But, of course, the guitar had actually debuted a year earlier as the Burns Double Six, before the London guitar maker was purchased by the big Cincinnati piano and organ company. (Clearly, being British and having an eye on The Beatles, Burns had noticed the impact of the Rickie 360/12 even before Fender and Gibson.)

Baldwin was eager to hop on the bandwagon in the midst of the guitar boom of the 1960s, and found a way to do so with the financially beleaguered Burns company, but never seems to have found a way to market guitars successfully. (Baldwin also acquired Gretsch two years later in 1967.) This in itself shouldn't be a comment on the quality of the Burns guitars; they were mostly pretty clever designs, were well made, played easily and smoothly, and often sounded very good. Perhaps their looks didn't catch fire with the market of the day, although they certainly earned a few devoted followers. The Burns Tri-Sonic pickups used on this guitar have some fans themselves, and are

perhaps better known as the pickups used by Queen's Brian May on his own homemade electric, the Red Special. They are fairly strong but bright single-coils in the medium-gain range, made with ceramic magnets instead of alnico, which was a little unusual for the day.

The Double Six is a pretty straightforward 12-string model, and therein lies its success, in design terms, if not in sales. Its body lines are only slightly modified from those of the Stratocaster, from which its sibling the Marvin Model had been derived – British guitar-instrumental star Hank Marvin of The Shadows having been a Strat devotee before being signed up to endorse Burns. In any case, the Double Six is a solid, stable 12-string with a somewhat wide yet comfortable neck, and three bright, punchy

single-coil pickups. As far as ringing, crystalline jangle goes, it is up there with the solidbody Fender Electric XII in rivaling the seminal Rickenbacker. Even so, Baldwin deleted the Burns range of guitars in 1970, and since then the fortunes of Burns has been up and down. The Double Six has recently been reissued as a Korean-made guitar under the Burns brand.

Of course, even before any of the above were ever available – the Bellzouki, the 360/12, all of them – Gibson had a very well-made solidbody electric 12-string available by custom order, but if you wanted to avail yourself of the refined jangle of the EDS-1275, you had to bend your back under the weight of the conjoined-twin-like six-string that was included in the package. The Double 12, which, in fact, had one six-string neck and one 12, was introduced in 1958, and became a showstopper for a few bold artists who wanted to stride the stage with something a little different. The guitar originally surfaced with a Les Paul-derived body with a forward-looking chambered, double-cutaway design, but is far more often seen in the 3G body style, which it took on in 1962.

> ### ⊙ 1965 Baldwin Double Six

> **Body:** offset double-cutaway body made from solid alder
> **Neck:** bolt-on maple neck with bound rosewood fingerboard, 21 narrow nickel-silver frets, 7¼" radius, 1¹¹⁄₁₆" nut width; 25½" scale length
> **Headstock:** symmetrical headstock with six-a-side tuners; zero fret
> **Bridge:** simple notched steel bar bridge, thumbscrew adjustment for height only; covered stop-bar type tailpiece
> **Electronics:** three single-coil Burns Tri-Sonic pickups with ceramic magnets; DC resistance approximately 6.5k to 7.5k; three-way switch to select each pickup individually, controls for master volume and individual tone for neck and middle pickups only
> **Sound:** bright and twangy, but with some body, depth, and sizzle; good power, clarity, and sustain

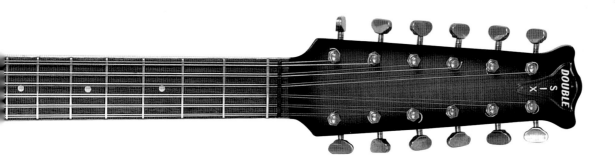

Only 110 of the EDS-1275 Double 12 were sold during its original run, which ended in 1968, although the model was reintroduced in 1977, no doubt on the back of its use by several big stadium-rock artists of the late 1960s and '70s: Jimmy Page of Led Zeppelin is probably the most famous Gibson double-neck player, but Alex Lifeson of Rush, Steve Howe of Yes, Charlie Whitney of Family, and a few other occasional double-neck users have wielded the Gibson over the years. Today, the guitar is also available in the more affordable Epiphone model, which puts similar quick-change rock thrills in the hands of many more players.

Given the coffee table-sized slab of mahogany and dual neck protrusions, this was one firm, fat, resonant electric 12-string, and you want to put one of these babies through an amp that can handle it. Whether carrying the PAF humbuckers that the 1958 to '61 models sported – a very collectable little stack of componentry on one guitar – or the Patent Number humbuckers of the later examples, these double-necks generated thick tones, yet possessed good sweetness and decent string definition, although the 12-string could certainly get a little muddy when switched to the neck pickup. Of course, the tone of the six-string neck is also affected by the vast expanse of wood required to make the EDS-1275's body, and these things ring and sustain a little more than the average SG when switched to the lower neck, too. It's an archetypal design in itself, a monster from the fringes of rockdom, but an instrument for which relatively few guitarists have a genuine need.

⌃ Charlie Whitney's 1966 Gibson EDS-1275 Double 12

> **Body:** solid mahogany double-cutaway body with concentric pointed horns, beveled edges, no binding; nitrocellulose finish

> **Neck:** two one-piece mahogany necks with (on each) bound rosewood fingerboards, 22 nickel-silver frets, 12" fingerboard radius, 1¹¹/₁₆" nut width; 24⅝" scale length

> **Headstock:** back-angled symmetrical headstocks; top neck has elongated headstock with six-a-side Grover tuners, bottom neck has standard Gibson SG-style headstock

> **Bridge:** two Tune-o-matic bridges, top unit with double-notched saddles; simple steel string-retainer tailpieces

> **Electronics:** four humbucking pickups with single alnico bar magnets mounted beneath, one coil with six steel-slug polepieces and one with six adjustable threaded steel polepieces for each neck; DC resistance approximately 7.5k; two-way toggle switch mounted between tailpieces to select upper or lower neck; three-way toggle switch for either pickup of selected neck independently or both together; individual volume and tone controls

> **Sound:** warm, full, and resonant, with some of the SG's characteristic sizzle, but a little more woody ring to it; excellent sustain and power

Meet The Makers

Author Dave Hunter talks to three top names in the guitar-making word:
Chris Fleming of the Fender Custom Shop, Don Grosh of Grosh Custom Guitars,
and Lindy Fralin of Fralin Pickups

Chris Fleming > Fender Custom Shop

A Fender Custom Shop Master Builder, Chris Fleming, 51, has played the guitar since his early childhood but only got into guitar making as a career in the early 1990s. From that point on he set about making up for lost time and progressed rapidly with his craft. Fleming was hired by Fender in 2000, and shortly thereafter was put in charge of overseeing the introduction of Guild electric models at the Fender Custom Shop in Corona, California. After two years as Guild production coordinator, Fleming was made a Master Builder of Fender Custom Shop guitars. One of his most notable recent projects at the time of writing was working on the prototype for the John Mayer Signature Stratocaster.

Tell us a little bit about tone woods and their importance in the instrument as a whole.

Part of my job, when I do custom pieces for individuals, is to help them understand what it is that they want, because there are often misconceptions about how woods really interact with each other and what the results are. Some of it's counterintuitive, and there's a lot of urban myth involved in how woods interact.

When somebody calls, the first thing I do is ask about their favorite music, who they listen to, what they play, and what they want to do with this guitar. Do they really want it to play, or do they just want to enjoy it as an object of art? I try to get as clear a picture as possible of what the person buying it actually wants from the guitar, and a lot of times that helps them reassess what they're into. Sometimes with an expensive instrument, what you're dreaming about is not exactly what's going to make you the happiest as a player. Also, I just like to get to know them a little bit, and that helps me in two ways: I get to steer them toward what they really want as opposed to what they just think they want, and I also get a sense of who the person is, so that when I make the guitar I have that in mind. I don't want to sound shmarmy or anything, but it's kind of a spiritual thing.

Sure, and I would hope there would be some element of that involved in building any high-end instrument.

Yeah, and musical instruments are unique objects. People use them as a therapeutic thing, as a means of expression, as a work of art – they take on so many more meanings than most other objects. An instrument is the next closest thing to your voice. So my approach to it isn't all that intellectual; I do intellectual things, of course, because I have to build the guitar properly, but the feeling for the work is a more intuitive and spiritual thing. So when I talk to people about their instruments, it's partly just getting aligned with them.

Then we start talking details. A lot of players, particularly professional players, can tell me exactly what they want to hear. Many times they're not necessarily clear about what's going to create that for them, and that's when we start talking about woods. Plenty of guys who buy guitars at this level, though, are pretty hip. They're well versed on woods and the years and eras of different types of Fenders, and they understand how those things determine the particular sound that an instrument will have.

Having said all that, we'll then pin down exactly what kind of guitar they want. Of course the earliest Spanish-style guitar Fender made was the Telecaster, which was made with an ash body and a one-piece maple neck with a walnut skunk stripe. So the most basic Fender sound is ash and maple.

What's the inherent character of that?

Generally speaking, ash can have a warm, round sound, with a bit of a focused cut to it. It can also be, depending on the guitar, a bit shrill, a bit snarly. But the best Teles sound wonderful; they're round sounding, they're rich, they're very loud, and they cut through a band very well. That's the point of them, too. The Telecaster was developed around country music originally, and those guys wanted to be able to cut through the band, so Leo voiced them to be clean and piercing. I'm sure he experimented with different things to see what worked the best, and also, being a very frugal and production-minded guy, he looked for woods that he could get cheaply and sustainably. At that time ash was a good candidate.

Is it a little easier to get good swamp ash today than it was for a few years?

It's fairly sustainable now. There's enough of it around to be able to get it. We buy a lot of ash and we're able to get it OK so far. The more difficult wood to get is alder, in clear and lighter pieces at least. A lot of the alder trees aren't as big any more, so they're harvesting trees that aren't as old and aren't as big, and they tend to be denser and heavier, and have more blemishes in them.

But at one point in the 1950s ash became very difficult to get. It became really heavy and more scarce, and that's one of the reasons Fender went toward alder, because it was another acceptable sounding wood and was more easily obtainable.

And you have to wonder if, when Fender made the move to alder, they could ever have predicted that some guitar players today would make such a big deal about the distinction between the two woods.
Probably not. Maybe some of those guys did, and Leo was really into figuring stuff out. For the most part, though, they were just doing what they needed to do to make their business work and to give the customer the best quality that they could along with it. I think it was more important to have a steady source of acceptable-quality wood to put into their products, and one of the main reasons that they went to alder was that it was probably cheaper and more readily available.

The first Strats in 1954 were also ash bodies with one-piece maple necks, and they have come of the same sound qualities as those Teles. A lot of the early country and early rock'n'roll has that Fender sound. Then in 1956 alder started coming in on Strats, and then often on Teles, too, and the character of the sound is a little different. It's very subjective and is difficult to characterize precisely, but the quality of the timbre changes a little with alder. Once again, though, between alder and ash so many other things come into play to determine the sound: the density of the wood and the grain patterns in the wood, how old the wood is, how dry it is.

Sure. It's important to be aware that even the same 'type' of wood won't always sound the same, and that in fact no two pieces of wood are ever exactly alike. It's a little like the old adage about snowflakes…
That's entirely correct. It's one of the things that can be frustrating when you're trying to make the best guitar you can, but it's also one of the things that makes it so wonderful. One of the things that gives a guitar its character is that each one of them is a unique and individual thing, just like every person is.

And even after each guitar is made, it's going to continue to age somewhat differently, too.

It is. And it's going to depend on the climate that it's in, how much it's played, the kind of conditions it finds itself in over the years.

How much difference is made by the mere fact of a guitar having been played or not played over the years?
That makes a big difference, probably more than anything, given the guitar was made right in the first place. A bad guitar probably will never be a great guitar, but it might get better over the years if it's played regularly. And by a 'bad guitar' I mean one that, if you put two of the same guitars up together, is less resonant and has poorer tonal qualities. But once again, that's all subjective, too. Some people's hearing leans toward warmer, rounder tones; other people, because of the way they hear, like things that are sharper and cut more.

So it's a real individual thing. But, generally speaking, a good guitar that's played a lot over a long period of time, it breaks down, it morphs, the cells break down in the wood. And I don't mean that they deconstruct, but they alter, they change, they get dryer and open up. The resonance that's going through the guitar over a long period of time changes the molecular structure of the guitar. That's why, for the most part, real expressive musicians tend to lean toward older instruments, and, if you look in the classical field, instruments that were made 200 or 300 years ago are the preferred instruments. A lot of it is the quality of the instrument, but also just the fact that it's had a long and rich life. Musical instruments are unique objects, in that because they get to express people's souls, they are altered.

I've played a lot of guitars, as you could imagine, and you can take two guitars made of wood from the same tree, and one will be better, it will have different qualities. You can take two guitars made on the production line in the Custom Shop on one day, right next to each other, and they're different. No two are alike. For the most part they're more similar than they are dissimilar, but no two are exactly the same. Then when you get one into the hands of a guy who plays country, that guitar's going to change because that's the kind of music that's played on it, and the one in the hands of the guy who plays jazz is going to change a little differently.

What's so cool is that guitars, like people, are kind of the sums of their experience. And they're kind of more than that, just because of the nature of spirit or whatever you want to call it. I think guitars, and instruments in general, are kind of metaphors for spiritual life. I don't mean to get heavy here, but when you come down to it, a scientist can cut something apart and analyze it and find out every single thing that he wants to know about it. He can run it through electronic tests and find out everything that a meter will tell about it, but it doesn't account for that spark of life or spirit or whatever that animates it.

So that's a big part of the variable behind guitar making.
Yeah. I can tell you that alder and maple are going to have a certain kind of a sound using X pickups with Y kind of a finish – I've made enough of these things and I'm sensitive enough to that stuff to be able to tell you generally how it's going to react – but once I put it together it does what it does, it is what it is. I've heard ash and maple guitars that are bigger and warmer sounding than alder and rosewood guitars, and vice versa. So when you get right down to it it's difficult to be certain about how it's going to end up.

And there sure are a lot of variables.
Sure, for something that seems as simple as a solidbody electric guitar such as a Tele. Even the materials in the magnets in the pickups, all of that stuff, will have its effect.

People talk a lot about the tonal properties of simply adding a rosewood fingerboard to a maple neck.
That's right. Although, interestingly, one of the reasons they went from maple neck to rosewood neck – and this is a story that I've heard (which I have to preface with the point that, naturally, a lot of the stories from those days are also folklore) – was because Leo didn't like the way the finish on the necks wore out on TV. They looked shabby. Back then Gibsons were considered 'real' guitars, and they all had rosewood fingerboards, so that's why Leo decided, as soon as he was able to, to start putting rosewood on the fingerboards.

Tonally, it definitely rounds the sound out and warms it up to some degree. A maple neck and an ash or alder body has kind of a brightness or edge to it that a rosewood guitar kind of doesn't, but, having said that, using different materials for the rosewood – Indian rosewood as opposed to Brazilian rosewood, or what we use a lot of now, which is Madagascan rosewood – makes a lot of difference in itself. My favorite rosewood to use now on a Fender is Indian. Fender used Indian and Brazilian fairly interchangeably. Most of it was Brazilian up until the early 1960s, and then it switched to mostly Indian because in the mid 1960s Brazilian began becoming a problem. But Brazilian, in my opinion, is a bit too bright. Once again, though, it depends

on the actual piece. Brazilian can be very dense and ringing, which is nice in some combinations. In my opinion, it works well with mahogany. I like acoustic guitars with a mahogany neck and a Brazilian rosewood fingerboard. I don't like ebony at all on maple, because it makes it – to my ear – harsh, and I'm not wild about Brazilian on maple for the same reason, although other guys will tell you I'm crazy.

Also, lately I've made a lot of slab-board rosewood fingerboards and what we call 'round lams' – the thinner laminated board – and I prefer round lams.

That's interesting, because many players and collectors go wild for slab-board Strats and so forth.
Well, somebody asked me why I thought Leo decided to do round lams [curved laminated rosewood fingerboards, adopted in 1963 to replace the previous flat-bottomed 'slab-board' fingerboards], and although I can't know for sure, I think it was for a couple of reasons. One is that he liked the idea of the maple being more of a majority of the wood, and he liked the idea that it was kind of a custom way to do it, it was proprietary. And I'd also like to think that he liked the sound of it.

I feel like the slab board was the way that they did it because they had to figure out how to do it quickly. Then they had to tool up to make the rounded board and never turned back.

Please tell us a little about how different types of finish can affect a guitar's sound.
The finish certainly makes a difference. Some of that, once again, is kind of a folklore thing, and some of it depends on the guitar itself. If you have a really great guitar, you could perhaps stifle it a little by putting polyester or another real hard type of plastic finish on, but it will probably still at least sound decent if it's good to begin with. I've heard guitars with really thick, polyester finishes that sound wonderful, and guitars with thin nitrocellulose lacquer on them that are real dogs.

The rule of thumb is, the thinner and more organic the finish on the guitar, the more resonance you're going to get out of it. Lacquer, being an organic material, continues to break down regularly and methodically over the years, so that in the 1950s when they made a brand-new guitar the finish was fairly thick, but by the time we see them now there's hardly any finish left on them. It's gassed out, so that the solids get thinner and thinner. Even on a mint, unplayed guitar, the finish will look really thin, like paper thin, whereas using finishes like polyurethane or acrylic lacquers or polyesters, they're much more durable, you can get them a lot flatter, a lot shinier, a lot prettier, and they last longer, but they tend to be a little more stifling. They tend to affect the sound of the guitar more.

But, once again, that doesn't necessarily mean that it's a bad thing. In fact, I've made plenty of guitars with polyurethane that sound great, and plenty of guitars with polyester that sound really good. Part of it is in how thick you put it on, and part of it is in the material itself. Generally speaking, though, if you want a vintage-style guitar to sound like a vintage guitar, you do the best you can to make it with the same materials and processes that were originally used to make the guitar. So my finish of choice is nitrocellulose lacquer. That's what I use on 90 per cent of what I make.

Let's talk a little bit about the vintage Stratocaster vibrato. Is it still one of the best things for the job, or can it be improved upon?
You know, if it's set up properly it works great. It was a real revolutionary design at the time, and it's the basis of most of what that type of bridge on electric guitar still does today. If you want it to float and be real loose and still stay in tune, it takes some adjusting, but it can be done. The less material touching [at the pivot points] – like the new American Standard-style bridges that are two-point bridges, whereas the old Strat bridge had six screws – the less there is to hamper the bridge coming back into tune. And of course Floyd Rose came up with the locking system and the floating tremolo and so forth…

All of them work well if they're set up properly, and some are preferable for specific styles of playing, but once again it comes down to individual guitars. This might sound funny, but there are some pieces of wood that don't want to be guitars, and I'm serious about that. It's not the design, it's not anything in particular, it's just that the wood doesn't cooperate.

It wanted to be a bench.
Yeah, or whatever. But I've worked on instruments [as a repairman] over the years that just do not do what they're supposed to do. Either the wood's too soft, or the grain pattern's interfering with what it has to do, or the wood's unstable in certain ways. And honestly, that's true of plenty of top-of-the-line guitars, too.

I guess that's one of the big variables about working with wood in the first place.

Yep. I'm kind of at the stage where I'm really intuitive about it. I don't think about it too intellectually: I look at the grain, I feel it, I feel how it responds to my touch and the sound that I hear when I rap my hand on it. I can tell what part of the body blank is heavier than the other part, so that when we cut the body out I tend to like to have the heavier part of the blank be towards the bottom of the guitar. But I don't think too hard about any of it, I just kind of intuit it. That doesn't mean it's always going to be OK, but I'd say 90 per cent of the time I can tell what's going to be good and what isn't. Sometimes a piece of wood might look really cool, but if it doesn't talk to me, I don't use it.

That has to come from just working with a lot of wood.
I've made lots of guitars now, and I've fixed lots of guitars, and messed around with lots of wood.

We talked a lot about how the weights and densities of different woods will affect a guitar, but how will different pieces of hardware shape its tone – tuners, for example?
Tuners will actually affect tone quite a bit. This is something I learned when I worked in a shop in Long Beach for a few years. The owner of the shop, John, is an expert in double basses and violin-family instruments, and he's an old-world craftsman, he uses all hand tools. He taught me a lot about that, and one thing I learned about the guitar or any stringed instrument is that it's a system, the different parts of the guitar work together to create what the guitar's going to do. I think not a whole lot of people understand how the mass of the headstock affects the guitar, but it's very important.

I learned this, because one time when John was setting up this double bass he said, "Hey, check this out." He played it with the bow, voooom. We'd listen to the quality of the sound, and it would resonate for a while then die slowly. Then what he did was, he took some plumber's putty and put some at a different spot under the fingerboard of the bass. He'd hit a string, and it would bloom, it would get bigger before it decayed. Then he'd put more putty on the headstock until he found the point where the bass just completely opened up, and would be super resonant and have a real beautiful quality of tone.

What he was doing was he was fiddling around with what's called a node, a focal point on the system. On a stringed instrument, the focal point should be on or very, very close to the nut. So by changing the density of the fingerboard, the neck material, and the headstock, you can change where that node ends up. A lot of times what will happen is, on a guitar that doesn't sound very good, it's because the node isn't where it should be. That's because the density of the headstock or the density of the fingerboard aren't working together to put the focal point of the system in the right spot.

So, having said all that, tuners are important in that they create mass on the headstock, and different tuners will do different things. I know this from a time that I was doing a repair on an old Gibson guitar. The guy who had brought it in had put Schaller tuners on it rather than the old open-backed Grover-type tuners. I changed the bridge on it – it was one of those old Gibson B-1 flat-tops – and he wanted to put it back to the original tuners, so I put them on, and the guitar didn't sound good. I put the much heavier Schallers back on, and the guitar sounded great. It changed the mass of the headstock, and on that guitar it made a huge difference.

Are there cases where you might want to lessen the mass of the headstock?
Yeah, sure. Or increase it. I found, for the best-sounding guitars, that the nodal point is on or right at the nut. I don't know that he consciously did it, but the designs that Fender came up with pretty much put that nodal point where it needs to be on the guitar.

Sure, you get that thick point on many Fender necks where, just beyond the nut, the neck curves down to the parallel plane of the headstock.
Yeah. Guitars are unlike violin-family instruments, of course, and putting putty there or something doesn't always do it. I know there have been products, such as a plate or something that will increase that mass for you.

Like the Fathead and Fat Finger that Aspen Pittman at Groove Tubes developed.
Yeah, that's right.

Although, as you say, at times you might equally want to lighten the headstock to help reposition that node.
Sure. And a lot of times, with hardware choices, there are practical considerations as much as tonal considerations. If you bend a lot you might want to put on locking tuners, or a graphite nut instead of bone. So there are practical questions, too.

That's right. It seems like there will always be some compromises between sound and playability.
To some degree the instrument is a tool, and it has to function the way the particular player needs it, so it becomes a matter of making the guitar work for the guy, and making him comfortable so he doesn't have to think about his guitar when he's playing. Having said that, a good guitar player, a guy who has his own style, will sound the same on any instrument. In fact, he can play a really shabby instrument and he'll still sound great, because it's the fool, not the tool.

You hear that case proved time and time again.
All the time. And the reverse of it, too. You get a lot of guys who think that if they get the best guitar in the world and they pay a lot of money for it, they're going to sound better or play better. That's just not so. I mean, on one level having a really great instrument can spur you on to play better and help you express yourself more fully, but it's not going to take the place of artistic expression or practice, obviously, even though we might like to think so.

Given your experience with Guild electrics, how do you get on with Bigsby vibratos?
I like Bigsbys. They do a certain thing that's unique, and I think they're cool. I've put a lot of Bigsbys on a lot of guitars.

They certainly look good.
They do look cool, and they sound cool, too. They do a very small change in pitch that is a very distinctive sound, and I like it a lot. I'm a very big fan of finger-style playing, Merle Travis and all those guys, Chet Atkins, and that was a big part of their sound.

One of my favorite vibratos, really, is the Jazzmaster and Jaguar vibrato. Leo always felt that the Jazzmaster vibrato was the pinnacle of his designs. A variation of that vibrato was going to be the original Strat tremolo, but they couldn't get it to work right so they saved it for later. As far as a really warm, pleasing, loose, expressive vibrato, I think the Jazzmaster and Jaguar are unsurpassed. If it's set up right, I think it's the smoothest vibrato there is.

It's often said that a Bigsby weakens the tone of a guitar somewhat.
I wouldn't say it weakens it; it changes it, you know, depending on the guitar you put it on. Some guitars were designed with that in mind so they sound the way they

sound, whereas other guitars, like Telecasters, weren't designed with them, and it changes the nature of them. I don't think it weakens them necessarily, it just changes the tone a little bit.

At least a Bigsby, and one with a roller bar in particular, is still a pretty solid anchor point down at the body end.
Very much so. And comes to the point that, as you know, for a period of time Fender used top-loading bridges on Telecasters, and some of those guitars are just killer sounding. Guys think that if the strings don't go through the back of the guitar it doesn't sound as good, but that's just not so. If you think about the P-Bass, the original P-Basses had the strings through the body, and they had their sound, and then they went to the top-loader and they had their own sound. It's really not a matter of one sounds better than the other, it's more a matter of either you like it or you don't. It's just another flavor.

Which brings up another important point for players searching for new guitars: as much information as a book like this or an expert such as yourself might be able to pass along, you still need to get out there and play as many guitars as you can.
Yeah, that's the thing. You know, I've just been getting into bass lately, so I went out to get a cheap bass to learn on, and one of the things that's great today is that for a couple of hundred bucks you can buy a guitar or a bass that works really well. When I was a kid, man, you couldn't. The cheap guitars were just really bad, and they weren't actually that cheap. You had to pay $300 or $400 to get a good guitar, and a crappy guitar was still $75 or $80 so, which was a lot of money for a kid. But now, every manufacturer has a guitar under $200 that's serviceable. So I got this cheap bass, made in Korea, and it's actually pretty well made, and it's got it's own sound. Eventually I'll probably make my own bass, when I know what I want out of a bass, and certainly it will be a lot better. But the bottom line is, it doesn't really matter what it's made out of, if it works for you and you like it.

A lot of guys – and I'm one of them – like weird and goofy and difficult instruments just because of their unique vibe and their quirky tones. I love old Silvertones and Danelectros. They're crummy Masonite guitars, but they're cool. And I like old plywood Harmonys and so forth, and sometimes guitars that are really hard to play still sound unique. With the job I have, people can sometimes get snobby about stuff, but, when it comes down to it, it's really kind of cool to just go play things and see what you like, see what you don't. That's the best way to find out about things. Then over a period of time you'll figure out what does it for you.

Don Grosh > Grosh Custom Guitars

Independent guitar-maker Don Grosh, 44, has been a respected name in electric lutherie since setting up a shop of his own in 1993. Grosh grew up north of Los Angeles, where he started playing the guitar at the age of 18. Being a self-confessed tinkerer and dissector of all things mechanical, he quickly delved into the innards of the instrument, and was soon repairing and then building guitars in earnest. Prior to starting his own business, Grosh worked for eight years for Valley Arts Guitars of California, where he had the opportunity to work on the instruments of many top-name players. Don Grosh Custom Guitars has recently relocated from California to Broomfield, Colorado.

Let's talk a little about body woods.
It definitely depends on the model. For Strats and Teles, the best-sounding wood is always going to be alder or swamp ash. If you're going to a maple-top Tele or a Set Neck, which is more of a Les Paul-sounding guitar, then the best-sounding wood for that guitar is going to be a mahogany back with a maple top, and a mahogany neck with a rosewood fingerboard. So there are some variances as far as woods go, but those are the best.

I know people have used more exotic or unusual woods and combinations, but it seems like the classic makers fell upon those standard woods pretty quickly, or maybe we just like them because they are what we're familiar with.

I think people have a reference as to what they want to hear. For an alder-body Strat it's going to sound a certain way, and if you try to use mahogany or poplar instead, it just doesn't seem to work with the pickups those guitars are using. Same thing with a Tele. If you deviate from what the standard woods are, you usually get something that isn't that appealing.

As you hear in some of the all-rosewood Telecasters that Fender made for a while. They are exotic and collectable, but often the sound can be rather harsh.
Actually, we did do an all-rosewood Tele-style guitar at Grosh, but it was a semi-hollow, and it sounded amazing. It still had a nice top end, but with more mids to round it out. But I wouldn't do that guitar in a solidbody. I don't think that would sound good at all.

And I believe Fender started to hollow out some of its rosewood Teles, although the classic one as made for George Harrison was solid.
Yeah. That would be just too harsh. But we only did a few of those, and the wood is very expensive, so that's definitely not the norm.

Have you tried any other more expensive or rare woods that proved interesting?
Sure, we've used some other things. Someone sent me some boxwood from Brazil. It's almost like maple, but it's really bright white, with hardly any visible grain to it. You know, it sounded good, a little more compressed than a maple neck, but I didn't think it sounded better than maple. So there's very little point in going to the trouble to use such a wood when a hard rock-maple neck will be just as good or better anyway.

You have to give credit to many of the early electric makers. It seems like they worked out pretty quickly what would sound and function the best.
Yeah. I think people are always looking for the next cool thing, and I did that when I first started. I was trying out woods like korina but I've been doing this now for about 13 years, and I'm coming back to the place where if the standard woods we are using are working really well, the job is more about fine tuning other aspects of the guitar.

Which is a good point. You do a wide range of guitar styles, and some of them are your versions of classics, but

they are all, as you say, fine tuned. What are some of the subtleties in making the Grosh version of a Strat-style guitar?
I'll give you a little rundown of what we do different from, say, a standard Fender Stratocaster. Starting with the neck, we use a completely different truss-rod. It's a strong, double-welded truss-rod that has round bar stock, and it's about twice the weight of the standard Fender truss-rod. That really helps to carry the overtones from the neck to the body. Also, we do the thickest headstock that we possibly can and still fit the locking tuners that we use. At the transition from the headstock to the neck, where the nut is, there is a lot more wood there on our guitars. The Fender is scooped out a lot more, and we actually go out the other direction so there's more mass there. The more mass you have on the headstock, the more tone you're going to have.

Why is that?
The more that the neck can resonate, the more it can pass through to the body. The test is, when you strum a guitar acoustically you want to hear it resonate and be very alive. Also, if you touch the tip of the headstock you will feel that vibrate, and at the strap button at the end of the body you should feel pretty much the same resonance. On our guitars, that's what you feel. So having a thicker neck or having more mass at the neck from the truss-rod really helps with that.

At the body, we're very particular about the woods we use. We buy the best grades we can find. We're really particular about selecting the right weight for particular bodies; same with the neck, a lot of times you can tap the fingerboard to test it for a particular tone to suit a particular guitar. With the bodies, it's a lot about the wood, but also we do some routings in particular ways. For a Strat-style body we do a universal rout, which a lot of people call a bathtub rout, and the reason we do that is because it actually brings a little more of an acoustic quality to the body, it opens the sound up, makes it more resonant, and it does lighten the body a little bit, too. So that's a little sound thing.

I know that was a derided technique as it applied to cheaper guitars, but it's interesting to hear that you use such a rout for tonal purposes on a high-end guitar.
Yeah, I think a lot of people think it's done because it's quicker or something, but it's not. It doesn't take me any more time to do a standard Fender-style rout versus that rout. I've done the traditional rout for a lot of guys who

wanted their guitars spec'd out with a six-point bridge and vintage routing, and I've had the particular customer that got the guitar ask why that guitar wasn't as resonant as the ones that he played in the store. Well, it's because of that routing! We're pretty accommodating, but there are reasons why we do things.

Are there other aspects of body shape that will affect tone?

I think as long as the same amount of wood's there it's not going to change a whole lot. With our bodies for the Strat and Tele-style guitars the contouring is completely different. I've always really been into Strats and liked the way they feel, but felt they could be improved upon, as far as the fret access, the contours on the body and so forth. Like, our back contour is not as deep, it's more rounded, so it fits your body a lot nicer. And we just have a slight heel cut, but nothing drastic; that's pretty critical, because if you do too much you're taking away too much wood from that part of the body. The overall shape is just a little rounder – it's more of a feel thing, in conjunction with trying to create the right sound.

What are some of the nuances that make your Set Neck model a little different from the classic of that genre?

What I did was I kept some of the things that I thought made the earlier Les Pauls really sound great, then I put in some of my own ideas that would make that guitar feel better and have more clarity.

Some of the things that I thought were important aspects of the early Les Paul were the long-tenon joint underneath the neck pickup, the thickness of the mahogany on the back, the thickness of the maple top, and the 17-degree headstock angle for string tension. Also, the neck on mine has a different truss-rod, a double-truss-rod that works both ways. One reason I use that truss-rod is because the access to the adjustment on the headstock involves taking out less wood. On the Les Paul, there's more wood being taken out in that routing, which creates a weaker area. Also, what I've done is I've put a volute on the back of the headstock for more mass for tone, and that also helps with the strength. And again, we make the headstock as thick as we can possibly get it and still keep the tuners working.

On the body, I always thought the neck angle on the Les Paul was way too steep; I designed the Set Neck so the strings are a little closer to the body, and in normal playing position your left hand isn't quite as far back as on a Les Paul, which to me always felt a little uncomfortable. There's still plenty of room for a Tune-o-matic bridge, but we just cut it back a little. And I always had a problem with the way a Les Paul would balance. So I've designed this body to be a little bit wider and a little bit shorter, so the waist is moved a little more forward, closer to where a Tele waist would be. It has better access to the upper frets, pretty much full access.

Using the design features that we do on this guitar, there's a nice, thick midrange – like on some of the better Les Pauls you've heard – but there's a lot more clarity and much better string balance. That's kind of what I went after, a guitar that would go head to head with some of the earlier Les Pauls, but with some improvements.

We're talking a lot about elements that create the right mass to get the best resonance out of different parts of the guitar, but I know that you and other builders usually use the lighter wood stocks when you can find them. There was a time, particularly in the 1970s, when Les Pauls and Telecasters were getting very heavy; people thought those dense, ton ton guitars had lots of sustain and power.

Tone and sustain don't have so much to do with the weight as they do with what's going on between the neck and the body. I think, for a Set Neck, if the body can even be a little bit lighter than average that helps. Like, we've even done some chambering, and that seems to help with the sustain and the sound. We've done chambered, semi-hollow, and full hollow, and even with the full-hollows there's still a lot of punch there. It's very open, very acoustic, but you can really drive that bridge pickup if you want to. For the neck, you can get some real nice jazz-box kind of tones out of it.

Is this a routed-out hollowbody, or a guitar built as an acoustic electric?

It's routed out. For me, that's the direction I wanted to go because I wanted a little more versatility, versus something too thin.

Tell us a little about the effect of scale length on tone.

To get that Les Paul tone the scale length has to be 24¾". There's no way around that. If you have a longer scale, it's just not going to reproduce that sound. Same with Strats and Teles and the 25½" scale. You're not going to get a great Strat sound with 24¾". We've made a few hybrid guitars, such as out Bent Top Custom, with 24¾" scale and hum-single-hum pickups, using the Fralin unmatched humbuckers – the Unbucker, with mismatched coils – in the bridge and neck and a Vintage Hot in the middle, and I'd say that guitar is as close as you're going to get to getting a great Strat tone and a great humbucker tone in one guitar. You're going to miss a little bit on the Strat sound with the shorter scale length, but having the maple top with the mahogany back does bring in a little more clarity and brightness. There are ways you can tweak things to bring in that snappiness, but it won't be exact.

What are your thoughts on some different bridge types, both tonally and in terms of feel?

The main difference between a Tune-o-matic with stop tail and a wrapover bridge is that the Tune-o-matic has a little bit sharper attack to it, whereas the wraparound has a little bit slower attack and maybe a little bit more warmth. So we use the wraparound with the P-90 guitars and the Tune-o-matic with the humbuckers.

Which, I guess, serves to balance out the characteristics of those two pickup types as used on a Set Neck. And, of course, you get a little bit of a different feel out of those bridges, too.

Yeah, there's a little bit better tension on the Tune-o-matic. The wraparound has a little bit less down-pressure on the saddles, so you could say it's got a little bit of a mushier feel.

You also use a different vibrato system for your Strat-top guitars.

We use the Gotoh 1088 tremolo system, and we also modify it. We modify the pivot points, and we also put a nylon bushing in the block to stabilize the arm. I like that bridge because it has the bent metal saddles, and I think that has a lot to do with the sound. I think it's more vintagey and open. And the way we modify it, the two-point fulcrum stays in tune as well as a Floyd. Tone-wise, I feel that's the best thing going, and having a bridge that is going to stay in tune is important. And what we do with the block takes that flop out of the arm and makes it a little bit more stable.

We also sometimes use the 1099 with the die-cast block saddles, and that's a little bit more of a modern sound. A Gotoh 1055 has the push-in arm, and that's even a little bit more of a modern feel.

I know some makers have been going to stainless-steel frets. Have you given that any thought?

Well, the way we do our fret ends is really labor intensive. We keep them more toward the outside of the neck, but we make them really round, so they feel very smooth but you don't have problems with strings dropping off the edge of the fingerboard. So rather than bringing those fret ends in so far like many companies do, we angle them at 30 degrees and then we really round 'em, so it looks like a hotdog on the end. The issue with the stainless-steel frets is, for us, it would be really time consuming to finish them the way that we do them. With stainless steel, it's so hard to do that rounding on the ends. You can pretty much just angle them the way you want and then clean them up a little, and that's about it. Also, until recently stainless-steel fret wire wasn't available in sizes I like to use. They have just come out with some in the sizes we put on our guitars, though, so we might give it a try in the near future. Even so, from what I've seen, if you just do decent maintenance on your [nickel-silver] frets and do a light dress of them every so often before they start getting grooves in them, they'll last a long time.

And perhaps the nickel-silver is still the traditional sound of frets, and of some other hardware, too.

Yeah. I know there's been a lot of hype with things such as stainless-steel blocks and stainless-steel saddles. I think maybe on a guitar that isn't very alive that might help. On our guitars, I haven't noticed any difference other than that the tremolo feel gets a lot heavier. The Gotoh bridge has a zinc block, but the guitar already has plenty of resonance so you don't need the steel block, and I like the overall feel of the tremolo bridge as it is. I've also tried stainless-steel saddles, and once again, I didn't hear much difference in tone on our guitars, but maybe on a guitar that didn't have that sustain or that clarity you might notice an improvement.

People talk a lot about the tone and sustain of set-neck guitars, but are there ways to build a bolt-neck that can come pretty close to that?

To me it all comes down to what sound you want. If you want a great Les Paul sound, it's not going to happen with a bolt-on neck. It all comes together with the way the neck is glued in, how much mass is there, the tenon joint and so forth. You can get similarities, but you just can't nail that sound. Just like gluing in a neck on a Strat-style body doesn't nail the best Strat sounds. Look at, let's say, a PRS Single Cut. It doesn't really nail that Les Paul thing because of the scale length and other details. Every little thing contributes.

When you set out to make your own guitars, was there something in particular that you sought to achieve, which perhaps was lacking in other designs?

I didn't buy into a lot of stuff that you hear out there. For instance, if you have a great-sounding Strat it's all about how old the alder was, or you have to do it 'this' way. I had a pretty good sense of sound and of what I wanted to hear, and I felt like I could reproduce that on our guitars. I really just set out to try to make the best guitar that we can, for playability, feel, and sound.

It's never been about trying to make the best 'vintage-sounding' guitar, it's been about trying to make the best-sounding guitar, period. That could be modern, vintage, whatever someone wants. It's a matter of understanding how all that stuff works and the principles behind it. It's not voodoo.

Plenty of players are stuck with the thinking that if something isn't vintage, or a very close reproduction of vintage, that it's no good. It's constantly surprising how conservative many guitar players can be at times.

Oh, they are. It's the only industry where the standards haven't been developed or changed much.

But you do get a few makers in your league, guys like John Suhr or Tom Anderson, who are willing to give a nod to the vintage classics, but also want to go back to the drawing-board with their own designs.

Yeah, to improve on some old ideas, but without getting anything too weird that it will scare those guitar players off.

Which is probably why your Retro Classic models do well. Players feel they've got a reference to something pretty familiar in those guitars, but they have been pretty heavily reworked.

It's not so different from what they're used to, but there are some new features there, certainly.

I know you are another believer in nitrocellulose lacquer finishes.

Yeah, we use all lacquer, and guitars definitely sound different with the lacquer. Polyester or urethane are all plastic based, so if you have a thin sheet of that and tap on it, you get a more plastic tone from that. Whereas the lacquer is very hard, very brittle, and you get more of a sharp, glassy tone. Plus it's a thinner material, so you don't have to have as much thickness build up on the wood, and you hear more of what the wood of the guitar is doing rather than hearing how a coating is affecting the wood.

Lindy Fralin > Fralin Pickups

Pickup manufacturer and rewinder Lindy Fralin, 49, has become known throughout the industry both for his high-quality reproductions of established designs – which often include thoughtful new twists – and his own new and original models. Lindy, himself a gigging guitarist, heads a small team of craftsmen in the Fralin Pickups shop in Richmond, Virginia, where all units are made by hand – as a matter of fact, Lindy was winding pickups as we spoke.

Please give us a little bit of an overview of how a magnetic pickup works.

A magnetic pickup needs a steel string to react, because it is typically a coil around a magnet. It can be six poles or one bar magnet, or it can also be a steel blade or a set of screws that are charged up by a magnet. But the point is, you've got a coil around a core, which is either charged-up steel or an actual magnet. And when steel moves above it, or of course

below it, it makes this field move, and the coil senses the movement of the field, and that's where your signal is created.

The field moves exactly corresponding to the string, which in the long run corresponds to the movement of a speaker cone. It doesn't produce a lot of voltage, and that's why amps are two- and three-stage amps. But that is the simplest pickup, a coil around a magnet.

It seems like the more you learn about pickups the more you discover there are an awful lot of variables between them, even if they all work on the same principles.

Of course, there are huge differences between magnet material, types of wire, the shape of the magnetic field, how many turns [of wire] you've put on there… There are all kinds of things you can vary for different effect. And, of course, the biggest difference is, if the magnet material is in the coil it's one school of pickup, and if it's steel [inside the coil] it's the other school.

That's the biggest division, because you can just picture how a P-90 sounds so different from a Jazzmaster pickup, and yet they have the same coil around them: 10,000 turns of 42-gauge plain, enamel-coated wire. And they are drastically different pickups, because anything with a magnet in it tends to give you a cleaner, clearer, but thinner signal; anything with steel in it tends to give you the bigger, beefier, more rounded but more distorted signal.

We're talking here about Fender-style pickups with magnetic polepieces, or Gibson types with the magnets mounted beneath the coil charging steel poles that run through the coil.

Well, that is the big difference. All pickups kind of fit in one of those two categories, whether it's a blade or a screw, that's that kind of pickup, and if it's alnico, whether it's a bar magnet or six polepieces, as in the Fender kind of pickup. So the similarities you hear between Rickenbacker, Danelectro, and Fender is that they're all pickups with the magnet in the coil. Or old DeArmonds, they're clean and clear. And then the beefy pickups are anything with a blade, from a Charlie Christian, or P-90s with screws, or humbuckers, Mosrite pickups, a lot of Nationals, anything with adjustable steel polepieces makes it a beefier, louder, more distorted kind of pickup.

What is it that makes the steel-in-the-coil pickup fatter sounding?

That gets us into some really heavy-duty physics, but it's partly that it's a more complicated magnetic field, because your bar magnets are sideways under everything. It also leads to a higher inductance, which just means more output for whatever movement of the string. Because, you see, a magnet is only 50 per cent iron; it's got other things in it: aluminum, nickel, cobalt. And a 100 per cent iron core is more efficient, but by the same token it's more distorted.

Why is it more distorted? I don't know – maybe for no other reason than that it gets more voltage and that distorts the tubes.

So even if the weight of the bar magnet and the weight of the six individual magnet polepieces are about the same, there's still going to be a difference in the output of that pickup?

There's a big difference, because there's a difference in inductance. And what you're creating here is a type of inductance, but any pickup's sound is an incredibly complex relationship of capacitance, inductance, impedance, and reluctance. This is why not just anyone can wind a pickup – or, anyone can make a pickup that makes noise, but it's actually much harder than people think to make good pickups that sound good consistently.

We have to go to a great deal of trouble to keep our pickups consistent. For example, instead of just making mass-produced pickups that might be stacked six-deep on a machine and machine-wound all at once, we have to stop each coil six times to check how it's winding, because the biggest thing that shapes tone is the distance between each layer of copper. Some of that's insulation, some of that's air. You hear about 'scatter wound' or 'randomly layered' pickups, and that's nothing but adding more air to the mix. If you get a batch of wire where the insulation's thicker then it needs less air, or if you get a batch of wire where the copper core is bigger you've got lower ohm readings.

You have to compensate constantly for whatever the wire's doing, because 42-gauge, by definition, means the copper core is between 2.1 thousandths and 2.4 thousandths of an inch in diameter. That's a big range, and there's a huge difference between the sound of those two extremes. So you learn that big-core wire winds good P-Basses, and small-core wire winds overwound pickups better than big-core wire. You just know what to do with it. We always wind a pickup or two off of each spool of wire, then decide, "All right, this is going to do that type of pickup." We'll write on it, "This is Strat bridges" or "This is Jazz Basses" or whatever. You know, Fender didn't do this, so that's why their pickups are so much less consistent. Any of your mass-produced pickups, they don't have time to do this. They stack 'em six-deep and crank 'em out. But a lot of the custom builders like me take a lot more time and a lot more care. So a ten-year-old Vintage Hot should sound like next year's Vintage Hot.

Of course, the likes of Fender set the templates for these designs, but everyone who has played more than one Strat or Tele knows there are good Strat pickups and there are less-good Strat pickups.

Of course. And they didn't count the turns, they just filled up the coils with wire. But Leo did know – and I've heard this from a good source, so I'm confident in quoting it – that hand winding was important. Because, you know, he had machinery and patents on every other kind of machinery, and he still hand-wound coils until he was not involved in the company any more. All the way up until 1964 they still hand-wound coils.

And when you say "hand-wound," you mean they hand guided the wire on to the coil?

Yeah, it was spun by a machine just like I'm doing, but I'm guiding – right now – the back-and-forth movement of the wire, and I'm in complete control of the tension. So, while Fender didn't care about making a hotter bridge then, or a reverse middle, they did know that it sounded better to have a hand-wound coil. All of the sloppiness that a human adds was important. Certainly you can get too sloppy and sound bad, or you can get too tight and too neat and sound bad. But Leo Fender knew this, just like he knew lighter wood sounded better than heavier wood.

Being a pickup maker, I'm very aware – because I've put together dozens of guitars – that the wood is every bit as important as the pickups. You can never discount the importance of how a particular piece of wood vibrates. If it either soaks up a certain frequency or resonates at a certain frequency, of course it comes out of the amplified instrument. I say this to people all the time, even on my web site: in Fenders, what you really don't want is a guitar that soaks up anywhere from 150Hz to 450Hz, that's essentially your treble strings. You've got to have a lot of resonance in the treble in particular, because the pickup itself doesn't boost that frequency or you see it as a ton of high end, but you don't want thin treble strings on your guitar. People love Fenders that are bright, so it's essentially a very hollow-midrange pickup. You can't have the guitar soaking up your midrange. You've heard bad Fenders that sound thin and clanky, and others with a set of 6k Strat pickups on them sound huge. And that's the wood just as much as the pickups.

It seems like there was a school of thinking for a time – maybe the late 1970s and '80s, if I recall – that held that

pickups mattered more than anything else. That you could pretty much bolt a good pickup to a plank of wood, and that would do the trick.

Yeah, and even Fender in the late 1960s and '70s thought that heavier wood was better because it would get longer sustain. Everybody was starting to use hotter pickups and fuzz boxes. But after a while everybody came back to liking the traditional sound, and I sell far more stock-output pickups than hotter stuff. There are pedals and amps and all these great ways to get easy hot tones. And Fender as a company has gotten very good at picking their wood correctly again. Considering how many guitars they ship a day, they're doing an amazing job at keeping their quality high and their company well run. I don't know how they do it.

It is pretty impressive, given the prices they sell things at today, which make decent guitars cheaper in real terms than they were back in the 1950s and '60s.

Sure, even the Mexican stuff is really pretty good, and I own some Korean stuff from other makers that I'm really very happy with. I've got a couple of Korean Danelectros and a Korean PRS, and I can't believe how good that is. A $500 guitar, and it's awesome.

You mentioned a minute ago that many players had come back around to liking more traditional sounds, and it seems to me that part of that involves a realization that the most powerful pickup available isn't always the best choice for your sound.

It totally depends on your style. One of the rules of pickups that I mention to people all the time is, hotter pickups are less dynamic, less articulate, but longer sustaining. What you tend to hear is, you can hit a note soft or hard, but it comes out of the amp about the same. Which is fabulous for really fast playing, hammer-ons with the double-handed thing on the fingerboard stuff, because you need to be less delicate in your touch. But if you want a real expressive, bluesy pickup, a weaker pickup – with your amp up louder – does a better job. Because now, when you hit it hard it gets louder, when you hit it soft it gets quieter, when you hit it near the bridge it sounds twangy, when you hit it near the neck it sounds mellow. You have much more control with a weak pickup, and that's another reason why people are coming back to the original, weaker outputs of these things, and just trying to get really good instruments and good amps and good pedals, and whatever makes them happy.

It's interesting to follow what a learning curve it has been for a lot of players. And when you talk about the expressiveness and dynamics available from weaker pickups, consider what a player like Jimi Hendrix was using most of the time.

Yeah, they didn't have hot pickups yet.

And even Eddie Van Halen was playing a standard PAF-style pickup.

Somebody told me it was only 8.2k, but that's not something I can say reliably.

Sure, I've heard it quoted as being something in the 8.5k region.

Yeah, and that's not all that hot for a humbucker. Just an average PAF. You heard him getting all his tweaks and whistles and wild stuff in the early days, and you don't get that stuff out of a really hot pickup.

And with a good distortion pedal into a Marshall you're going to get a pretty heavy sound anyway.

Of course. Unless your amp's on ten all the time and you're still wishing for more power, you don't always need a hotter pickup. But, then again, it depends on the guy's style and his amp. I tended for years to play blackface Fender Princetons and other amps of that size, and they don't like a whole lot of input from a hot pickup. But a Twin Reverb maybe, or a Marshall, responds better to a much louder pickup. It overwhelms the Princeton, it just doesn't need it.

For years, the main way people judged pickups was by their DC-resistance readings, but it seems there is actually a lot more to it than that.

Well, that's actually one of the least important numbers. The crucial things for tone are the number of turns – that directly relates to your voltage – and the strength of the magnetic field, then capacitance and inductance shape treble and bass. So balancing all of those things is important, as is also 'reluctance,' the term for the magnetic field's resistance to change. You're getting way complex here, and none of this is stuff that someone listening to a guitar needs to know. They need to know if the sound pleases them.

I used to have all this fancy test equipment – inductance bridges and frequency analyzers – and I learned to use it all, and then I would go listen to the pickups. So I know now, by just listening, what kind of Q and resonant peak I've got

going. I don't use any of that equipment any more. I have a test guitar and a little amp in the shop, and I can listen to anything I want – and we do all day long.

Another thing that's often talked about is the difference between different types of alnico.

That stuff does matter, particularly when the magnet is in the coil. Then it really matters which magnet material you're using, because of something called 'hysteresis.' Hysteresis is a graph of the resistance to change of any magnetic material. You can have the exact same coil on a pickup that you can slide rod magnets in and out of like the plastic Fender pickups, and you can totally change the sound of it by switching magnets.

Just between an alnico II and an alnico V, for example?

Oh yeah. We even mix them in some pickups, although I don't know that that helps a whole lot. It [a coil with mixed magnet types] doesn't always treat strings differently, it kind of averages out the sound of the whole sound of the pickup. I think hysteresis affects the coil, and not just the sound of that one string, but we still do it when people insist. To me, the biggest reason to mix magnets is not to achieve some tone, but if you put a weaker magnet under that E string, you tend to get rid of some of that detuning trouble from the magnetic pull. When we mix the magnets, we tend to put them under E, A, and G. They're always the ones that respond worst to that lack of sustain that you hear from a real strong magnet pulling on the strings. The weak-magnet pickups do have a longer sustain on the guitar, or backing your pickups off – lowering them down from the strings a little – can also help to increase your sustain.

Which is interesting to note. I think that fact is confusing to some players when they first discover it: that lowering your pickups can actually increase the sustain of your guitar, even though it lessens the output a little, too.

Sure. Personally, I have always liked brighter-sounding guitars, too – I have always liked to twang. That's why I could never play the old-fashioned humbuckers. We developed this new humbucker recently that sounds like a single-coil all the way. It's the Split Single, it's on my web site. One is just a two-coil P-90, and the other is a two-coil pickup that's somewhere between a Strat and a Jazzmaster. It's got shorter magnets than a Strat, but longer magnets than a Jazzmaster, and I have room for anywhere from 8,000 to 11,000 turns. Jazzmasters had 10,000 and Strats had

8,000 so we can really get any Fender sound you want, but out of a humbucker. They're quiet, they're drop-in humbucker replacements, and they're for people who just want cleaner wound-string sounds, like me.

Is there anything in this talk of magnets aging?
Yeah, there's something in it, but there's a lot of bunk, too, a lot of misinformation. Alnico in itself has a 300,000 year half-life, but you see, anything can demagnetize it. A strong field nearby it will demag it. The transformers on your amp, or speaker magnets, or who knows what else. Banging on the polepiece with the string repeatedly will gradually weaken it. So magnets do degauss [weaken], but it's all to do with their environment, what they have experienced over the years, that determines how much they have degaussed. I'm not convinced that they sound better degaussed, though, because I like my high-end. Also, I've degaussed them on purpose, and they don't really get much different. You can feel a little bit of a weaker magnet, but it doesn't seem much duller or much quieter. The magnet is incredibly forgiving.

So that's another pretty complex issue.
Yeah, and I certainly wouldn't recommend people trying to demag their own pickups, because it's hard to mag 'em again.

And if the change is so subtle, you're going to find a desired change by tweaking something else in your guitar or rig.
I feel it's much more important to get the right number of turns on there, and get the right piece of wood. What we offer with our exchange policy is that you can try something else to get the sound you're looking for if the first one you order isn't right. If you get a Vintage Hot and you still go, "Man, I was looking for something darker and warmer…" Well, what you need is more turns, because you can't change the wood. I can't make a pickup that's perfect for everyone's guitar and taste, so we offer an exchange policy.

I have always been interested to see that you offer both over-wound and under-wound pickups, which is something you don't often hear about.
It's my job to wind a pickup correctly so that it has its full output. If you wind it too tight or too loose or choose the wrong magnets or wire, it's going to sound bad, even though it has X number of turns on it. But picking the right number

of turns for each person, that's a very personal thing, and I can't be the guy that tells them, "Oh, you need this," unless a guy says, "I've had four different sets of Tele pickups and my Tele is still really bright." But if he's only tried the set his guitar came with, we really don't know anything.

Speaking of which, I know you have put a lot of thought into Telecaster pickups, and in particular the function of the plate under it.
A Tele pickup really is a Strat pickup, except you've added a steel plate under it. Also, the bridge is a piece of steel on old Teles, and that becomes part of the pickup. So a Telecaster is a different animal, and the body being different, too, is why they don't sound the same as Strats. You don't have the routing for a whammy bar or a middle pickup, and the strings go into the wood instead of a huge steel block. But the bridge is the main difference: you've got a piece of steel under the pickup, and a piece of steel around the pickup. Both of those focus the magnetic field in a positive way, to get the most output out of that coil. So they really seem louder than the same number of turns on a Strat pickup.

Is the magnetic field otherwise a little different, because it's a slightly different coil shape?
It's really not much different, and the way Leo designed them they both would have had the same turns on the same magnets. The Tele is a tiny bit taller and wider, but those are insignificant factors.

I know you also use a Tele-style bottom plate on some Strat pickups.
Yeah. That gets you 20 per cent closer to sounding like a Telecaster, but it doesn't get you all the way.

Which, I guess, might be just enough for someone who wants their bridge pickup to be just a little hotter.
Part of our success is because I still play bars, and I still know what a good guitar sounds like versus a bad one. We work really hard to make our sets for Strats. The neck and middle are essentially the same pickup, but the bridge is totally different. It's wound with a different type of wire for a little bit bigger midrange, and it has more turns, and we recommend that steel plate, because the biggest thing you hear with that steel under it is the pickup's louder and bassier even without having any more turns. So, hopefully, between

those things we get a bridge pickup that is usable on the same amp setting as the neck and middle. That's why I got into coil winding in the first place, because all my Strats had an unusable bridge pickup.

Do you have any unsung heroes of older undiscovered pickups?
I've always been a huge Danelectro fan. Of all my instruments, my Danelectros have always been the ones I've never modified. I've monkeyed with everything I've ever bought, but with my Danelectros I've never even replaced the cheap toggle switch that always breaks. Danelectros are just so cheap and so functional. I've bought a lot of cheap guitars over the years, because I usually bought guitars that had something wrong with them so I could monkey with them and modify them.

My favorite guitar right now is a Gibson ES-225 that a friend of mine found for me in a music store for $350 that was painted black and stripped of all its hardware. So he stripped it for me and I put new everything on it, and it plays like a dream. But I never would have bought a $2,000 or $3,000 guitar and put my pickups on it.

You wouldn't want to devalue the thing.
I just couldn't afford it. It was much easier to buy a $350 guitar and fix it up.

What do you think of the pickups on the reissue Danelectros?
I have two of those, and I think they're fine. I own a lot of old ones, too, several U-2s and a couple of old basses. But they're pretty sweet-sounding little pickups.

One pickup that gets a bum rap from a lot of people is the Gretsch HiLo'Tron. What's your opinion on those?
They're very weak and clean, and if that's not what you want, don't play them. I think they're great, because I am a fan of clarity. I owned an Anniversary, and the reason I sold it was not the sound, it was just because I couldn't keep it in tune.

Certainly the Dynasonics – the DeArmond 200 model – was a punchier pickup, despite being single-coil.
Oh, they're great.

I know you have also put a lot of thought into P-90s.
I love P-90s, but I didn't like them for years. It took a lot of experimenting with them to realize that I could underwind them, and they were still loud as hell. Gibson intended that pickup to have 10,000 turns, but in that blond ES-225 I mentioned it has 8,000 on the neck and 9,500 on the bridge, so they're cleaner. They still break an amp up like crazy if you push it, but you can now twang your low E string and play Duane Eddy and rockabilly on them, too.

It comes back to one of the first things we talked about: you have more control over a weaker pickup. You can dig in and make it nasty, you can twang it close to the bridge to get brighter, and in every way – with that P-90 for example – you have more control than a 10,000-turn pickup, which tends to be just muddy all the time. I sell them overwound too, but I think more people buy 10 per cent-underwound and stock bridge [pickup sets] than any other set we sell. I mention to people that I'm using 20 per cent-underwound neck pickup and five per cent-underwound bridge as a set, and people try that, and they always like it. If you get brave enough to try a weaker pickup, you'll find that you can turn your amp up, and you've got pedals, so you've got plenty of control over your sound.

Any final tips?
Match your pickup to your guitar, because the pickup can only pick up what the guitar is doing.

CD Track Listing And Notes

The sample tracks on the accompanying CD are not intended to precisely mirror the guitars covered in the chapters, but are instead offered as a representative selection of diverse makes and models to provide a broad range of sounds that exemplifies the diversity of tones available to the electric guitarist. The author's playing here is occasionally a little 'rough'n'ready' because the intention is to give a glimpse of the natural character of the guitar rather than the guitarist. Similar riffs are used for similar types of guitars, and some guitars are employed in different genres for comparative purposes (a Telecaster included in the Jazz Boxes group, for example). Even so, some of the riffs used even for different categories are extremely similar, with the intention of enabling the listener to make cross-comparisons of different styles of guitars.

The repetition isn't intended in the name of monotony, but rather for ease of comparison and a certain uniformity. For the same reasons, I didn't see fit to vary the riffs greatly according to genre – playing 'shred licks' on a 'shred guitar' such as the Ibanez JS100 for example – but partnered humbuckers together, or thinlines together, and so forth, so the listener could hear the difference between a Les Paul and a JS100 under similar playing conditions. Note also that there is an intentional mixing of both very expensive and very inexpensive guitars (an original 1964 Fender Stratocaster compared with a new Mexican-made Fender Strat for example, or a $12,000 1954 Gibson L-5 compared with a $369 Ibanez AFS-75). That said, all of the guitars will obviously sound a little different played by your hands through your amplifier, so it still pays to get out and play as many guitars as you can before making any purchase decisions.

Tracks were recorded through two different high-end, all-tube amplifiers and miked live in the room, rather than DI'd, in a manner intended to exhibit as closely as possible how any given guitar is likely to sound if you were to plug it in yourself at similar amp settings. Recordings were made dry with no effects and no EQ, compression or other processing in the recording or mastering process, although a vintage Ibanez TS9 Tube Screamer overdrive pedal was used on certain takes, as indicated by OD in the track listings. This is a fairly universal overdrive sound, and provides a good example of how guitars sound with mild distortion added.

The Jazz Boxes riffs were recorded through a Dr Z Z-28 1x12″ combo with Celestion G12H-30 speaker, set to (in o'clock scale):
Volume 9:00
Bass 11:30
Treble 12:30

The remaining riffs were recorded through a TopHat Club Royale 2x12″ combo with one Celestion G12H-30 and one Celestion G12 Alnico Blue (the latter speaker was the one miked), set to:
Volume 9:30
Treble 10:30
Mid 2:00
Bass 11:00
Cut 12:00
Master full
Boost off

An Ibanez TS9 Tube Screamer overdrive, used where 'OD' is indicated, was set to
Drive 12:00
Tone 12:00
Level 2:00

A Beyer Dynamic M160NC dynamic ribbon microphone was placed approximately 12″ from the speaker, slightly off center, in each case, and routed through a MOTU 828 digital interface (Input Gain 3:00) and recorded direct to disc.

All musical excerpts © Dave Hunter 2006. To be sampled or copied with permission only.

CD Track Listing

Telecasters & T-types

Track #	Guitar	Settings/Notes
01	1957 Fender Telecaster	Bridge pickup, OD in at 00:16
02	1978 Fender Telecaster	Bridge pickup, OD in at 00:16
03	'78 Tele with DiMarzio	DiMarzio Fast Track dual-rails humbucker, OD in at 00:16
04	1999 G&L ASAT Z-3	Bridge pickup, OD in at 00:16

Stratocasters & Jazzmasters

Track #	Guitar	Settings/Notes
05	1964 Fender Stratocaster	Bridge pickup
06		Neck pickup
07		Neck pickup with OD
08	'56 Fender Stratocaster American Vintage Reissue	Bridge pickup
09		Neck pickup
10		Neck pickup with OD
11	Mexican Fender Standard Strat	Bridge pickup
12		Neck pickup
13	Fender Jazzmaster American Reissue	Bridge pickup
14		Neck pickup
15		Surf riff, one pass on bridge pickup, one on neck, through Fender Reissue Tube Reverb
16	Jazzmaster	Vibrato unit action
17	1964 Fender Stratocaster	Vibrato unit action
18	1999 G&L ASAT Z-3	Bigsby vibrato unit action

Humbuckers

Track #	Guitar	Settings/Notes
19	2001 Gibson Les Paul Standard	Bridge pickup, OD at 00:20
20		Neck pickup
21		Bridge and neck pickups on lower gain amp setting
22	2005 Epiphone Les Paul Elitist '57 Goldtop	Bridge pickup, OD 00:20
23		Neck pickup

Humbuckers (continued)

Track #	Guitar	Settings/Notes
24	2001 Gretsch Duo Jet	Bridge Filter'Tron, OD 00:20
25		Neck Filter'Tron
26	2002 PRS McCarty	Bridge pickup, OD 00:20
27		Neck pickup
28	2004 Parker Nitefly (bolt-on neck with carbon-fiber fingerboard, solid mahogany body)	Bridge pickup, OD 00:20
29		Neck pickup
30		Piezo pickup alone, then with neck humbucker added, then final strum alone
31	2005 Ibanez JS100	Bridge pickup, OD 00:20
32		Neck pickup
33	2003 Ibanez SZ270	Bridge pickup, OD 00:20
34		Neck pickup

Semis, Thinlines, P-90s and Friends

Track #	Guitar	Settings/Notes
35	1961 Gibson ES-330TDC with Bigsby	Bridge pickup
36		Neck pickup, OD 00:18
37	1965 Epiphone Casino	Bridge pickup
38		Neck pickup, OD 00:18
39	1998 Gibson ES-335	Bridge pickup
40		Neck pickup, OD 00:17
41	2000 Danelectro U-2	Bridge pickup (lipstick tube)
42		Bridge and neck together
43		Neck pickup, OD 00:17
44		Jangle on bridge pickup
45	Reverend Rick Vito Special with Bigsby (semi-solid body with aluminum-faced phenolic top and back, solid mahogany center core)	Bridge pickup (P-90-style)
46		Neck pickup, OD 00:17
47	Reverend Rick Vito Signature (same construction, but through-body stringing with no vibrato unit)	Bridge pickup (P-90-style)
48		Neck pickup, OD 00:17

Semis, Thinlines, P-90s, and Friends (continued)

Track #	Guitar	Settings/Notes
49	Reverend 'Contour control'	Tonal difference achieved by rotating the Contour control from bright to fat
50	c1960 Supro Dual-Tone	Bridge pickup (single-coil)
51		Neck pickup, OD 00:16
52	PRS SE Soapbar II	Bridge pickup (P-90-style)
53		Neck pickup, OD 00:16

Jazz Boxes (and a little Rock'n'Roll)

Track #	Guitar	Settings/Notes
54	2005 Benedetto Bravo	Neck pickup (humbucker)
55	1954 Gibson L-5 CES with dual alnico pickups	Neck pickup
56	1958 Guild X-50	Neck pickup (P-90-style)
57	1961 Gibson ES-330	Neck pickup (P-90)
58	1955 Gibson ES-135	Neck pickup (P-90)
59	c1960 Kay N-50	Neck pickup (single-coil)
60	2005 Ibanez AFS-75	Neck pickup (humbucker)
61	1957 Fender Telecaster	Neck pickup
62	2001 Gibson Les Paul	Neck pickup
63	1954 Gibson L-5 CES	Rockabilly on bridge pickup
64	2005 Ibanez AFS-75	Rockabilly on bridge pickup

INDEX

ACKNOWLEDGEMENTS

The author wishes to extend a heartfelt "Thank you" to the following for their help and support through the course of this project: Morgan Ringwald and Fender Musical Instruments for assisting with loan samples; Dave Maddux of the Fender Custom Shop for taking the photograph of the Benedetto Bravo, and Cindy and Bob Benedetto for arranging it; Don Grosh for talking with me and supplying photography; Chris Fleming of the Fender Custom Shop for taking the time to chat; Lindy Fralin for convivial conversation and critical pickup information; David McLaren of G&L for information and photography; Dave Burrluck, author of *The Player's Guide To Guitar Maintenance*, for laying the groundwork for many of the photographs used in Chapter 1; Armando Vega at Yamaha U.S.A. and *Guitar Magazine* (U.K.) for supplying images; Tom Ferry for lending his 1978 Telecaster; Gary Traversy of Gary's Guitars in Portsmouth, New Hampshire, for unchaining his vintage Gibson L-5CES and other jazzboxes for the CD recording; Brian Fischer of Earcraft Music in Dover, New Hampshire, for allowing me to put much of his stock under the microphone; and all at Backbeat U.K. for putting the book together.